Maldives

Northern
Atolls p91

North & South
Male Atolls p64

Ari
Atoll
p82

Male p44

Southern
Atolls
p104

THIS EDITION WRITTEN AND RESEARCHED BY

Tom Masters

PLAN YOUR TRIP

ON THE ROAD

SHOPFRONTS ON
MAAFUSHI P75

TOBIAS HELBIG/GETTY IMAGES ©

LAGOON PIER, SOUTH MALE
ATOLL P75

MATTEO COLOMBO/GETTY IMAGES ©

MICHELE FALZONE/GETTY IMAGES ©

Contents

UNDERSTAND

SURVIVAL GUIDE

SPECIAL FEATURES

FILITHEYO ISLAND RESORT
P107

Welcome to the Maldives

Unrivalled luxury, stunning white-sand beaches and an amazing underwater world make the Maldives an obvious choice for a true holiday of a lifetime.

Unbelievable Beaches

The Maldives is home to perhaps the best beaches in the world; they're on almost every one of the country's nearly 1200 islands and are so consistently perfect that it's hard not to become blasé about them. While some beaches may boast softer granules than others, the basic fact remains: you'll find consistently whiter-than-white powder sand and luminous cyan-blue water like this almost nowhere else on earth. This fact alone is enough to bring over a million people a year to this tiny, remote and otherwise little-known Indian Ocean paradise.

Resorts for All

Every resort in the Maldives is its own private island, and with over 100 to choose from the only problem is selecting where to stay. At the top end, the world's most exclusive hotel brands compete to attain ever-greater heights of luxury, from personal butlers and private lap pools to in-room massages and pillow menus. It's not surprising that honeymooners and those seeking a glamorous tropical getaway have the country at the top of their wish lists. But there's choice beyond the five- and six-star resorts. Other islands cater for families, for divers, for those on a (relative) budget, and anyone wanting a tranquil back-to-nature experience.

Underwater World

With some of the best diving and snorkelling in the world, the clear waters of the Maldives are a magnet for anyone with an interest in marine life. The richness and variety is astonishing; dazzling coral walls, magnificent caves and schools of brightly coloured tropical fish await you when you get down to the reef. In deeper waters lurk manta rays, turtles, sharks and even the world's largest fish, the whale shark. The best bit? The water is so warm many people don't even wear a wetsuit.

Independent Travel

In the last few years, these incredible islands have finally started to open to independent travellers, meaning you no longer have to stay in resorts and remain separate from the local population, something that has kept backpackers away for decades. Intrepid individuals can now make their own itineraries and travel from island to island by public ferry, staying among the devout but friendly local population. With a fast-growing number of privately run guesthouses on inhabited islands, the Maldives and its people are now more accessible than ever.

Why I Love the Maldives

By Tom Masters, Author

I first came to the Maldives with no idea how different it was to the rest of the world, how fragile or challenging life seems here at the mercy of the sea, with so few resources locally available. I instantly formed a bond of respect and friendship with the people who make these inhospitable coral islands home. It's such a contradiction that this is also where to find some of the world's most luxurious hotel properties, and this is a paradox – among many – that I continue to enjoy every time I return to this astonishing, beautiful country.

For more about our author, see page 192

Above: Swimming with the fish at Soneva Fushi (p101)

Maldives

DEPTHS & ELEVATION

	approximate values
0m+	
200m	
1000m	
2000m	
3000m	
4000m+	

Ⓝ 0 ___ 100 km
0 ___ 60 miles

INDIAN OCEAN

IHAVANDHIPPOLHU ATOLL

HAA ALIFU
NORTH THILADHUNMATHEE ATOLL

Dhidhdhoo

HAA DHAALU
Kulhuduffushi
SOUTH THILADHUNMATHEE ATOLL

MAAMAKUNUDHOO ATOLL

NORTH MILADHUNMADULU ATOLL

SHAVIYANI Funadhoo

SOUTH MILADHUNMADULU ATOLL

RAA NOONU Manadhoo

Ugoofaaru

NORTH MAALHOSMADULU ATOLL

Naifaru
LHAVIYANI

FAADHIPPOLHU ATOLL

SOUTH MAALHOSMADULU ATOLL

BAA
Eydhafushi

GOIDHOO ATOLL

RASDHOO ATOLL

NORTH MALE ATOLL

KAAFU Thulusdhoo

MALE ✪ Ibrahim Nasir International Airport

ALIFU

ARI ATOLL

Mahibadhoo

SOUTH MALE ATOLL

FELIDHOO ATOLL

VAAVU Felidhoo

Male
Explore the fascinating Maldivian capital (p44)

Maafushi
The centre of independent travel in the Maldives (p75)

Rasdhoo Atoll
Meet hammerhead sharks at dawn (p83)

Ari Atoll
Swim with a whale shark (p83)

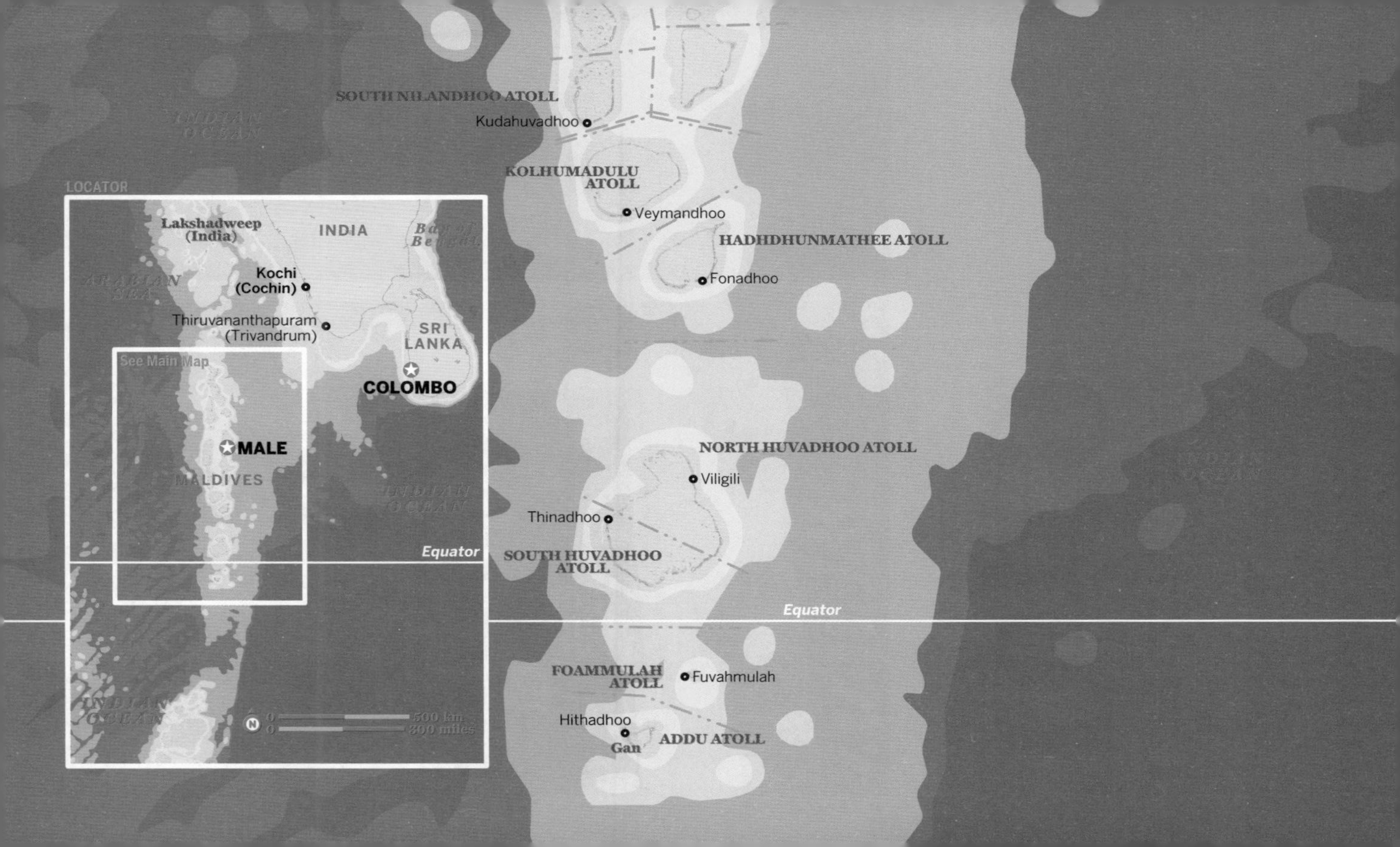

SOUTH NILANDHOO ATOLL
Kudahuvadhoo
KOLHUMADULU ATOLL
Veymandhoo
HADHDHUNMATHEE ATOLL
Fonadhoo
NORTH HUVADHOO ATOLL
Viligili
Thinadhoo
SOUTH HUVADHOO ATOLL
Equator
FOAMMULAH ATOLL
Fuvahmulah
Hithadhoo
Gan
ADDU ATOLL
LOCATOR
Lakshadweep (India)
INDIA
Kochi (Cochin)
Thiruvananthapuram (Trivandrum)
SRI LANKA
COLOMBO
See Main Map
MALE
MALDIVES
Equator
0 500 km
0 300 miles

The Maldives'
Top 9

Male

1 The Maldivian capital (p45) is definitely the best place to get to know locals and see what makes them tick. The brightly painted houses, crowded markets and convivial teashops where you can chat to regulars and share plates of delicious 'short eats' are just some of the highlights of this unusual capital city – and perfectly complement the resort experience.

Male market stall

Breakfast with the Hammers

2 Hammerhead sharks, definitely one of the weirdest-looking creatures in the sea (and that's saying something), can be seen in abundance in Maldivian waters – if you know where to look for them. There are few more thrilling experiences than a dawn dive, descending free fall into the deep blue to 30m, before suddenly coming upon a huge school of hungry hammerhead sharks waiting to be fed. The best place to do this is at the world-famous Hammerhead Point (p83; aka Rasdhoo Madivaru) in Rasdhoo Atoll.

IAN SCOTT/DREAMSTIME.COM ©

JOHN BORTHWICK/GETTY IMAGES ©

R EISELE-REMOVE IT/GETTY IMAGES ©

FELIX HUG/GETTY IMAGES ©

Watch a Bodu Beru Performance

3 Whether you're in a resort or staying on an inhabited island, the cultural highlight of almost any trip to the Maldives is seeing a dance and drum performance (p153) known as *bodu beru,* which means 'big drum' in Dhivehi. These traditional all-male performances are a thrilling and genuine experience, even if they can feel rather contrived in your resort's restaurant. The drum ceremony starts off slowly and builds gradually to an incredible climax, during which some dancers enter a trance-like state.

Take a Seaplane

4 There are few destinations where the mode of transport by which you arrive could be called a highlight, but that's because there are few places in the world where you need seaplanes to reach your hotel. These zippy Twin Otters function like taxis in a country with no roads, and taking off from the water is an unforgettable experience, as is observing the spectacular coral atolls, blue lagoons and tiny desert islands from above.

Stay at a Guesthouse

5 The guesthouse phenomenon in the Maldives has only been around for a few years, and yet it's led to the creation of some truly unique places in which to experience the 'real' Maldives on an inhabited island: interact with locals, eat traditional food and experience something totally different to life in a resort. The best guesthouses are those on remote atolls, far from the modernity of Male, where friendly local families will literally treat you like one of the family, take you to desert islands, let you fish, dive and snorkel.

Learn to Dive

6 You simply *have* to get beneath the water's surface in the Maldives; the corals, tropical fish, sharks, turtles and rays all make up an unforgettably alien world, which is best experienced by diving (p27). All resorts and many guesthouses have diving facilities, and you won't regret deciding to learn here. The Maldives boasts excellent safety standards, modern equipment, passionate and experienced dive staff and – best of all – the water is so warm many people don't even bother diving in a wetsuit.

Be a (Luxurious) Castaway

7 Nearly every resort offers some variation on this theme: you and your partner or family are given a picnic basket (in the most luxurious resorts it may be a full meal set up for you by staff) and dropped off on an uninhabited, pristine island by dhoni. The crew then jump back on the boat and leave you to your own devices on a white-powder beach surrounded by a turquoise lagoon. Explore the island, dine on great food, sunbathe and swim – this is the modern castaway experience.

Swim with a Whale Shark

8 The largest fish in the world, the whale shark (p87) is prevalent in Maldivian waters, especially in the south of Ari Atoll and during a full moon when the currents between the atolls are at their strongest. Swimming with one of these gentle giants is an incredible experience – they average almost 10m in length – and it's also totally safe, as despite their immense size, whale sharks feed only on plankton.

Maafushi

9 Maafushi (p75) is the first inhabited island in the Maldives to become a big traveller centre, with some 30 guesthouses and hotels now operating. It's probably the best place for a cheap beach holiday in the Maldives, with lots of competition and low prices for accommodation, diving, snorkelling and other excursions. There's also a good private beach, which means visitors can swim without offending the local population. What's more, at just a couple of hours away from the international airport, it's also very easy to reach.

Need to Know

For more information, see Survival Guide (p162)

Currency
Maldivian rufiyaa (Rf)

Language
Dhivehi; English is
widely spoken.

Visas
Nobody coming to the
Maldives requires a visa
for a stay of 30 days
or less.

Money
Credit cards can be used
in resorts and most
guesthouses. ATMs are
only reliably found in
Male.

Mobile Phones
Local SIM cards can be
bought in Male or other
inhabited islands, but
not at resorts. Most
phones will automatical-
ly roam in the Maldives.

Time
GMT plus five hours

When to Go

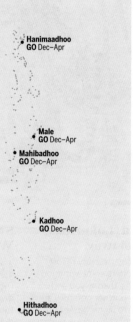

Tropical climate, wet/dry seasons

Hanimaadhoo
GO Dec–Apr

Male
GO Dec–Apr

Mahibadhoo
GO Dec–Apr

Kadhoo
GO Dec–Apr

Hithadhoo
GO Dec–Apr

High Season
(Dec–Feb)

➡ The Maldives
enjoys its best
weather.

➡ Expect little rain,
low humidity and
blue skies.

➡ Christmas and
New Year involve
huge price hikes and
often minimum stays
of five days or more.

Shoulder
(Mar–Apr)

➡ Great weather
continues until the
end of April, when
temperatures are at
their hottest.

➡ The surf season
begins in March
and continues until
October.

➡ Prices jump
during Easter.

Low Season
(May–Nov)

➡ Storms and rain
more likely, but
weather warm and
resorts at their
cheapest.

➡ Prices rise in
August for European
summer holidays.

➡ Marine life is more
varied on the western
side of atolls at this
time.

Websites

Lonely Planet (www.lonely-planet.com/Maldives) Info, bookings, traveller forums.

Visit Maldives (www.visitmaldives.com) Official tourism site.

TripAdvisor (www.tripadvisor.com) Resort reviews.

Minivan News (www.minivannews.com) Balanced English-language newspaper.

Guesthouses in Maldives (www.guesthouses-in-maldives.com) A great resource.

Maldives Directory (www.maldivesdir.com) A useful database of Maldives resources.

Important Numbers

Country code	☑960
International access code	☑00
Ambulance	☑102
Fire	☑118
Police	☑119

Exchange Rates

Australia	A$1	Rf12.63
Euro zone	€1	Rf17.84
Japan	¥100	Rf13.16
New Zealand	NZ$1	Rf12.01
Switzerland	CHF1	Rf17.55
UK	UK£1	Rf23.33
US	US$1	Rf15.34

For current exchange rates, see www.xe.com.

Daily Costs

**Budget:
Less than US$300**

➡ Budget resorts cost US$150 to US$400 per night.

➡ Guesthouses are cheaper at around US$100 per night.

➡ Reach guesthouses cheaply by taking public ferries for US$5 to US$10.

**Midrange:
US$400-850**

➡ Midrange resorts start from US$300 per night.

➡ Full board or all-inclusive options can save money.

➡ Speedboats to resorts cost around US$200.

**Top end:
More than US$850**

➡ Top-end rooms start at US$750.

➡ Seaplane transfers generally cost around US$400 return.

➡ Dine at the best restaurants in Male for around US$20.

What to Bring

As nearly all visitors head directly to their accommodation on small, remote islands, it's important to bring everything you'll need for the duration of your stay. Going to the nearest supermarket to pick up something you've forgotten is not an option, and while all resorts have small shops selling essentials, they're generally overpriced and the selection tends to be limited.

Some obvious things to pack include sunscreen and after-sun products, a sun hat, flippers, mask and snorkel, three-pin UK-style adaptors if you're coming from outside the UK, any birth control or medication you'll need, plenty of reading material and a good pair of UV-blocking sunglasses.

Arriving in Maldives

Male Ibrahim Nasir International Airport

Speedboat Resorts in South and North Male Atoll transfer guests by speedboat (10 to 70 minutes).

Seaplanes Chartered transfers operate daily until around 5pm (seaplanes cannot fly after dark) to resorts outside South and North Male Atoll. Late arrivals need to overnight in Male and take a seaplane the next day.

Male ferry The ferry leaves 24 hours a day to the capital (Rf10, five minutes, every 10 minutes).

Getting Around

Transport in Maldives is either fast and expensive, or reasonably priced and very slow. However, whether it's seaplane, speedboat or public ferry, travelling around is always an exciting experience.

Air Internal flights connect Male to nine regional airstrips at least daily. Chartered seaplanes run by Trans Maldivian Airways collect arrivals at Male Airport and fly them direct to their resorts; a pricey but beautiful and very convenient way to travel.

Boat Most transport in Maldives is by boat, for obvious reasons. Resorts collect guests from Male or regional airstrips by speedboat, a fast and comfortable way to travel. Independent travellers will need to use the slow but cheap public ferry system to get around.

Car Most islands are totally car free, with the exception of Male and a few other larger inhabited islands, where taxis are a good way to get around. On resorts, you'll often be driven to your room in a golf cart.

For much more on **getting around**, see p171

If You Like...

Romance

Cocoa Island by COMO Simple luxury with little fuss, this gorgeous island is perfect for high-end romance. (p80)

Makunudu Island Back-to-nature triumphs in a refreshingly unfancy resort designed for honeymooners. (p69)

Anantara Kihavah Villas Sumptuous rooms and one of the best beaches in the country – heaven for couples. (p100)

Gili Lankanfushi There are few things more romantic than spending the day in your giant over-water villa here. (p72)

Soneva Fushi With stunning beaches, beautiful private villas and thick jungle vegetation, this is a totally romantic destination. (p101)

Luxury

Cheval Blanc Randheli The Louis Vuitton resort that has everyone talking, as well as the highest room rates in the country. (p96)

One & Only Reethi Rah An old time classic, this superlative place is the playground of billionaires and royalty. (p72)

Four Seasons Landaa Giraavaru Less bling and more class, the Four Seasons has the feel of a giant social club. (p99)

Velaa Private Island The personal creation of one individual, VPI effortlessly competes with the best international hotel chains. (p97)

Six Senses Laamu With its wooden structures and sustainable ethos, this is barefoot luxury at its relaxed best. (p113)

Diving & Snorkelling

Equator Village Some of the cheapest and best diving in Maldives is available at this former British naval base. (p119)

Adaaran Select Meedhupparu The remote location in Raa Atoll means that divers have 30 dive sites essentially to themselves. (p98)

Chaaya Lagoon Hakuraa Huraa A remote location means pristine dive sites where you're highly unlikely to be bothered by other divers. (p106)

Chaaya Reef Ellaidhoo Attracts divers with over 100 sites within easy reach, as well as the finest house reef in the country. (p85)

Reveries Diving Village One of the most diving-focused guesthouses in the country, this is a great mixture of diving resort and boutique hotel. (p113)

Surfing

Chaaya Island Dhonveli The most surf-focused resort in the country, Dhonveli has access to perfect left Pasta Point. (p71)

Cokes Surf Shack A popular guesthouse on the island of Thulusdhoo, with access to two great breaks. (p74)

Six Senses Laamu This top end resort is also the best place to access Ying Yang, one of the biggest breaks in Maldives. (p113)

Reveries Diving Village A great base for divers, also excellently located to access six surf spots in Laamu Atoll. (p113)

Family Holidays

Conrad Maldives Rangali Island This mega resort on two islands has everything imaginable to keep kids entertained. (p89)

Four Seasons Landaa Giraavaru High-end option popular with families, with great kids club and numerous activities. (p99)

Kurumba Maldives Set up more like a grand country club, here you'll find a great kids club and boundless entertainment options. (p67)

Shangri-La Villingili Resort & Spa Has a kids club and Cool Zone for teenagers. (p119)

Kuredu Island Resort & Spa
One of the best midrange resorts for families, Kuredu has a great range of activities, a kids club and lots of excursions. (p103)

Good Food

Maalifushi by COMO This brand new luxury resort has some mind-blowingly good food in its many restaurants, including excellent in-villa dining. (p111)

Six Senses Laamu Superb Japanese, Vietnamese and Mediterranean cuisine, and the best breakfast buffet in the country. (p113)

Huvafen Fushi This luxurious island has an enormous range of excellent eating options. (p73)

Jumeirah Vittaveli Whether it's lobster on the beach or fine dining at Finesse, this resort offers top-notch menus. (p79)

One & Only Reethi Rah This gorgeous place has so much going for it, but its cuisine, from Middle Eastern to Japanese, is definitely a highlight. (p72)

Cool Design

W Retreat & Spa This refreshingly modern and chic place redefines the Maldives resort into something contemporary. (p87)

One & Only Reethi Rah Perhaps the best rooms in the country: all the villas look like Balinese palaces. (p72)

Shangri-La Villingili Resort & Spa With water villas twice the size of those normally found in other luxury resorts, this place is a stunner. (p119)

Cheval Blanc Randheli The Jean-Michel Gathy–designed public areas and rooms here are the latest in cutting-edge Maldivian style. (p96)

PLAN YOUR TRIP IF YOU LIKE...

Top: Spa treatments are increasingly popular in the Maldives (p22)
Bottom: Island in Laamu Atoll (p111)

Choosing a Resort

Don't worry about being swayed by the judicious use of Photoshop in brochures – almost every resort in the Maldives will get you a superb beach, amazing weather and turquoise waters overlooked by majestic palms. Indeed, so uniform is the perfection, it's often hard to take memorable photographs here – they all just look like they've been lifted from a holiday brochure. The standard of facilities and accommodation in Maldivian resorts varies enormously, from budget and extremely average accommodation to the best of everything – if you can afford to pay through the nose for it. Your choice of resort or guesthouse is absolutely key to getting the holiday you want. Take plenty of time and weigh up as many options as possible before settling for the place or places you'll book into. There are plenty of factors you need to take into consideration when selecting a resort.

Best Rooms

Jumeirah Vittaveli (p79) Huge and sumptuously furnished villas with enormous outdoor bathrooms, surrounded by lap pools and enjoying direct beach access.

Best Pool

Anantara Kihavah Villas (p100) Simply our favourite pool in the country, long enough for swimming lengths and fun for kids too.

Best Beach

Kanuhura (p103) The endless white-sand beach is unbeatable, and the resort owns a private desert island for you to boat over to for a picnic lunch.

Best Restaurant

Six Senses Laamu (p113) You're spoiled for choice here, but our favourite of Six Senses restaurant is Leaf, where sublime Vietnamese cuisine is served at lunch, and Mediterranean fare is served for dinner.

Atmosphere

Every resort has cultivated a distinct atmosphere to appeal to its guests. Before choosing a resort decide on the type of holiday you want and the atmosphere most conducive to providing it. Honeymooners who find themselves surrounded by package-tour groups and screaming children may quickly come to regret booking into the first resort they looked at. Similarly, divers and surfers may find the social-life vacuum in a resort popular with honeymooners and couples a little claustrophobic after a week on a liveaboard.

Back to Nature

The Maldives has built much of its tourism industry on the desert-island ideal: the fantasy of simplicity, tranquillity, beach and sea. Of course, the fact that many places also provide a butler, a gourmet restaurant and a fleet of staff who cater to your every whim makes the whole experience somewhat more luxurious than being a real castaway. These resorts tend to be well designed, use imported woods and natural fibres and have little or no air-conditioning outside the bedroom. The simplicity of such places (even at top-end resorts, which admittedly add supreme style and comfort to the mix), not to mention their peacefulness and relaxed feel, is what attracts people. These 'no shoes, no news' resorts are great for a romantic break, a honeymoon or total escape.

High Style

Few countries in the world have such a wealth of choice in the luxury market as the Maldives. Most major luxury-hotel brands have or hope to have a presence here, and at times things can look like a never-ending glossy travel magazine, bringing ever higher levels of comfort and pampering.

And the pampering on offer here is almost legendary. You'll have your own *thakuru,* Man Friday or Guest Experience Manager (all various terms for personal butler), who will look after you during your stay. And you'll nearly always have a sumptuous villa stuffed full of beautifully designed furniture and fabrics, a vast, decadent bathroom (often open air) and a private open-air area (in a water villa this is usually a sun deck with a direct staircase into the sea). Now most resorts in this category also include private plunge pools – some big enough to do lengths in, but all a wonderful way to cool off or wash off the salt after a dip in the sea.

Food in these resorts is almost universally top notch. There will be a large choice of cuisine, with European and Asian specialist chefs employed to come up with an amazing array of dishes day and night. Social life will be quiet, and will usually revolve around one of the bars. Most of the market here are honeymooners, couples and families, but kids will certainly not run riot (most resorts impose a limit on the number of children), and even if they do, there will be enough space to get away from them. Despite the general feel being romantic and stylish, activities will not be ignored – everything from diving to water sports and excursions will be well catered for. Essentially, if you can afford this level of accommodation (and you're looking at a minimum of U\$1000 per room per night, plus food), you are guaranteed an amazing time, whatever your interests.

Romance

Romance is big business in the Maldives, where more than a few visitors are on their honeymoon, renewing their vows or just having an indulgent break. Almost anywhere is romantic. That said, the more budget the resort, the more families and groups you'll get, and the intimacy of the romantic experience can be diminished if it's peace, quiet and candlelit dinners you're after. Nonetheless, romance doesn't necessarily mean huge cost. It's hard to think of anywhere more lovely than little Makunudu Island, for example, where there's no TV or loud music, just gorgeously simple and traditional houses dotted along the beach, and vegetation thick with trees planted by past honeymooners. However, the maxim of getting what you pay for is still true here – the loveliest, most romantic resorts are usually not the cheaper ones.

Be aware that you cannot at present get married in the Maldives, although this may change in the near future. However, if you really want to, you can organise non-legally-binding services and effectively have your wedding here even if the legal formalities are completed elsewhere. Nearly all midrange and top-end resorts can organise such ceremonies, so check websites for details and special packages. Honeymooners are often eligible for special deals and some added extras, but you'll need to prove your recent marriage with a certificate and let the resort know in advance that you're newlyweds.

Diving

All resorts have their own diving school and every resort has access to good diving. It's very hard to say that one resort has better diving than another, but when in fact all the sites are shared, but there are a few resorts that have obvious advantages, such as remote Helengeli, which offers access to some 40 dive sites, many of which are not used by any other resorts. You'll find a similar situation in and around Ari Atoll, where the dive sites are excellent, including Kuramathi and Chaaya Reef Ellaidhoo. But above all, divers should go for resorts that are focused on diving, as prices will be lower, and there will be more enthusiasm for the activity than elsewhere.

Ecotourism

Ecotourism can so often be a gimmick that it's important to know who's serious and who's just trying to attract a larger number of visitors. Despite the lip service paid by many resorts, relatively few of them have genuine ecotourism credentials. Look for resorts that offer educational programs, sustainable development, environmentally friendly building practices, minimal use of air-conditioning and electricity in general, and a resort ethos that fosters environmental awareness and care (ie offering you not only Evian when you ask for water, but also water that has been desalinated on-site). The resorts we recommend in this category are leading the way in the use of materials, their interaction with the local ecosystem and the activities they offer guests. Those that are serious about their commitment to ecotourism include Gili Lankanfushi (p72), Soneva Fushi (p101), Rihiveli Beach Resort (p77) and Six Senses Laamu (p113).

Guesthouses

Guesthouses are a relatively new initiative in a country where tourism and the local population were always kept scrupulously apart. There are now scores of these small hotels dotted around the country, and the experience offered here is one totally different to that found in resorts. Forget the infinity pool and cocktails – you're on a dry local island here and swimming costumes aren't culturally acceptable save in a few places with enclosed swimming pools or screened-off beaches – but you can still enjoy the beach on nearby uninhabited islands, do lots of diving, snorkelling, surfing, fishing, island hopping and cultural tourism. This is the best option for anyone who finds being separate from the local population in a self-contained resort an unappealing idea.

Activities

Few people will want to spend an entire holiday sunbathing and swimming, so resorts are careful to provide a program of excursions and activities for guests. Bear in mind that this is the only way you'll be able to leave the island during your stay, public transport from resort islands being nonexistent and opportunities for sightseeing almost as scarce.

While all resorts have a diving centre, the uniformity ends there; you'll have to check to see if the resort you're planning to visit has a water-sports centre or its own spa, organises guided snorkelling, lays on marine biology lectures or morning yoga sessions or has a resident tennis coach. For example, only Kuredu Island Resort (p103), Velaa Private Island (p97) and Shangri-La Villingili (p119) offer golf courses, while Soneva Fushi (p101) is the only resort to offer an observatory.

RESORT TIPS

➡ It's always worth checking a resort website yourself and even contacting the resort for specific, up-to-date information, as things change regularly. Is there construction work happening on the island? Is the spa finished yet? Does it still offer kite-boarding? Also, be aware that many resort websites are not regularly updated. While there are exceptions, it's never a good idea to take the information there as fact – check when the page was last updated and also read up on the resort online.

➡ Check the dive centre website. It might provide a discount if you block book your dives before your arrival. Email them for specific dive information and to check that they will definitely be visiting any site you want to dive at during your stay.

➡ If the trip is a honeymoon, or second honeymoon, or if you will be celebrating an anniversary or birthday, let your resort know – there's usually something laid on in such circumstances. Some resorts require a wedding certificate before they do anything, though.

Top: Resort outdoor dining

Bottom: Water-villa room at Jumeirah Vittaveli Resort (p79)

DAVID EVANS/GETTY IMAGES ©

Day Trips

Day trips from your resort are one of the very few ways you'll be able to see something of the 'real' Maldives occupied by ordinary Maldivians. Even if you are an independent traveller, this is still a good way to see otherwise inaccessible islands.

Almost all the resorts in North and South Male Atolls offer day trips to Male. There's enough to see and enough shopping to make this trip worthwhile, and it's a great way to get a feel for Maldivian culture, as terrifyingly polite resort staff are replaced by a friendly and down-to-earth city populace.

Another popular excursion is a trip to an inhabited island, which allows you to see a small island community, traditional housing, craftwork and lifestyle. The trips inevitably feel rather contrived, but can still be immensely enjoyable depending on how friendly the locals are and how many people are around (with children often in school or studying in Male, and menfolk away for work, some islands feel like ghost towns). While it's often more enjoyable to explore an island on your own, the resort guides will at least know all the locals and can be helpful in making contacts and telling you in detail about local life.

Fishing

Just about any resort will do sunset, sunrise or night-fishing trips, while many resorts can also arrange big-game fishing trips. These work out cheaper if there are several participants, as costs are high: from $450 for a half-day trip for up to four people. Large boats, fully equipped with radar technology, are used to catch dorado, tuna, marlin, barracuda and jackfish among others.

Snorkelling & Diving

All resorts cater for divers and snorkellers, and most organise twice-daily diving excursions and sometimes snorkelling trips too, especially if there's not good snorkelling on the house reef. If you're keen on diving, it's always cheaper to bring your own equipment, including snorkel, mask and fins, plus buoyancy control device (BCD) and dive computer. Most top-end resorts supply free snorkelling equipment to guests, but it normally attracts a charge at budget and midrange places. Dive schools are generally of an exceptionally high safety standard, as regulated by Maldivian laws. Most resorts have at least 10 sites nearby and visit them in rotation. If there's a particular dive site you want to visit, you should contact the dive school at the resort and check it'll be running a trip there during your stay.

Spa Treatments

As a destination that has become synonymous with relaxation, the Maldives unsurprisingly offers a huge array of treatments in purpose-built spas. These include many different types of massage, beauty treatments, Ayurvedic (Indian herbal) medicine, acupuncture and even traditional Maldivian treatments. All midrange and top-end resorts have a spa, and even some of the budget resorts now have them. The best are sometimes booked up in advance, so plan ahead if you're interested in certain treatments. With staff often from Bali, Thailand, India and Sri Lanka, you're in safe (if expensive) hands. Resorts well known for Ayurvedic therapy include Adaaran Select Meedhupparu (p98), Taj Exotica (p81), Vivanta by Taj Coral Reef (p69), Four Seasons Landaa Giraavaru (p99) and Olhuveli Beach & Spa (p79).

Surfing

The best resorts for surfing are Chaaya Island Dhonveli (p71) and Adaaran Select Hudhuran Fushi (p37), which are both blessed with their own surf breaks and are very popular with surfers during the season. The popularity of surfing is increasing in the Maldives, with surfer arrivals going up massively in the past few years. However, it's really only these two resorts that are perfectly located near good breaks, although nearby resorts, such as Four Seasons Kuda Huraa (p73) and Paradise Island (p71) can organise boat trips. Meemu Atoll is also great for surfing, and is largely unvisited by travellers, despite there being two nearby resorts making access fairly easy. Another fantastic option to avoid the crowds and explore a pristine region of the country is to join a 'surfari' – check with your resort or travel agent.

Water Sports

In addition to diving schools, most resorts have a water-sports centre. These vary enormously. Some offer the most basic

RESORT BASICS

On meeting you at the airport, your resort representative will usually take your ticket and/or passport for the duration of your stay, which is quite normal in the Maldives.

Unless you arrive in the late afternoon or evening, you'll soon be transferred to your resort – either by a waiting dhoni, speedboat, airplane or seaplane from the nearby lagoon airport. You may have to wait for other passengers to get through customs. You can use US dollars or euros at the airport cafe, and change cash into rufiyaa at the bank.

Travellers arriving after dark may have to spend a night at the airport hotel or at a hotel in Male; seaplane transfers are not carried out after dark for obvious reasons, and so they generally do not leave Male after 4pm. Speedboat transfers can be done at any time of day or night.

On arrival at the resort you'll be given a drink, asked to fill out a registration form and taken to your room. Resort staff will bring your luggage separately.

Room Types

Most resorts have several types of room, ranging from the cheapest 'Superior Garden Villas' to the 'Deluxe Over-Water Suites'. A 'Garden Villa' will not have a beach frontage, and a 'Water Villa' will be on stilts over the lagoon at a big cost hike.

More expensive rooms tend to be bigger, newer and better finished, and can have a bathtub as well as a shower, a minibar instead of an empty fridge, tea- and coffee-making facilities (even an espresso machine), a sound system and maybe even a Jacuzzi. More and more often in top-end resorts a private plunge pool (or even a lap pool) is part of the set up; these are now de rigeur in newly built resorts.

Seasons & Supplements

High-season room rates are December to March for single/double occupancy. Rates also spike over Easter and in August. The cheapest time to visit the Maldives is from April to July and from September to November.

Extra people can usually share a room, but there's a charge for the extra bed, which varies from resort to resort, as well as additional costs for meals and the obligatory US$8 per person per night 'bed tax', which is collected by the government for each tourist. This was supposed to be retired in 2013, but was still being charged in 2015.

For children two years and younger, usually just the US$8 bed tax is payable. From two to 12 years, the child supplement will be more, though usually less than a full adult rate.

Be aware that most resorts in the Maldives quote their prices exclusive of taxes, which are significant. In general all resorts add on a 10% to 12% service charge as a tip for staff and a 12% general sales tax (GST). Therefore bear these extras in mind when you're totalling up a trip's cost – the 'plus pluses', as they're known, essentially add around an extra 25% of all your resort costs, as they're added to food, drinks, activities and transfers too!

Pricing Periods

Pricing patterns vary with the resort and the demands of its main market – some are incredibly detailed and complex with a different rate every week. The basic pattern is that Christmas–New Year is the peak season, with very high prices, minimum-stay requirements and huge surcharges for the obligatory Christmas and New Year's Eve dinners. Early January to late March is high season, when many Europeans take a winter holiday. The weeks around Easter may attract even higher rates (but not as high as Christmas). From Easter to about mid-July is low season (and the wettest part of the year). July and August is another high season, for the European summer holidays. Mid-September to early December is low season again.

Beach bar at Eriyadu Island (p67)

array of kayaks and windsurfing, while others run the gamut from water skiing to kite-boarding and wakeboarding. The best resorts for sailing and windsurfing have a wide lagoon that's not too shallow, and lots of equipment to choose from. Non-motorised water-sports tend to be free in better resorts, while they're all charged in budget and midrange ones in general. Good resorts for sailing and windsurfing include: Kanuhura (p103), Four Seasons Landaa Giraavaru (p99), Kuredu (p103), Sheraton Maldives Full Moon Resort & Spa (p67), Villingili Resort & Spa (p119), Ayada Maldives (p115), Four Seasons Kuda Huraa (p73), LUX* Maldives (p86), Vilu Reef (p110), W Retreat & Spa (p87), Kurumba Maldives (p67) and Meeru Island Resort (p70).

Food & Drink

What you eat in Maldives varies tremendously, but essentially boils down to your budget and your choice of resort. At the top end, you'll be cooked for by Michelin starred–chefs, while at the lower end the buffet – the standard dining option – is still in evidence, and quality is extremely variable. The usual truism that you get what you pay for is especially relevant here.

Alcohol is also becoming more of a feature at resorts – many have spent years building up wine cellars. Reethi Rah claims to have over 8000 bottles of wine in its cellar, while Huvafen Fushi's wine cellar is a work of art itself, buried deep below the island and hired out for private dinners at great expense.

Meals

Typically, breakfast is a buffet wherever you stay in the Maldives. At the bottom end, there will be a fairly limited selection of cereals, fruit, pastries and yoghurts. At the midrange and top end you'll have an enormous spread, usually including omelette stations, fresh fruit, good coffee, freshly baked pastries, curries, rice dishes, full English-style breakfast, meat platters and oodles of sweet cakes.

In budget resorts, lunch and dinner will usually be a buffet as well. This can quickly become repetitive, and while you'll never go hungry, you may find yourself craving some variety. Some budget resorts have à la carte restaurants where you can dine to have a change of cuisine and scenery – if you're on an all-inclusive deal, meals like this will be charged as extras. However, for the most part there's little or no choice at the budget end. Dinner will usually have the biggest selection, and may be a 'theme night' specialising in regional cuisines such as Italian, Asian, Indian or Maldivian.

If you're in a midrange or top-end resort, you'll have a totally different experience. Almost all resorts in these categories have at least two restaurants, with a few exceptions for small islands where the restaurants are à la carte and have sufficiently long or changing menus to keep you satisfied for a couple of weeks or more. The larger resorts will have multiple choices.

Another alternative to the usual buffet is a 'speciality meal'. This might be a barbecue or a curry night, served on the beach and open to anyone who pays an extra charge. Or it can be a much pricier private dinner for two in romantic surroundings – on an uninhabited island, on the beach, or on a sandbank a short ride from the resort island. Most resorts will do special meals on request, and nearly all top-end places offer in-room dining for those enjoying themselves too much to leave their villas.

Meal Plans

Many guests are on full-board packages that include accommodation and all meals. Others take a half-board package, which includes breakfast and dinner, and pay extra for lunch. Some resorts offer a bed-and-breakfast plan, and guests pay separately for lunch and dinner. The advantage of not paying for all your meals in advance is that you permit yourself the freedom to vary where you eat (assuming your resort has more than one restaurant). However, at good resorts your full-board plan is usually transferable, meaning you can eat a certain amount at other restaurants, or at least get a big discount on the à la carte prices.

Room-only deals are also sometimes available, but they're rarely a great idea. Never underestimate the sheer expense of eating à la carte in the Maldives at any level, although at the top end it's positively outrageous – think US$75 per head without alcohol for a decent lunch.

Self-catering is of course not possible, and there's nothing worse than being unable to eat properly due to financial constraints. Unless you're very comfortable financially and want to eat in a variety of different places, it's definitely a good idea to book full-board or at least half-board meal plans.

All-inclusive plans are some of the best value of all, although in general they're associated with the core package-tourist market and tend to be available only in budget resorts. These typically include all drinks (non-brand-name alcohol, soft drinks and water) and some activities and water sports/diving thrown in for good measure. Always investigate carefully exactly what's on offer meal-wise before you make a decision – the meal plan can make an expensive package worthwhile or a cheap one a rip-off. One upmarket all-inclusive resort is Lily Beach (p89) in Ari Atoll, where you'll get good wines and brand-name spirits for your (not inconsiderable) daily rate.

HOW TO SPOT A TOP RESORT

In case you have any doubts about where you're staying, this checklist should help you confirm you're in the very smartest of Maldivian resorts:

➡ You will not be given a fruit cocktail on arrival, but rather an iced ginger tea, homemade ice cream or fresh melon juice served in a dainty earthenware cup.

➡ The staff line up on the jetty when you arrive and you have to work the line shaking their hands and feeling like a minor royal.

➡ You have your own lap pool so you don't have to mix with the hoi polloi in the main one.

➡ You have more towels than you know what to do with in your room, and more brand-name bath products than you can actually be bothered to swipe.

➡ Staff members you have never even seen magically address you by your first name.

➡ Every time you leave your room a fleet of staff will swarm in to clean it.

Luxuries

You've come to the right place if this is your main interest. The Maldives' top-end resorts (and even some of its midrange options) offer an eye-watering range of treatments, pampering and general luxury.

Currently indispensible in the luxury industry is the personal *thakuru*, or butler, otherwise known as a 'man Friday' or 'villa host'. The *thakuru* is assigned to you throughout your stay. He's your point of contact for all small things (restocking the minibar, reserving a table for dinner), but given that one *thakuru* will often be looking after up to 10 rooms at a time, the term 'personal' is pushing it a bit, especially when even in the best hotels in the country there are often language problems and some service issues.

The home of pampering at most resorts is the spa. Until recently they were considered optional for resorts, whereas now they are usually at the very centre of the luxury experience. Expect to pay from about US$100 for a simple massage at a budget or midrange place to US$500 for a long session of pampering at a top-end resort.

Beaches

Very few resorts in the Maldives do not have an amazing beach. Some beaches suffer a great deal from erosion, but resorts work very hard to redress this with sandbags and seawalls in certain places. These can of course be unsightly, but they are necessary to hold the islands' beaches in place. Obviously, the more expensive the resort, the more effort is made to ensure that sandbags are never visible

For the record, here are a list of our favourite beaches in the country: Anantara Kihavah Villas (p100), Sun Siam Iru Fushi Maldives (p96), Kanuhura (p103), One & Only Reethi Rah (p72), Kuredu Island Resort & Spa (p103), Soneva Fushi (p101), Reethi Beach (p99), Coco Palm Dhuni Kolhu (p99), Eriyadu Island Resort (p67), Angsana Ihuru (p70), Bandos (p71), Baros (p74), Banyan Tree Vabbinfaru (p74), Gili Lankanfushi (p72), Rihiveli (p77), Paradise Island (p71), Hideaway Beach Resort & Spa (p92), W Retreat & Spa (p87), Veligandu Island Resort & Spa (p86), Vilu Reef (p110), Huvafen Fushi (p73) and Conrad Maldives Rangali Island (p89). This doesn't mean that resorts not on this list don't make the grade – these are just our very top choices!

Children

If you're bringing children to the Maldives, it's very important to get your choice of resort right, as only some resorts have kids clubs or babysitters available, and activities for older children can be limited at resorts more used to welcoming honeymooning couples. If you aren't looking for kids clubs and your offspring are happy to spend the day on the beach, then almost every resort will be suitable. Note that Komandoo Island Resort doesn't accept children aged under six and W Retreat & Spa doesn't accept children under 12.

In general kids will love the Maldives, although more than a week might be pushing it unless you're staying in a big family resort where there are plenty of other children for them to play with and lots of activities. Nowadays nearly all top-end resorts have kids clubs, and these can be impressive places, with their own pools and a host of activities, which mean parents can drop off kids (usually under 12) at any time, for free during the day.

Surfing off Hudhuran Fushi (p37)

Plan Your Trip

Diving, Snorkelling & Surfing

Unless you explore the magical world beneath the water in Maldives, you're seeing just one part of this incredibly diverse country. Glance into the deep blue all around and you'll see why Maldives is a favourite destination for divers from around the world.

Top Diving Sites

These are some of the best dive sites in Maldives:

Bodu Hithi Thila (p65), North Male Atoll

British Loyalty Wreck (p118), Addu Atoll

Dhidhdhoo Beyru (p83), Ari Atoll

Embudhoo Express (p76), South Male Atoll

Fish Head (p83), Ari Atoll

Fushifaru Thila (p103), Lhaviyani Atoll

Guraidhoo Kandu (p76), South Male Atoll

Halaveli Wreck (p83), Ari Atoll

Hammerhead Point (p83), Rasdhoo Atoll

Hanifaru Huraa (p98), Baa Atoll

Helengeli Thila (p65), North Male Atoll

HP Reef (p66), North Male Atoll

Kakani Thila (p99), Baa Atoll

Kuredhoo Express (p102), Lhaviyani Atoll

Maa Kandu (p119) & **Kuda Kandu** (p119), Addu Atoll

Maaya Thila (p83), Ari Atoll

Manta Reef (p83), Ari Atoll

Shark Point (p119), Addu Atoll

Diving in Maldives

Taking the plunge into the deep blue is one of the most exciting things imaginable and the rewards are massive, especially in the Maldives, which is rightly known as a world-class scuba-diving destination. The enormous variety of fish life is amazing, and there's a good chance you'll see some of the biggest marine creatures – a close encounter with a giant manta or a whale shark is unforgettable.

Where to Dive

There are hundreds of recognised and named dive sites, with dozens accessible from nearly every resort. In general there are four types of dive sites in the Maldives.

Reefs Along the edges of the reef, where it slopes into the deep water, is the best part of the reef to dive on. There's lots of life, including small tropical fish, and bigger creatures often swim by.

Kandus These are channels between islands, reefs or atolls. The strong current makes them a breeding ground for plankton, which attracts whale sharks, and they're also a place where soft corals thrive.

Thilas & Giris Thiras are coral formations that rise from the atoll floor and reach to between 5m and 15m before the surface of the water, while a giri rises almost to the surface. Both brim with life.

Wrecks Maldives' treacherous shallows have made it a rich place to do wreck dives, even if most of those regularly visited are purposely sunk craft where coral has subsequently grown.

Learning to Dive

Diving is not difficult, but it requires some knowledge and care. It doesn't require great strength or fitness, although if you can do things with minimum expenditure of energy, your tank of air will last longer.

There's a range of courses, from an introductory dive in a pool or lagoon to an open-water course that gives an internationally recognised qualification. Beyond that, there are advanced and speciality courses, and courses that lead to divemaster and instructor qualifications. Courses in the Maldives are not a bargain, but they're no more expensive than learning at home and this way you are assured of high standards, good equipment and extremely pleasant conditions. On the other hand, if you do a course at home, you'll have more time for actual diving when you get to the Maldives.

The best option for learners is to do an open-water referral course in their home country (ie all the theory and basics in the pool), allowing you to complete the course in the Maldives in just two days rather than the four or five needed for the full course. After all, you didn't fly halfway around the world to sit in a room watching a PADI DVD, did you? If you do this, ensure you have all your certification from the referral course with you; otherwise you'll have to start from scratch.

If you're at all serious about diving, you should do an open-water course. This requires nine dives, usually five in sheltered water and four in open water, as well as classroom training and completion of a multiple-choice test. The cost in the Maldives is from US$500 to US$850. Sometimes the price is all-inclusive, but there are often a few extra charges. You can do the course in as little as five days, or take your time and spread it over a week or two. Don't try it on a one-week package – transfers and jet lag will take a day or so, and you shouldn't dive within 24 hours before flying. Besides, you'll want to do some recreational dives to try out your new skills.

The next stage is an advanced open-water course, which involves five dives (including one night dive) and costs from US$350 to US$500, depending on the dive school. Then there are the speciality courses in night diving, rescue diving, wreck diving, nitrox diving and so on.

Dive Schools & Operators

Every resort has a professional diving operation and can run courses for beginners, as well as dive trips and advanced technique courses that will challenge even the most experienced diver. The government requires that all dive operations maintain high standards, and all of them are affiliated with one or more of the international diving accreditation organisations.

Certificates

When you complete an open-water course, you receive a certificate that is recognised by diving operators all over the world.

Diving instruction, Ari Atoll (p82)

Certificates in the Maldives are generally issued by the Professional Association of Diving Instructors (PADI), the largest and the best-known organisation, but certificates from Confédération Mondiale des Activités Subaquatiques (CMAS; World Underwater Federation), Scuba Schools International (SSI) and a number of other organisations are also acceptable.

Diving Safaris

On a diving safari, a dozen or so divers cruise the atolls in a live-aboard boat fitted out for the purpose. You can stop at your pick of the dive sites, visit uninhabited islands and local villages, find secluded anchorages and sleep in a compact cabin. If you've had enough diving, you can fish, snorkel or swim off the boat.

The massive expansion in the market for safari cruises has meant an increasingly sleek approach from the tour companies that run them. A typical, modern boat is air-conditioned and spacious, and serves varied and appetising meals. It should have hot water, a sun deck, fishing and diving gear, a mobile phone, a full bar, a DVD player and cosy, comfortable cabins.

REINHARD DIRSCHERL/GETTY IMAGES ©

DIVING SEASONS

January to April Generally considered the best months for diving, with fine weather and good visibility.

May and June Can have unstable weather – storms and cloudy days are common until September.

October and November Tend to have calmer, clearer weather, but visibility can be slightly reduced because of abundant plankton in the water. Some divers like this period because many large fish, such as whale sharks and mantas, come into the channels to feed on the plankton.

December Can have rough, windy weather and rain.

Diving course at Meemu Atoll (p105)

Costs start at around US$100 per person per day, including the US$8 per day per bed tax and all meals, plus roughly US$60 per day for diving trips. There's usually a minimum daily (or weekly) charge for the whole boat, and the cost per person is lower if there are enough passengers to fill the boat. You'll be charged extra for drinks, which are priced comparably to most resorts.

The most basic boats are large dhonis with a small galley and communal dining area, two or three cramped cabins with two berths each, and a shared shower and toilet. The bigger, better boats have air-conditioning, more spacious accommodation, and a toilet and shower for each cabin.

Choosing a Safari Boat

There are over 100 safari boats operating in the Maldives, so you'll need to do some research. When you're considering a safari-boat trip, ask the operator about the following:

➡ Boat size – Generally speaking, bigger boats will be more comfortable, and therefore more expensive, than smaller boats. Most boats have about 12 berths or less. Few boats have more than 20 berths, and those that do may not be conducive to the camaraderie you get with a small group.

➡ Cabin arrangements – Can you get a two-berth cabin (if that's what you want)? How many cabins/people are sharing a bathroom?

➡ Comforts – Does the boat have air-con, hot water and desalinated water available 24 hours?

➡ Companions – Who else will be on the trip, what language do they speak, have they done a safari trip before? What are their interests: diving, sightseeing, fishing, surfing?

➡ Food and drink – Can you be catered for as a vegetarian or vegan? Is there a bar serving alcohol, and if so, how much is a beer and a bottle of wine etc?

➡ Recreation – Does the boat have iPod jacks, fishing tackle or a sun deck? Does the boat have sails or is it propelled by motor only?

Safari Boat Operators

Safari boats often change ownership, or get refitted or acquire a new name. The skipper, cook and divemaster can change too, so it's hard to make firm recommendations. The following boats have a good reputation, but

⇒ **MV Carina** (www.seamaldives.com.mv) Boat 33m, 11 cabins, 33 berths, hot water.

⇒ **Sting Ray** (www.maldivesboatclub.com.mv) Boat 31m, nine cabins, 22 berths, hot water.

⇒ **Sultan of Maldives** (www.sultansof theseas.com) Boat 30m, eight cabins, 16 berths, hot water.

Equipment

Dive schools in the Maldives can rent out all diving gear, but most divers prefer to have some of their own equipment. It's best to have your own mask, snorkel and fins, which you can also use for snorkelling. The tank and weight belt are always included in the cost of a dive, so you don't need to bring them.

Wetsuit

The water may be warm (27°C to 30°C) but a wetsuit is often preferable for comfortable diving. A 3mm suit should be adequate, but 5mm is preferable if you want to go deep or dive more than once per day. Alternatively, it's possible to dive in a T-shirt if you don't feel the cold too much.

Regulator & BCDs

Many divers have their own regulator (the mouth piece you breathe through), with which they are familiar and therefore confident about using. BCDs (Buoyancy Control Devices) are the vests that can be controlled to inflate and deflate and thus increase or decrease your buoyancy, a vital tool for safe diving. Both pieces of equipment are usually included in full equipment packages, though serious divers will usually bring their own.

Dive Computer

These are now compulsory in the Maldives. They're available for rent, for US$5 to US$10 per dive, or as part of a complete equipment package. Again, many serious divers have their own that they bring with them.

Logbook

You'll need this to indicate to divemasters your level of experience, and to record your latest dives, which are then authenticated by the divemaster and stamped by the school.

Other items you might need are an underwater torch (especially for cave and night dives), a waterproof camera,

Dhoni at pier with coral reef in the foreground

there are many others offering decent facilities and services. The boats listed here all have a bar on board, oxygen for emergencies, and some diving equipment for rent. Universal's *Atoll Explorer* is like a mini cruise ship with a swimming pool on deck, while the *Four Seasons Explorer* is the most luxurious and expensive. The official Maldives tourism website (www.visitmaldives.com) has reasonably up-to-date details on almost every safari and cruise boat.

⇒ **Adventurer 2** (www.maldivesdiving.com) Boat 31m, eight cabins, 20 berths, hot water.

⇒ **Atoll Explorer** (www.atollexplorer.co) Boat 50m, 20 cabins, 40 berths, hot water.

⇒ **Dive Masters** (www.guraabu.com.mv) Boat 30m, eight cabins, 19 berths, hot water.

⇒ **Eagle Ray** (www.maldivesboatclub.com) Boat 26m, seven cabins, 14 berths, hot water.

⇒ **Four Seasons Explorer** (www.fourseasons.com/maldivesfse) Boat 39m, 11 cabins, 22 berths, hot water and ultimate luxury.

⇒ **Gulfaam** (www.voyagesmaldives.com) Boat 20m, five cabins, 12 berths.

⇒ **Manta Cruise** (www.tripconcept.com) Boat 31m, nine cabins, 20 berths, hot water.

MICHAEL AW/GETTY IMAGES ©

Above: Diving among pennant butterflyfish

Left: Manta rays

a compass, and a safety buoy or balloon, most of which are available for rental. Some things you won't need are a spear gun, as spear-fishing is prohibited, and diving gloves, which are discouraged since you're not supposed to touch anything anyway.

Diving Costs

The cost of diving varies between resorts, and depends on whether you need to rent equipment. A single dive, with only tank and weights supplied, runs from US$50 to US$120, but is generally around US$60 (night dives cost more). If you need to rent a regulator and a BCD as well, a dive will cost from US$50 to US$150. Sometimes the full-equipment price includes mask, snorkel, fins, dive computer and pressure gauge, but they can cost extra. A package of 10 dives will cost roughly from US$300 to US$600, or US$400 to US$700 with equipment rental. Other possibilities are five-, 12- and 15-dive packages, and packages that allow you as many dives as you want within a certain number of consecutive days.

The best diving operators will bill you at the end of your stay, having worked out which tariff is most economical for you based on the diving you've done. In addition to the dive cost, there is a charge for using a boat, which can be as much as US$20 per dive. There may also be a service charge of 10%, plus a general sales tax of 12% if diving is billed to your room, so the prices do add up. Ideally book your dives ahead of time, confirming the total price, and shop around between resorts to find the best deals.

Marine Environment Protection

The waters of the Maldives may seem pristine but development and commercial activities have had adverse effects on the marine environment. The Maldivian government recognises that the underwater world is a major attraction, and has imposed many restrictions and controls on fishing, coral mining and tourism operations. Twenty-five Protected Marine Areas have been established, and these are subject to special controls, while the country's first ever National Marine Park is being created in Noonu Atoll at present, although progress is slow.

The following rules are considered necessary for conservation, and most of them apply equally to snorkellers and divers.

REEFS IN BRIEF

An overview of some of the best and most popular reefs in the country:

REEF	ATOLL	REEF TYPE	PAGE
Banana Reef	North Male	reef & kandu	66
Devana Kandu	Vaavu	kandu & thila	105
Embudhoo Express	South Male	kandu	76
Fotteyo	Vaavu	kandu	105
Fushifaru Thila	Lhaviyani	kandu & thila	103
Kuda Giri	South Male	giri & wreck	76
Kuda Kandu	Addu	kandu	119
Kuredhoo Express	Lhaviyani	kandu	102
Maa Kandu	Addu	reef & kandu	119
Macro Spot	Dhaalu	giri	109
Manta Reef	Ari	reef & kandu	83
Milaidhoo Reef	Baa	kandu	98
Orimas Thila	Ari	thila	83
Panetone	Ari	kandu	85
Rakeedhoo Kandu	Vaavu	kandu	105
Rasdhoo Madivaru	Ari	outer-reef slope	83
Two Brothers	Faafu	giri	107
Vaadhoo Caves	South Male	kandu	76

PLAN YOUR TRIP DIVING, SNORKELLING & SURFING

Snorkelling off Kurumba Island (p67)

➡ Do not use anchors on the reef, and take care not to ground boats on coral. Encourage dive operators and regulatory bodies to establish permanent moorings at popular dive sites.

➡ Avoid touching living marine organisms with your body or dragging equipment across the reef. Polyps can be damaged by even the gentlest contact.

➡ Never stand on corals, even if they look solid and robust. If you must hold on to prevent being swept away in a current, hold on to dead coral.

➡ Be conscious of your fins. Even without contact the surge from heavy fin strokes near the reef can damage delicate organisms. When treading water in shallow reef areas, take care not to kick up clouds of sand. Settling sand can easily smother the delicate organisms of the reef.

➡ Collecting lobster or shellfish is prohibited, as is spearfishing. Removing any coral or shells, living or dead, is against the law. All shipwreck sites are protected by law.

➡ Take home all your rubbish and any litter you may find as well. Plastics in particular are a serious threat to marine life. Turtles can mistake plastic for jellyfish and eat it. Don't throw cigarette butts overboard.

➡ Resist the temptation to feed fish. You may disturb their normal eating habits, encourage aggressive behaviour or feed them food that is detrimental to their health.

➡ Practise and maintain proper buoyancy control. Major damage can be done by divers descending too fast and colliding with the reef.

➡ Take great care in underwater caves. Spend as little time within them as possible as your air bubbles may be caught within the roof and thereby leave previously submerged organisms high and dry. Taking turns to inspect the interior of a small cave will lessen the chances of damaging contact.

Snorkelling

Snorkelling is the first step into seeing a different world. Anyone who can swim can do it, it's cheap (and often free) to use the equipment and the rewards are immediately evident. The colours of the fish and coral are far better at shallow depths, because water absorbs light. This means a visual feast awaits any snorkeller on any decent reef.

Paddling out to catch a wave

Surfing

Surfing has been slow to take off in the Maldives, but in recent years, particularly since the development of independent tourism, there's been a strong growth in surfer numbers. There's some great surf throughout the country, although breaks are generally only surfable from March to November.

The period of the southwest monsoon (May to November) generates the best waves, but March and April are also good and have the best weather. June can have bad weather and storms, and is not great for boat trips, but it is also a time for big swells. The best breaks occur on the outer reefs on the southeast sides of the atolls, but only where a gap in the reef allows the waves to wrap around.

North Male Atoll

This is where the best-known breaks are, and they can get a bit crowded, especially if there are several safari boats in the vicinity.

➡ **Chickens** A left-hander that sections when small, but on a bigger swell and a higher tide it all comes together to make a long and satisfying wave. It's named for the old poultry farm onshore, not because of any reaction to the conditions here.

➡ **Cola's** A heavy, hollow, shallow right-hander; when it's big, it's one of the best breaks in the area. This is a very thick wave breaking hard over a shallow reef, so it's definitely for experienced, gutsy surfers only. Named for the Coca-Cola factory nearby on the island of Thulusdhoo, it's also called Cokes.

➡ **Honky's** During its season, this is the best wave in the Maldives. It's a super-long, wally

Where to Snorkel

Usually an island is surrounded firstly by a sand-bottomed lagoon, and then by the reef flat *(faru),* a belt of dead and living coral covered by shallow water. At the edge of the reef flat is a steep, coral-covered slope that drops away into deeper water. These reef slopes are the best areas for snorkelling – around a resort island this is called the 'house reef'. The slope itself can have interesting features such as cliffs, terraces and caves, and there are clearly visible changes in the coral and marine flora as the water gets deeper. You can see both the smaller fish, which frequent the reef flats, and sometimes much larger animals that live in the deep water between the islands but come close to the reefs to feed. You can also take a boat from your resort to other snorkelling sites around the atoll.

The best resorts for snorkelling have an accessible house reef around at least part of the island, where deep water is not far offshore. There are usually channels you can swim through to the outer-reef slope. To avoid grazing yourself or damaging the coral, always use these channels rather than trying to find your own way across the reef flat.

SNORKELLING SAFELY

Don't snorkel alone, and always let someone else know where and when you'll be snorkelling. Colourful equipment or clothing will make you more visible. Beware of strong currents or rough conditions – wind chop and large swells can make snorkelling uncomfortable or even dangerous. In open water, carry a safety balloon and whistle to alert boats to your presence.

Surf Breaks

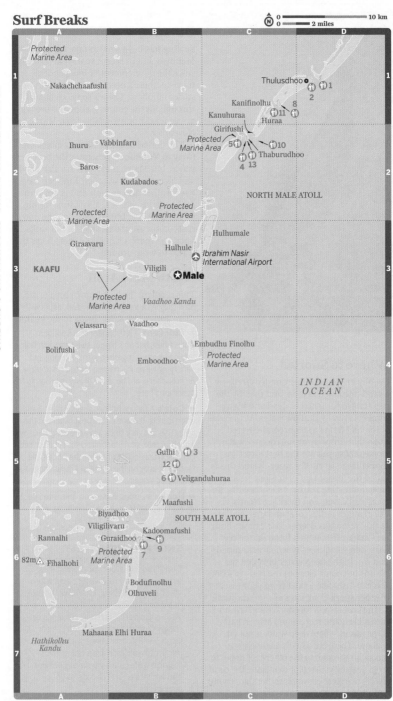

Surf Breaks

lefthander that wraps almost 90 degrees and can nearly double in size by the end section.

➜ **Jailbreaks** A right-hander that works best with a big swell, when the three sections combine to make a single, long, perfect wave. There used to be a prison on the island, hence the name.

➜ **Lohi's** A solid left-hander that usually breaks in two sections, but with a big enough swell and a high enough tide the sections link up.

➜ **Pasta Point** A perfect left that works like clockwork on all tides. There's a long outside wall at the take-off point, jacking into a bowling section called the 'macaroni bowl'. On big days the break continues to another section called 'lock jaws', which grinds into very shallow water over the reef. It's easily reached from the shore at the Chaaya Island Dhonveli resort, whose guests have exclusive use of this break.

➜ **Piddlies** A slow, mellow, mushy right-hander, a good Malibu wave. It's also called Ninja's because of its appeal to Japanese surfers. It's off the island of Kanifinolhu.

➜ **Sultan's** This is a classic right-hand break, and the bigger the swell, the better it works. A steep outside peak leads to a super-fast wall and then an inside section that throws right out, and tubes on every wave.

South Male Atoll

The breaks in South Male Atoll are smaller than those in North Male Atoll and generally more fickle.

➜ **Guru's** A nice little left off the island of Gulhi; it's good for manoeuvres and aerials when conditions are good.

➜ **Kate's** A small left-hander, rarely more than a metre.

➜ **Last Stops** This is a bowly right-hander breaking over a channel reef. It's a Protected Marine Area, and can get very strong currents when the tides are running.

➜ **Natives** A small right-hander, rarely more than a metre.

➜ **Quarters** Another small right-hander, rarely more than a metre.

Resort-Based Surfing

The most accessible surf breaks are in the southeastern part of North Male Atoll. Half a dozen resorts and a few guesthouses are within a short boat ride, but check with them if you plan to surf, as only a few of them cater for surfers by providing regular boat service to the waves.

Chaaya Island Dhonveli (p71) is the resort that's best set up for surfers – the reliable waves of the 'house break', Pasta Point, are just out the back door, while Sultan's and Honky's are close by. A surfside bar provides a great view of the action. Surfing packages here include unlimited boat trips to the other local breaks with surf guides who know the conditions well, leaving and returning on demand.

Adaaran Select Hudhuran Fushi, a few kilometres northeast of Dhonveli, is a bigger, more expensive resort with more facilities and it also has its own, exclusive surf break at the southern tip of the island. A bar and a viewing terrace overlook the wave, which has hosted international surfing competitions.

Outer Atolls

Only a few areas have the right combination of reef topography and orientation to swell and wind direction. Laamu and Addu both have surfable waves on occasions, Laamu in particular has regular surf visitors staying at Reveries Diving Village (p113) and Six Senses Laamu (p113).

South of Male, Meemu Atoll has several excellent surf breaks on its eastern edge including Veyvah Point, Boahuraa Point and Mulee Point, which are gradually being explored by more adventurous surfers.

In the far south, Gaaf Dhaal has a series of reliable breaks that are accessed by safari boats in season. From west to east, the named breaks are Beacons, Castaways, Blue Bowls, Five Islands, Two Ways (also called Twin Peaks; left and right), Love Charms, Antiques and Tiger.

Plan Your Trip

Independent Travel

A mini-revolution has occurred in Maldivian travel in the past few years, stemming from the 2009 decisions of the Nasheed government to lift all travel restrictions on foreigners, allow the building of hotels on inhabited islands and create a national ferry network. These three factors have combined to mean that Maldives is for the first time open for business as an independent travel destination. Despite the change of government since then – and the far less liberal approach to integration of tourists with the local population – the genie is now out of the bottle, and there seems to be no going back.

Best Islands for Independent Travellers

Maafushi (South Male Atoll)

The centre of the Maldivian independent travel scene has lots of accommodation options, a good beach and low diving and excursion prices.

Thulusdhoo (North Male Atoll)

A popular destination for surfers with two excellent breaks; also easily accessible from Male.

Haa Dhaalu (Northern Atolls)

This remote, totally undeveloped island is a great place to see life on a traditional Maldivian island.

Fuvahmulah (Southern Atolls)

An interesting combination of urban island and remote community, Fuvahmulah also has some excellent beaches.

Gan (Laamu, Southern Atolls)

Connected to three other islands by a causeway and itself the largest single island in Maldives, Gan offers lots to see and do and a great diving guesthouse to boot.

A Total Rethink

Maldivian tourism developed in a very unusual way. From the inception of the first resorts in the 1970s, the government ensured that the devout and conservative local population was kept entirely separate from the alcohol-drinking, bikini-wearing Westerners frolicking on the beaches. Amazingly, until 2009, a permit was needed for foreigners to stay overnight anywhere outside a resort island or the capital, meaning that the only contact that most island populations had with the outside world were the occasional tour group from a nearby resort visiting to buy souvenirs before disappearing back to the infinity pool. Now tourists are free to travel and overnight wherever they please, so options beyond the resorts are enormous.

While this is exciting, it's not totally problem free. The Maldives isn't overflowing with great sights or cultural events to attend – indeed, save the incredible underwater world and various water-sports there's very little to do here except sunbathe and enjoy the beauty and tranquillity of the islands, and even this has to be done in accordance with fairly strict local customs. Yet for those who itch to enjoy the magnificent snorkelling, beaches, diving, surfing and fishing of the Maldives, but can't imagine anything worse than being confined to a resort, your hour to visit the country has finally come.

The National Ferry Network

Another persistent problem facing independent travellers was always the lack of transport infrastructure in a country where even the shortest journey must be done by boat. While there have always been public dhoni ferries connecting the islands, their timetables were guesswork and journeys achingly slow, so it was totally unrealistic for most people to journey around the country this way. Now there is a national ferry network based on Male and in the individual atoll capitals that somewhat regularly (and cheaply) connects all the inhabited islands in the country. Timetables can still be infuriatingly difficult to obtain, but as in most cases you'll be travelling from one guesthouse to another, staff will be able to tell you what time the ferries go and from where.

The ferries themselves remain as slow as ever, and you still need to give yourself plenty of time to get around: while most places in the central atolls have connections to Male daily except Fridays, local ferries that connect inhabited islands within the atolls themselves normally only run every other day.

Taking a local ferry is a fascinating cultural experience, and you'll often find yourself the only non-Maldivian on the creaking old dhonis and *vedhis* (large dhonis) that make the journeys between islands and atolls – a great way to meet people and get a feel for local life.

Travelling by ferry is remarkably cheap in the Maldives. Short journeys within an atoll cost only Rf20, rising to Rf53 for longer journeys between atolls, while even huge inter-atoll trips will set you back only Rf100 (around US$7).

Ferry schedules for planning your journey into the atolls from Male can be found at www.mtcc.com.mv. Bear in mind that it may take you 24 to 48 hours to reach far-flung destinations, often involving an overnight in Male or an atoll capital, depending on where you're heading.

Arriving by Air

The domestic air network in Maldives has improved dramatically in the past few years, with several new airports opening to make access to the outer atolls far easier. Maldivian and FlyMe are the two domestic airlines, and there's also Maldivian Air Taxi, which operates sea plane charters – a good option if you're travelling in a group and keen to get somewhere really remote.

LOCAL CUSTOMS & HOW TO AVOID CAUSING OFFENCE

When you decide to travel independently outside the resorts, it's important to realise that you're entering a very conservative Muslim country. You will be visiting the country on the locals' terms, and so should respect this. Maldivians are tolerant people, but even if nothing is said overtly, dressing in ways that they consider immodest (particularly for women), will definitely cause offence or unease.

Of course in places such as Maafushi, where the island is almost totally reliant on tourism, these strictures are not so absolute, but if you are staying on a small island with just one guesthouse, and are one of the few foreigners to visit, it's doubly important to be sensitive to your environment. This means that women should wear long skirts, cover their shoulders and avoid low-cut tops. Men get away with showing more flesh: shorts are totally fine, but don't walk about bare-chested. Beaches on inhabited islands cannot be swum at in the normal way – a woman stripping down to a swimming costume or a bikini, for example, would be a big scandal: when women swim at all, they do so fully clothed, and even men wear T-shirts. Some islands now have enclosed foreigner beaches where you can swim just as you would anywhere else in the world, but these are still relatively rare. For this reason, guesthouses are very focused on day trips to uninhabited islands where tourists can strip down without fear of offending.

DRY ISLANDS

Travelling independently among the inhabited islands of the Maldives means that you'll need to be prepared to adapt to local standards of dress and behaviour, many aspects of which don't exactly gel with most people's idea of a holiday. Perhaps the most restrictive of all is the total lack of alcohol anywhere in the country outside the resorts. You can't even bring alcohol with you, as its import is banned and all luggage is X-rayed on arrival. You'll be limited to widely available non-alcoholic beer for the duration of your stay, unless you're lucky and a passing live-aboard dive boat is accessible: this is one legal way to have an evening of drinking when you're staying on a local island, and live-aboards often call guesthouses to let them know they're nearby in case any guests would like to be picked up. Another, far pricier option, is arranging with a nearby resort to come for the day, or for the evening just for drinks. With increased independent traveller numbers, many resorts – particularly those in South Male Atoll, get a lot of business from independent travellers who want a day at the resort and the alcohol privileges this entails.

Island Guesthouses

There is an ever-growing number of independently run guesthouses in the villages and towns that make up the Maldives beyond the resorts. These are most prevalent in the atolls near to the capital, making a ferry ride from Male a maximum of three or four hours, although they can be found as far away as Haa Dhaalu Atoll, on the island of Hanimaadhoo, an hour's flight north of the capital.

In general the guesthouses are similar. They tend to be modest and fairly small (normally between four and six rooms), but comfortable, aiming at budget and mid-range travellers. They generally offer full-board accommodation (usually as there are few or no other suitable eating options on the island) and a full list of excursions and activities to ensure that boredom doesn't encroach. The latter is important, as there is often relatively little to do on a small, conservative island.

Activities are pretty similar across the country: desert-island visits, beach barbecues, snorkelling, diving and fishing expeditions. Staff members at guesthouses tend to be a highlight. Young, enthusiastic and entrepreneurial, they are pioneers of local tourism and, for the most part, speak great English and have a real passion for showing foreigners the very best of their country.

Many guesthouses are still strangers to the internet, and many emails can go unanswered. For easy booking, try www. guesthouses-in-maldives.com, a website that arranges stays on local islands with guesthouses for you, and who offer some good package deals, including help with your transfers.

Where to Go

While essentially the islands of Maldives are extremely similar to one another, that doesn't mean that it's not going to make a difference where you go as an independent traveller. Most travellers head instinctively to the popular traveller island of Maafushi, as it's close to Male and reachable by daily or twice-daily ferry. Indeed this is probably the best choice if you want a budget sun, sand and diving holiday with plenty of other travellers around, and lots of competition between hotels, ensuring some of the lowest hotel prices in the country.

However, Maafushi is probably not the bet if you want to have a genuinely local experience; in this case, it's far better to chose an island with a small tourist presence, where you'll be as much of a novelty for the local population as they are for you. The best islands for this are outside North & South Male Atolls, and in general, the more remote the island (ie without airports or big resorts nearby), the easier it is to make local connections. Guesthouses will often help you meet locals, inviting you into private houses or to various social events, such as a family meal or a beach or fishing trip with locals, and many independent travellers say that the human element is a real highlight of any backpacking adventure in Maldives.

Regions at a Glance

Male

History
Eating
Shopping

Mosques & Museums
Male has an array of historic mosques, as well as a first-class National History Museum that is essential for anyone interested in the unusual history of this island nation. Don't miss the superb Old Friday Mosque.

Varied Dining
The capital has a great range of places to eat and, after being in a resort, the low prices and wide choice will seem like thrills in themselves. Even on a budget there's plenty of choice: don't miss traditional Maldivian 'short eats' at any local teashop – delicious!

Shop Till You Drop
Male is all about trade and commerce, and its mercantile atmosphere is infectious. Don't miss the catch being sold off at the fish market, or the crowds at the produce market. But for a real slice of the shopping action, head down Chandhanee Magu for souvenir shops and then wander the main avenue of the city, Majeedee Magu.

p44

North & South Male Atolls

Luxury
Surfing
Independent Travel

Superb Resorts
Few atolls have the concentration of excellent, world-class resorts that can be found in North and South Male Atolls. Whether it's small and romantic (Cocoa Island by COMO), super-glamorous (One & Only Reethi Rah) or back-to-nature luxury (Gili Lankanfushi), you'll find the right resort here.

Surf Breaks
North Male has several excellent surf breaks on the eastern side of the atoll. There are a few nearby resorts and guesthouses that cater to surfers, and the best thing of all is that surf season coincides with Maldivian low season!

Independent Travel
The small island of Maafushi in South Male Atoll has become the centre of Maldives' thriving independent traveller scene. Here you'll find scores of guesthouses, a foreigners' beach and cheap diving.

p64

Ari Atoll

Wildlife
Island Hopping
Beaches

Whale Sharks & Hammerheads

There are two utterly amazing wildlife-watching opportunities in Ari Atoll, unfortunately at opposite ends of the atoll. In the south, swim with whale sharks, the largest fish in the world, while in the north, feed hammerhead sharks at Hammerhead Point.

Paradise Found

Don't forget your PADI certification or at least your mask and fins for some snorkelling in North and South Ari Atolls. You'll see an incredible array of marine life on the reef, from sharks and moray eels to turtles and rays.

Mind-Blowing Beaches

When it comes to beaches, you'll be spoiled for choice. Every single one of the dozens of resorts and guesthouses here has access to perfect white sand and amazing turquoise lagoon water.

p82

Northern Atolls

Diving
History
Beaches

Pristine Underwater World

The lack of resorts and a new National Marine Park in Noonu Atoll makes the Northern Atolls one of the best places to dive in the country. Live-aboard dive boats can take you to even more remote locations than the resorts.

Maldivian Heritage

Take a trip to Utheemu in the country's very far north if you'd like to see some real Maldivian cultural heritage. The island is home to Utheemu Palace, a perfectly preserved nobleman's 16th-century mansion.

Perfect White Sand

The beaches in the remote Northern Atolls are some of the most extraordinarily perfect you'll ever come across. What's more, the relative lack of resorts means that even beyond your resort you'll find plenty of perfect uninhabited islands with equally brilliant sands.

p91

Southern Atolls

Snorkelling
Fabulous Resorts
Independent Travel

Unbleached Corals

Addu Atoll managed to escape the ruinous coral bleaching that followed El Niño in 1997–98 and thus has the most dazzlingly colourful coral in the country. Don't miss snorkelling here.

Lap of Luxury

The Southern Atolls are home to some of the most impressive new luxury resorts, including the amazing Shangri-La Villingili, Six Senses Laamu, Jumeirah Dhevanafushi and Niyama, all setting new standards for pampering and style.

Culture

For the truly intrepid independent traveller, the south is a great place to explore alone. Check out the island of Fuvahmulah with its two inland lakes and traditionally isolated community, or visit the Maldives' second largest city, Hithadhoo.

p104

On the Road

Northern
Atolls p91

North & South
Male Atolls p64

Ari
Atoll
p82

Male p44

Southern
Atolls
p104

Male

AREA 1.95 SQ KM / POP 105,000

Best Places to Stay

➡ Hotel Jen Male (p53)

➡ Sala Boutique Hotel (p53)

➡ House Clover (p51)

➡ LVIS Hotel (p51)

➡ Marble Hotel (p51)

Best Places to Eat

➡ Aïoli (p55)

➡ Sala Thai (p56)

➡ Royal Garden Café (p54)

➡ Newport (p55)

➡ Irudhashu Hotaa (p54)

Why Go?

The pint-sized Maldivian capital is the throbbing, mercantile heart of the nation, a densely crowded and extraordinary place, notable mainly for its stark contrast to the laid-back pace of island life elsewhere in the country.

Male (*mar*-lay) offers the best chance to see the 'real' Maldives away from the resort buffet and infinity pool. Overlooked by tall, brightly coloured buildings and surrounded by incongruously turquoise water, Male is a hive of activity, the engine driving the Maldives' economy and the forum for the country's political struggles.

Male is also pleasant and pleasingly quirky – alcohol-free bars and restaurants jostle with shops and lively markets and the general hubbub of a capital is very much present. This city island offers a chance to get a real feel for the Maldives and what makes its people tick, and to meet Maldivians on an equal footing.

When to Go

➡ **Jul** Independence day celebrations on July 26 see floats and dancing children in Republic Sq.

➡ **Nov** Parades and marches mark Republic Day on November 11, when the capital celebrates.

➡ **May-Nov** Marginally cooler than the rest of the year, Male isn't as sweaty during these months.

History

Male has been the seat of the Maldives' ruling dynasties since before the 12th century, though none left any grand palaces. Some trading houses appeared in the 17th century, along with a ring of defensive bastions, but Male didn't acquire the trappings of a city and had a very limited range of economic and cultural activities. Visitors in the 1920s estimated the population at only 5000. Despite this, Male has always been the heart of the nation, and it is even from where the Maldives' name derives.

Growth began with the 1930s modernisation, and the first banks, hospitals, high schools and government offices appeared in the following decades. Only since the 1970s, with wealth from tourism and an expanding economy, has the city really burgeoned and growth emerged as a problem.

And a problem it has definitely become; despite extending the area of the city through land reclamation over the island's reef, Male is unable to extend any further and so the government is looking to projects such as nearby Hulhumale to accommodate the future overspill of the city. Overcrowding, pollution, traffic and meeting basic human needs are all problems Male residents are familiar with. This was underscored in late 2014, when the city's one desalination plant caught fire and the capital was left without running water for seven days; a real problem in a city with no fresh water sources.

Dangers & Annoyances

The main danger in Male is posed by the mopeds that seem to appear from nowhere at great speeds. Keep your wits about you and look around before crossing the road.

One other danger to bear in mind is that of gang or mob violence. Most are linked to crime but there have been occasional flare-ups of anti-Western feeling in Male, exploited by Islamist organisations with a very specific political agenda. Don't be overly concerned about this, but do keep an eye on the news.

The principal annoyance in Male for most visitors is the lack of alcohol. If you really want a drink, take the approximately hourly ferry from Jetty No 1 to the Hulhule Island Hotel near the airport, or take the airport ferry and walk the 10 minutes to the hotel for a cold beer by the pool.

◉ Sights

Male is more of an experience than a succession of astonishing must-sees. The best thing to do is enjoy a stroll and absorb the atmosphere of this oddest of capitals. Do remember that you are not in a tourist resort, and dress accordingly: women in shorts and low-cut tops may feel uncomfortable here and are likely to offend local sensibilities, though it's rare for anything to be said. Only ask to enter mosques if you are respectably dressed, which means trousers and sleeves for men, and long skirts, long sleeves and head coverings for women.

★ **Old Friday Mosque**   MOSQUE
(Hukuru Miskiiy; Map p54; Medhuziyaarai Magu) This is the oldest mosque in the country, dating from 1656. It's a beautiful structure made from coral stone into which intricate decoration and Quranic script have been chiselled. Visitors wishing to see inside are supposed to get permission from an official of the Ministry of Islamic Affairs. Most of the staff are officials of the ministry, however, and if you are respectful and well-dressed they will usually give you permission to enter the mosque on the spot.

Even though an ugly protective corrugated-iron sheet now covers the roof and some of the walls, this is still a fascinating place. The interior is superb and famed for its fine lacquer work and elaborate woodcarvings. One long panel, carved in the 13th century, commemorates the introduction of Islam to the Maldives.

The mosque was built on the foundations of an old temple that faced west rather than northwest towards Mecca. Consequently, worshippers have to face the corner of the mosque when they pray – the striped carpet, laid at an angle, shows the correct direction.

Overlooking the mosque is the solid, round, blue-and-white tower of the *munnaaru* – the squat minaret. Though it doesn't look that old, it dates from 1675. To one side of the mosque is a cemetery with many elaborately carved tombstones. Stones with rounded tops are for females, those with pointy tops are for males and those featuring gold-plated lettering are the graves of former sultans. The small buildings are family mausoleums and their stone walls are intricately carved. Respectably dressed non-Muslims are welcome to walk around the graveyard; you don't require permission for this.

(Continued on page 48)

PATRIK ENGSTROM SCUBAMALTA/GETTY IMAGES ©

1. Anemonefish
Also called clownfish, these fish have a symbiotic relationship with sea anemones, and are protected from the anemone's poisonous stings by a film of mucous.

2. Parrotfish
There are many species of parrotfish, recognisable by their beak-like mouths. Almost all of them are sequential hermaphrodites, being born as females and maturing into males.

3. Pennant Butterflyfish
Commonly found at a range of depths, these fish feed mainly on algae.

4. Red Lionfish
Adults can grow as large as 45cm and the spines are poisonous.

FRANCO BANFI/GETTY IMAGE ©

(Continued from page 45)

★ **National Museum** MUSEUM
(Map p54; ☑ 332 2254; Chandhanee Magu; adult/
child Rf100/20; ⊙10am-5pm Sun-Thu) The National Museum may be a ferociously ugly
building recently gifted by China, but it
nevertheless contains an excellent and well-
labelled collection of historic artefacts that
serve to trace the unusual history of these
isolated islands. Sadly, the museum was
broken into by a mob of religious extremists
during protests against former President
Nasheed in 2012, and its most precious
items, some 30 ancient Buddhist coral stone
carvings from the country's pre-Islamic period, were destroyed for being 'idols'.

The display begins downstairs with galleries devoted to the ancient and medieval periods of Maldivian history. Items on display include weaponry, religious paraphernalia and
household wares as well as many impressively carved Arabic- and Thaana-engraved pieces of wood commemorating the conversion
of the Maldives to Islam in 1153.

Upstairs is a display representing the
modern period and including some prized
examples of the lacquer-work boxes for
which Maldives is famous, and various
pieces of antique technology including the
country's first gramophone, telephone and
a massive computer. Quirkier relics include
the minutes of the famous underwater cabinet meeting held under President Nasheed
in 2009 and an impressive marine collection, the highlight of which is the 6m-long
skeleton of the very rare Longman's Beaked
Whale, which is yet to have been sighted
alive in the sea.

**Grand Friday Mosque
& Islamic Centre** MOSQUE
(Jumhooree Maidan) The golden dome of this
impressive modern mosque dominates the
skyline of Male and has become something
of a symbol for the city. Opened in 1984,
and built with help from the Gulf States,
Pakistan, Brunei and Malaysia, the Grand
Friday Mosque is striking in its plainness,
built in white marble and virtually free
from decoration. Set back off the main
square, Jumhooree Maidan, and opposite
the National Security Service Headquarters, it is the biggest mosque in the country.

Entering Male's harbour by boat, you
can still see the gold dome glinting in the
sun, although the gold is actually ano-
dised aluminium. The *munnaaru*, with
its space-age shape and distinctive zigzag
decoration, was supposed to be the tallest
structure in Male, but that title now goes to
the telecommunications towers.

Tourists wanting to enter the mosque
can only visit between 9am and 5pm, and
outside of prayer times. The mosque closes to all non-Muslims 15 minutes before
prayers and for the following hour. Before noon and between 2pm and 3pm are
the best times to visit. Invading bands of
casual sightseers are not encouraged, but
if you are genuinely interested and suitably dressed, you'll be welcomed by one of
the staff members who hang out by the entrance. Men must wear long trousers and
women a long skirt or dress.

The main prayer hall inside the mosque
can accommodate up to 5000 worshippers
and has beautifully carved wooden side
panels and doors, a specially woven carpet
and impressive chandeliers. The Islamic
Centre also includes a conference hall, library and classrooms.

Fish Market MARKET
(Map p54; Boduthakurufaanu Magu) Although
the squeamish may well object to the buck-
ets of entrails or the very public gutting of
fish going on all around, the Fish Market
should not be missed. This is the soul of
Male – and it's great fun watching the day's
catch being brought in from the adjacent
fishing harbour. Look out for some truly
vast tuna, octopus and grouper. Maldivian

MALE HIGHLIGHTS

➡ Gape at historic artefacts, giant fish
and other quirky relics at the superb
National Museum.

➡ Admire the beautiful exterior of the
Old Friday Mosque (p45), the oldest in
the country.

➡ Watch the morning's catch being
brought in, gutted and sold at the
fascinating Fish Market, one of Male's
busiest places of trade.

➡ Join locals for 'short eats' at any
traditional teashop (p53), a delicious
way to spend time outside the tourist
bubble.

➡ Make a trip to Hulhumale (p61)
and discover the modern face of the
Maldives on this manmade island.

Male

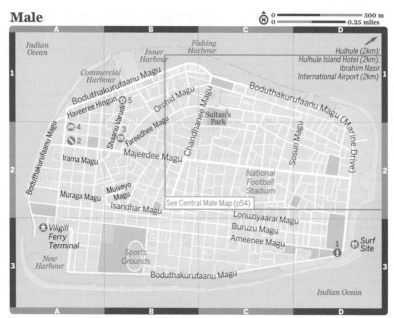

women don't usually venture into these are-as, although foreign women walking around won't cause any raised eyebrows.

Produce Market   MARKET
(Haveeree Hingun; ☉ dawn-dusk) The busy pro-duce market gives you a sense of the real flavour of the Maldives – people from all over the country gather here to sell home-grown and imported vegetables. Coconuts and bananas are the most plentiful produce, but look inside for the stacks of betel leaf, for wrapping up a 'chew'. Just wandering around, watching the hawkers and the shop-pers and seeing the vast array of products on display is fascinating and as real a Maldivian experience as possible.

National Art Gallery   MUSEUM
(Map p54; ☎ 333 7724; www.artgallery.gov.mv; Medhuziyaarai Magu; ☉ 9am-6pm Sun-Thu) FREE
The Museum Building, in one corner of Sul-tan's Park, houses the National Library, var-ious cultural centres from countries around the world and this exhibition space, which has regular displays of Maldivian art. There is sadly no permanent collection on display, but group and individual shows are regu-larly held and the biennial Maldives Con-temporary exhibition is a great chance to see the varied art produced in the country,

from photography to painting and concep-tual works.

**Muleeaage
& Medhu Ziyaarath**   PRESIDENTIAL PALACE
(Map p54) Muleeaage was built as a palace for the sultan of Maldives in the early 20th century, though he was deposed before he could move in and the building was used for government offices for about 40 years. It became the president's residence in 1953 when the first republic was proclaimed, but lost the honour in 1994 to **Theemuge**, a lavish residence on Orchid Magu favoured by President Gayoom. Muleeaage became

the presidential residence again in 2009, and remains so today.

At the eastern end of the building's compound, behind an elaborate blue-and-white gatehouse, the Medhu Ziyaarath is the tomb of Abul Barakat Yoosuf Al Barbary, who brought Islam to Male in 1153.

Tomb of Mohammed Thakurufaanu   TOMB

(Neelafaru Magu) In the back streets in the middle of town, in the grounds of a small mosque, is the tomb of Mohammed Thakurufaanu, the Maldives' national hero who liberated the country from Portuguese rule and was then the sultan from 1573 to 1585. Thakurufaanu is also commemorated in the name of the road that rings Male, Boduthakurufaanu Magu (*bodu* means 'big' or 'great').

Artificial Beach   BEACH

(Map p54) The eastern seafront of Male is the city's recreational centre. Here a sweet little beach has been crafted from the breakwater tetrapods and there's a whole range of fast food cafes next to it, as well as open fields for ad hoc games of soccer and cricket. Further up towards the airport ferry there are fairground attractions at the Majeediyya Carnival (Map p54), including a bowling alley and more eateries.

🏃 Activities

There is some excellent diving within a short boat ride of Male, even though the water here is not as pristine as it is elsewhere in the country. Some of the best dives are along the edges of Vaadhoo Kandu (the channel between North and South Male Atolls), which has two Protected Marine Areas. There is also a well-known wreck.

Hans Hass Place   DIVING

Hans Hass Place is a wall dive beside Vaadhoo Kandu in a Protected Marine Area. There is a lot to see at 4m or 5m, so it's good for snorkellers and less-experienced divers when the current is not too strong. There's a wide variety of marine life, including many tiny reef fish and larger species in the channel. Further down are caves and overhangs with sea fans and other soft corals.

Lion's Head   DIVING

Lion's Head is a Protected Marine Area that was once a popular place for shark feeding, and although this practice is now strongly discouraged, grey-tip reef sharks and the occasional turtle are still common here. The reef edge is thick with fish, sponges and soft corals; although it drops steeply, with numerous overhangs, to over 40m, there is still much to see at snorkelling depth.

Maldive Victory   DIVING

The wreck of the *Maldive Victory* is an impressive and challenging dive because of the potential for strong currents. This cargo ship hit a reef and sank on Friday, 13 February 1981 and now sits with the wheelhouse at around 15m and the propeller at 35m. The ship has been stripped of anything movable,

---

THE MAGNIFICENT TETRAPOD

The installation of tetrapod walls around much of Male saved it from potential devastation by the Indian Ocean tsunami in 2004. Tetrapods are concrete blocks with four fat legs, each approximately 1m long, sticking out like the four corners of a tetrahedron. These blocks can be stacked together in rows and layers so they interlock together to form a wall several metres high, looking like a giant version of a child's construction toy. A tetrapod breakwater has gaps that allow sea water to pass through, but collectively the structure is so massive and its surface so irregular that it absorbs and dissipates the force of the waves and protects the shoreline from the physical impact of a storm. As Male has expanded through land reclamation to cover its entire natural coral reef, its natural buffer from the force of strong waves has disappeared.

A severe storm in 1988 prompted the construction of the walls. Huge waves broke up tonnes of landfill that was part of a land-reclamation scheme, and much of this land was re-reclaimed by the sea. The solution was to protect the whole island with a rim of tetrapod breakwaters, constructed as part of a Japanese foreign-aid project. In some places the tetrapod walls are used to retain landfill, and have a path on top forming an attractive seaside promenade. In other places, tetrapod walls enclose an artificial harbour that provides a sheltered anchorage for small boats, and a safe spot for kids to swim. So beloved are these curious structures to locals, there's even a Tetrapod Monument (Map p49; Boduthakurufaanu Magu) in the southwestern corner of town.

but the structure is almost intact and provides a home for a rich growth of new coral, sponges, tubastrea and large schools of fish.

Sea Explorers Dive School
DIVING

(Map p49; ☑ 331 6172; www.seamaldives.com.mv; H Asfaam 1st fl, Bodufungadhu Magu; dives per person from US$84) The Sea Explorers Dive School is a very well-regarded operation that does dive courses and organises regular day trips to nearby dive sites.

Whale Submarine
SUBMARINE

(☑ 333 3939; www.whalesubmarine.com.mv; adult/child US$120/60) The Whale Submarine can hardly be described as a sight of Male, but it's a popular excursion. This is not a submarine for whale watching but for observing life on a reef. It's hard to recommend for divers, as the trip can't really compare to a real dive, but for kids (under-threes are not allowed) and those who don't dive, this is a great, if overpriced, little excursion. Book online or by phone, and then you'll be picked up by boat from the airport or from Jetty No 1 in Male 30 minutes beforehand and transported to the embarking platform.

🛏 Sleeping

Male makes Hong Kong look spacious, and as you'd expect on this densely populated island, space is at a premium. Compared to the rest of Asia prices are very high here, though a night in Male still costs peanuts compared to one in most resorts. One cheaper option than staying in Male itself is to stay on Hulhumale (p61), a 10-minute boat ride away from the capital, and the place where Maldives' nascent backpacker scene is concentrated.

LVIS Hotel
BOUTIQUE HOTEL $

(Map p49; ☑ 766 3223; www.lvishotels.com; Jahaamuguri Goalhi; s/d from US$55/65; ❋ 🛜) This small 10-room property on a side street looks anything but boutique from the outside. The staff, too, seem rather easily confused, but providing you can make yourself understood, you'll find gleaming rooms here, each with minibar, safe and flat-screen TV. Not a place to consider if you're looking for service, but otherwise a decent and stylish choice.

Skai Lodge
GUESTHOUSE $

(Map p54; ☑ 332 8112; www.skailodge.com.mv; Violet Magu; s/d US$65/79; ❋ 🛜) This attractive and well-maintained townhouse full of plants boasts 13 clean and well-maintained

MALE FOR CHILDREN

Male isn't particularly child-friendly. The narrow streets and rush of moped traffic make walking with kids or pushing a pram a fairly stressful experience; however, most hotels above two storeys have lifts and some restaurants have changing facilities. The Whale Submarine will appeal to kids of all ages (although be aware that those under three aren't allowed), while the Artificial Beach is also a great place for them to swim, and older kids might be able to join in soccer or cricket matches with local children at the recreational areas nearby. The nearby Majeediyya Carnival also has some fun activities for children, including the Slam Bowling Alley.

rooms (those upstairs are bigger and brighter) with good bathrooms, hot water, phone and TV; some even have balconies, which makes this a good deal by local standards.

Real Inn
BUDGET HOTEL $

(Map p54; ☑ 300 0822; realinn@dhinet.net.mv; off Ameer Ahmed Magu; s/d from US$35/40; ❋ 🛜) Tucked away on a side street just a block back from the airport ferry, this place is the cheapest deal in town. The rooms are simple but have all you need, including fridge, cable TV and hot water. There are just two singles, so it's best to reserve in advance for these. Little English is spoken at the front desk.

House Clover
GUESTHOUSE $$

(Map p54; ☑ 300 5855; www.houseclovermaldives. com; Shaheed KTM Hingun, off Chandhanee Magu; s/d US$89/99; ❋ @ 🛜) Set over several floors of a high-rise building in the centre of the island, this 20-room guesthouse is sparkling new, with bright and spacious rooms. The rooms have cable TV and decent bathrooms, while each floor shares basic kitchens and common areas. Staff members are super-helpful and reserving accommodation in advance is advised.

Marble Hotel
HOTEL $$

(Map p49; ☑ 330 2678; www.marble.mv; Kanba Aisa Rani Higun; s/d from US$73/100; ❋ 🛜) On the far side of the island with some great views towards neighbouring Viligili from its higher rooms, the Marble Hotel offers good quality, spacious accommodation with TV and fridge. It's not particularly convenient

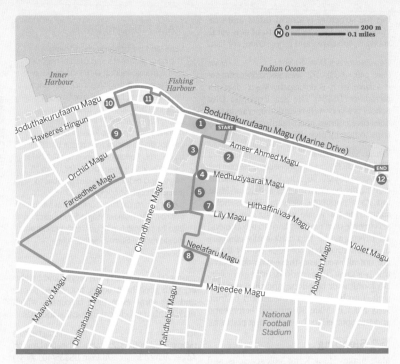

🏃 Walking Tour
Male

START JUMHOOREE MAIDAN
FINISH NEWPORT
DISTANCE 3KM
DURATION ONE HOUR

Start from the waterfront near ❶ **Jumhoo-ree Maidan**, the main square, conspicuous for the huge Maldivian flag flying on its eastern side. All around here is the apparatus of government and you'll notice that it's a well-guarded place, with the police station on one side and the white ❷ **National Security Service (NSS) Headquarters** to the south.

To the right of the NSS is the ❸ **Grand Friday Mosque** (p48). Walk down the gravel street past its main entrance and you'll arrive at the ❹ **Republican Monument**, a modern-style roundabout centrepiece unveiled in 1999 to commemorate 30 years of Maldivian independence. Cross over to the ❺ **Sultan's Park** and walk through, noting the new ❻ **National Museum** (p48) to your right. Exit the park and turn left, where you'll see a charming coral stone ❼ **mosque** at the corner of the park, typical of the intricate 17th-century Maldivian design. Continue south from here through streets that are far more typical of the crowded capital until you reach the ❽ **Tomb of Mohammed Thaku-rufaanu** (p50), honouring the man who liberated the Maldives from the Portuguese in the 16th century.

Cut down to Majeedee Magu, the city's main thoroughfare, and the cut up through Fareedhee Magu and Orchid Magu, passing the striking ❾ **Theemuge**, previously the official residence of the president and now the seat of the supreme court.

From here head north towards the ❿ **produce market** (p49). Continue along the seafront to the ⓫ **fish market** (p48), a must-see for any visitor to Male. Wander along the seafront, which is always fascinating as people crowd on and off boats. Finish up with a cool drink at ⓬ **Newport** (p55) with a view of the harbour and the bustle of Male's main road.

for the airport ferry, but it's very handy for the Viligili Ferry Terminal if you're heading to the atolls.

Baani Hotel HOTEL **$$**
(Map p54; ☑330 3530; www.baanihotels.com.mv; Filigas Hingun; s/d incl breakfast US$86/96; ❄☎) Overlooking one of Male's two football fields, the Baani offers spacious, bright rooms (avoid the dark ones at the back of the building) with pleasant views. It's centrally located yet relatively quiet and well-located for the airport ferry. The downside is that the breakfast sucks – eat out.

Park House HOTEL **$$**
(Map p54; ☑330 6600; info@theparkhouse.com.mv; Lily Magu; s/d incl breakfast US$70/93; ❄☎) The brightly painted Park House offers 24 large yellow-and-green rooms with dark-wood furniture and rock-hard mattresses. It's not a particularly great place, but it's good value by Male standards, and has a pizza restaurant downstairs and a convenient location in the centre of town. Breakfast, though unexciting, is brought to your room each morning.

★**Hotel Jen Male** LUXURY HOTEL **$$$**
(Map p54; ☑330 0888; www.hoteljen.com; Ameer Ahmed Magu; r from US$268; ❄☎☀) By far Male's best hotel is this smart Shangri-La-run property a block back from the harbour. A little slice of glamour in the heart of town, this stylish temple of orchids, doormen and minimalist furnishings has 117 slick and stylish rooms, a rooftop gym, bar and lap pool, a spa and sumptuous breakfast buffet.

Sala Boutique Hotel BOUTIQUE HOTEL **$$$**
(Map p54; ☑334 5959; www.salafamilymaldives.com; Buruneege; r from US$169; ❄☎) Set above Male's most celebrated restaurant, Sala Thai (p52), these six boutique rooms are of a very high standard, although like most Male non-high-rise hotels, there's little or no natural light in them. On the other hand there are real spring mattresses, mahogany furniture, flat-screen TVs, Nespresso machines and minibars. An excellent bet for a high-end experience that doesn't break the bank.

Mookai Hotel HOTEL **$$$**
(Map p54; ☑333 8811; www.mookai.com.mv; Meheli Golhi; s/d US$125/155; ❄☎☀) With a good location just seconds from the waterfront, rooms with great views on the higher floors, and a tiny but effective rooftop swimming pool to cool down in, the Mookai is a solid choice. Rooms are small but clean and well furnished, and the feel is upmarket.

Eating

You'll eat decently in Male, with restaurants typically offering several different cuisines – most popular are Thai, Indonesian, Indian, Italian and American-style grills. Male restaurants don't serve alcohol, but many serve nonalcoholic beer. By contrast nearly every restaurant has now acquired an espresso machine, and you can get a good cup of coffee almost anywhere.

VISITING A MALE TEASHOP

Maldivians don't have a particularly rich culinary history, due to obvious limitations of what's available on this isolated group of islands. The standard local eatery is known as a teashop, where little morsels known as *hedhikaa* ('short eats') are served up, and Male is full of them.

Teashops are frequented by Maldivian men, and while it's not the done thing for local women to visit one, foreign women accompanied by men will not normally raise eyebrows. Some traditional teashops have in recent years broadened the menus, installed air-conditioning and improved service – you should feel quite comfortable in these places and they're a great way to meet locals. A bigger and slightly better teashop might be called a 'cafe' or even a 'hotel'.

Teashops have their goodies displayed on a counter behind a glass screen, and customers line up and choose, cafeteria style – if you don't know what to ask for, just point. Tea costs around Rf2 and the *hedhikaa* range from Rf2 to Rf10. You can fill yourself for under Rf30. At meal times teashops also serve 'long eats', such as soups, curried fish and *roshi* (unleavened bread). A good meal costs from Rf20 to Rf50.

Teashops open as early as 5am and close as late as 1am, particularly around the port area where they cater to fishermen. During Ramazan they're open till 2am or even later, but closed during the day.

Central Male

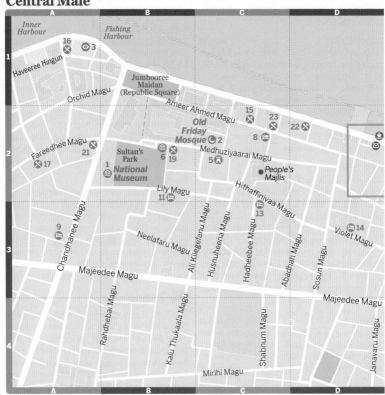

★ **Irudhashu Hotaa** TEASHOP **$**
(Map p54; Filigas Hingun; short eats from Rf5;
⊙7am-10pm) Our favourite 'short eats' place
in town is this perennially busy meeting
place by the Henveiru football field. After
prayers at the next-door mosque, it's always
jammed, and the spicy fish curries and selection of *hedhikaa* are delicious.

Royal Garden Café INTERNATIONAL **$**
(Map p54; ☑332 0288; Medhuziyaarai Magu;
mains Rf50-150; ⊙8am-1am Sun-Thu, from 2pm
Fri; 🛜) This great little place, with a charming garden and an air-conditioned, stylish
dark-wood interior, is housed in a rare surviving example of a *ganduvaru,* a nobleman's house. The menu is a combination of
Italian, Indonesian, American and Indian
cuisines – try the delicious satay chicken or
the ever-good nasi goreng.

Shell Beans INTERNATIONAL **$**
(Map p54; ☑333 3686; Boduthakurufaanu Magu;
mains Rf50-100; ⊙8am-11.30pm Sun-Thu, 3pm-
12.30am Fri; 🛜) This useful spot on the
seafront serves up tasty sandwiches, full
breakfasts, sandwiches, burgers, good coffee
and pastries. It's a great spot for lunch on
the run, although there's seating both upstairs (which includes a great balcony with
harbour views) and downstairs for a less
hurried meal.

Dawn Café TEASHOP **$**
(Map p54; Haveeree Hingun; short eats from Rf3;
⊙24hr) This is one of the best teashops in
the area, and due to its fish-market location it's popular with fishermen and open
around the clock. You can get a brilliant and
very cheap meal here. Try it on Friday afternoon when people come in after going to the
mosque.

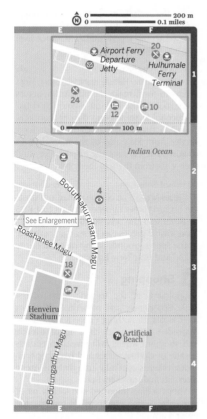

including fresh fruit and veg. It's handy for self-catering, which can be a sensible option during Ramazan.

Watercress
TEASHOP $

(Map p54; Ameer Ahmed Magu; short eats from Rf5; ⊙ 7am-11pm, from 1pm Fri) A popular place right in the centre of things, this friendly and somewhat upmarket teashop serves up a delicious selection of 'short eats'.

Sea House
INTERNATIONAL $

(Map p54; ☑ 333 2957; Boduthakurufaanu Magu; mains Rf50-150; ⊙ 24hr, closed 10am-1pm Fri) This breezy (and sometimes downright windy) place above the Hulhumale ferry terminal has expansive harbour views and a large menu that runs from pizza and sandwiches to full meals. It's a popular meeting place, and while the food won't amaze you (avoid the decidedly average breakfast), it's a reliable option and full of locals.

Fantasy Store
SUPERMARKET $

(Map p54; Fareedhee Magu; ⊙ 9am-10pm Sat-Thu, 2.30-10pm Fri; ❄) The city's best-stocked supermarket sells a great range of products,

★ Newport
INTERNATIONAL $$

(Boduthakurufaanu Magu; mains Rf130-225; ⊙ 6am-1am; ☏) This cool spot on Male's busy seafront road is a godsend to anyone travelling through Male. Sleek and minimalist, Newport feels very different to Male's other restaurants, and the food is excellent. The iPad menus are enormous and run from good breakfasts to falafel, seared tuna cubes, sandwiches, giant prawns and burgers. There's also good coffee.

Aïoli
INTERNATIONAL $$

(Map p54; ☑ 330 4984; Lotus Goalhi; mains Rf100-500; ⊙ 9am-11.30pm Sun-Thu, from 4pm Fri; ❄ ☏) This stylish restaurant, decked out in dark wood and cream furnishings, has the feel of a boutique hotel more than a dinner spot. The menu is just as fabulous, with Black Angus fillet steak, coconut chilli crab and baked mussels on offer, all served up on an attractive outdoor terrace or in one of two dining rooms.

Thai Wok THAI $$
(Map p54; ☑ 331 0007; Hithaffivinivaa Magu; mains Rf100-150; ☉ noon-3.30pm Sun-Thu, 7pm-midnight daily; ✱) The Thai food here is good value and authentic, though the best reason to visit is for the thrice-weekly buffet (R140 per person), where you can take your pick of lots of great dishes. The interior of the place is rather charmless, and it's fearsomely popular with Chinese tour groups, but the food makes it worth the trip.

Seagull Café House INTERNATIONAL $$
(Map p54; ☑ 332 3792; cnr Chandhanee Magu & Fareedhee Magu; mains Rf70-250; ☉ 8am-midnight Sun-Thu, 4pm-midnight Fri) The Seagull boasts an impressively designed space complete with a charming downstairs garden and a 1st-floor terrace with a tree growing through it. The menu is extensive and includes sandwiches, burgers, curries, wraps, pasta, fish and grills. There's also a popular gelataria attached, serving up the city's best ice cream – perfect for dessert.

★ Sala Thai THAI $$$
(Map p54; ☑ 334 5959; Buruneege; mains Rf250-600; ☉ noon-midnight Sat-Thu, 5-11.30pm Fri; ☎) This very smart restaurant is generally held to be the best on the island, and it should be at these prices. The Thai menu is sumptuous, and thoroughly authentic, with a huge choice of soups, noodles and curries. Meals are served al fresco in a charming walled terrace, or inside in a plush dining room.

☆ Entertainment

Nobody comes to a dry town for the nightlife, let's face it, but there's still a surprising amount of life on Male's streets after dark. The evening is popular with strolling couples and groups of friends who promenade along the seafront and Majeedee Magu until late. Thursday and Friday nights are the busiest, after prayers at sundown. There are even sporadic club nights put on, although there's nothing regular. Keep your eye out for notices along the seafront, as such events are usually advertised.

Jazz Café CAFE
(Map p49; Haveeree Hingun; ☉ 7am-1am Sat-Thu, from 2pm Fri) This friendly cafe takes a thoroughly un-Maldivian concept (jazz) and marries it to another (good coffee) to create

one of the capital's nicest hangouts. It offers a full menu as well as good pastries, to be enjoyed to the taped (and sometimes live) jazz accompaniment.

Hulhule Island Hotel BAR
(www.hih.com.mv; Hulhule island; ☉ 24hr) Most expats in town make the pilgrimage across the lagoon to the Hulhule Island Hotel bar for alcohol at some point during their stay. There's a dedicated though irregular ferry service from Male run by the hotel, but it's usually faster to take the airport ferry and then walk from there to the hotel.

National Stadium SPECTATOR SPORT
(Majeedee Magu) The National Stadium hosts the biggest soccer matches (tickets cost Rf15 to Rf50) and the occasional cricket match. More casual games can be seen any evening in the sports grounds at the east end of the island and near New Harbour.

🛍 Shopping

Shopping is at the frenetic heart of the Male experience, and sometimes it seems as if locals do nothing else – a walk down Majeedee Magu, the city's main avenue and shopping street, will reveal an endless parade of clothes, shoes and bag shops, although there's generally little that will excite international travellers here.

Shops selling imported and locally made souvenirs, which are aimed at tourists, are on and around Chandhanee Magu. Many of the tourist shops have a very similar range of tatty stock, and it's hard to recommend any in particular.

Male is definitely the best place to shop for more unusual antiques and Maldivian craft items – come here for old wooden measuring cups, coconut graters, traditional lacquer boxes, ceremonial knives and finely woven grass mats. The best places to find such items are along Chandhanee Magu, behind the Grand Friday Mosque.

ℹ Information

EMERGENCY
Ambulance (☑ 102)
Fire (☑ 118)
Police (☑ 119)
Police Station (Boduthakurufaanu Magu) On the corner of Jumhooree Maidan.

INTERNET ACCESS
There are no internet cafes in Male – you'll need a laptop or smart phone to get online here, or

HOUSE NAMES

Street numbers are rarely used in Male, so most houses and buildings have a distinctive name, typically written in picturesque English as well as in the local Thaana script. Some Maldivians prefer rustic titles like Crabtree, Forest, Oasis View and Banana Cabin. Others are specifically floral, like Sweet Rose and Luxury Garden, or even vegetable, like Carrot, or the perplexing Leaf Mess. There are also exotic names like Paris Villa and River Nile, while some sound like toilet disinfectants – Ozone, Green Zest, Dawn Fresh.

Some of our quirkier favourite house names include Hot Lips, Subtle Laughter, Remind House, Pardon Villa, Frenzy, Mary Lightning and Aston Villa.

Shop names and businesses, on the other hand, often have an overt advertising message – People's Choice Supermarket, Bless Trade, Fair Price and Neat Store.

ask at your hotel if you need to use a terminal. All hotels in Male have free wi-fi, while only some cafes and restaurants do, including Newport (p55), Shell Beans (p54), Aïoli (p55), and Sala Thai.

LAUNDRY

Nearly all hotels will take care of your laundry for a couple of dollars per item. Another option is **The Laundry** (Ameer Ahmed Magu; ⊘ 8am-1pm & 2-7pm), where you can drop off clothes and pick them up the next day. It also offers a four-hour express service and dry cleaning.

LEFT LUGGAGE

There are no dedicated left-luggage facilities in Male itself. The only option is taking a day room at a hotel, or asking nicely at reception if you can leave your bags. There is a left-luggage service at the airport that costs US$5 per item, per 24 hours.

MEDICAL SERVICES

Both the following will make arrangements with travel insurance companies, and both have doctors trained to do a diving medical check. There are a large number of well-stocked chemists outside both establishments.

ADK Private Hospital (☑ 331 3553; www.adk-hospital.mv; Sosun Magu) Private facility with Western-trained doctors and dentists, excellent standards of care and quite high prices.

Indira Gandhi Memorial Hospital (☑ 333 5211; www.mhsc.com.mv; Buruzu Magu) Modern public facility, well equipped and staffed with English-speaking doctors.

MONEY

International banks line the waterfront Boduthakurufaanu Magu near the airport ferry dock. All have ATMs that accept international cards.

More local banks are clustered near the harbour end of Chandhanee Magu and east along Boduthakurufaanu Magu. They all change travellers cheques, usually for a small transaction

fee. Bank of Maldives doesn't charge a fee if you change travellers cheques for Maldivian rufiyaa, but does charge if you want US dollars. There are also change facilities and ATMs at the airport.

POST

Main Post Office (Map p54; ☑ 331 5555; Boduthakurufaanu Magu; ⊘ 9am-7.30pm Sun-Thu, 10am-3.30pm Sat) The main post office is just opposite the airport ferry dock. There's a post office at the airport too.

TELEPHONE

Anyone staying in the Maldives for a while will save a lot of money by getting a local SIM card for their mobile phone.

Dhiraagu (www.dhiraagu.com.mv; Chandhanee Magu)

Ooredoo (www.ooredoo.mv; Majeedee Magu)

TOILETS

The most conveniently located public toilets (Rf2) are on the back street between Bistro Jade and the small mosque on Ameer Ahmed Magu. However, you can also pop in and use the toilets of most cafes or restaurants; the owners are almost universally polite and don't seem to mind.

TOURIST INFORMATION

There is a tourist information desk at the airport, which is supposedly open when international flights arrive, but sometimes this isn't the case. Even when it's not staffed, look on the shelf out the front for some useful booklets. Otherwise, the best places to start are the following:

www.lonelyplanet.com/maldives/male For planning advice, author recommendations, traveller reviews and insider tips.

www.visitmaldives.com The country's official tourism portal.

TRAVEL AGENCIES

Few travellers use a travel agency in the Maldives, as most people book their holidays from

(Continued on page 60)

Big Creatures of the Deep

Marine life on the reef is fabulous, colourful and fascinating, but what divers and snorkellers really want to see are the big creatures of the deep. Indeed, an encounter with an enormous whale shark can be the experience of a lifetime.

Sharks

1 If you're lucky, you'll see a wide range of sharks in the Maldives. Reef sharks are commonly seen, but one of the most impressive sights in the country is a school of hammerheads at Rasdhoo Madivaru (aka Hammerhead Point; p83) in Rasdhoo Atoll.

Moray Eels

2 The moray eel and its slightly manic expression as it leans out of its protective hole are standard sights on almost any Maldivian reef, and some can be playful with divers. Be careful of its bite, though – once it closes its teeth, it never lets go.

Turtles

3 Turtles often swim around the reefs and can be curious around snorkellers and divers. Five different types of turtles swim in Maldivian waters. The most common are green and hawksbill turtles.

Rays

4 These creatures are a favourite with divers. Smaller stingrays and eagle rays often rest in the sand, while enormous manta rays can have a 'wingspan' of around 4m, and seeing one swoop over you is an extraordinary experience.

Whale Sharks

5 These gentle giants eat nothing but plankton and the odd small fish, but somehow have evolved to be the biggest fish in the world, measuring up to 12m long. They can often be spotted cruising Dhidhdhoo Beyru (p83) on the edge of Ari Atoll.

Clockwise from top left
1 Grey reef shark 2 Spotted morays 3 Green sea turtle
4 Manta rays

(Continued from page 57)

home and have little need to arrange anything in the country. Even independent travellers can usually book everything themselves. However, the following are experienced Male-based travel agencies that can make arrangements throughout the Maldives. A full list of Male travel agents can be found at www.visitmaldives.com/en/travel_agents.

Crown Tours (☑ 332 9889; www.crowntoursmaldives.com; 5th fl, Fasmeeru Bldg, Boduthakurufaanu Magu) With 30 years' experience, this agency can book resorts, weddings, transfers and organise live aboards, diving and fishing trips.

Elysian Maldives (☑ 773 8889; www.elysianmaldives.com; Viligili) Elysian specialises in independent travel and guesthouses, and is one of a number of newer agencies that is squarely aimed at the independent travel market. It can also arrange surf cruises, live aboards and book resorts. The company's office is on the island of Viligili, so everything is done by phone or email.

Inner Maldives (☑ 300 6886; www.innermaldives.com.mv; Ameer Ahmed Magu) Highly regarded local operator with plenty of experience with independent travellers and a good network of partners throughout the country.

Sultans of the Sea (☑ 332 0330; www.sultansoftheseas.com; ground fl, Fasmeeru Bldg, Boduthakurufaanu Magu) This agency is all about luxury water travel, and charters yachts of all sizes.

Voyages Maldives (☑ 332 2019; www.voyagesmaldives.com; Chandhanee Magu) With over three decades of experience, Voyages Maldives specialises in live-aboard dive boats, sailing and surfing trips, and can also book resorts and arrange transfers.

ⓘ Getting There & Away

AIR

All international flights to the Maldives use Male's **Ibrahim Nasir International Airport** (☑ 331 5366; www.macl.aero), which is on a separate island, Hulhule, about 2km east of Male island. Domestic flights and seaplane transfers to resorts also use the airport, although the seaplane terminal is on the far side of the island, involving a free five-minute bus ride around the runway.

Male is linked by daily flights to Colombo, Doha, Dubai, Kuala Lumpur and Trivandrum, and regular flights to Abu Dhabi, Bangalore, Bangkok, Beijing, Chennai, Frankfurt, Hong Kong, Istanbul, Kuala Lumpur, London, Milan, Moscow, Muscat, Paris, Shanghai, Singapore, Tokyo, Vienna and Zürich.

BOAT

Male is the boat transport hub for the entire country, and it's possible to connect by boat from here with all neighbouring atolls and most nearby islands.

All long-distance public ferry services depart from the New Harbour on the southwest corner of Male, including those to nearby Viligili. Some short-hop ferries depart from the **Hulhumale Ferry Terminal** (Map p54) on the city's northeastern corner, including services to Hulhumale. Various other private services go from different jetties along the waterfront between the Hulhumale Ferry Terminal and the produce market, so always check exactly where the ferry you're supposed to be taking leaves from. Ferries to the airport depart from outside the main post office on Boduthakurufaanu Magu.

In terms of reaching resorts, the airport harbour functions as the biggest transport hub in the country. In general, if you want to travel by boat to a resort from Male, you'll usually need to take the **airport ferry** (Map p54) and get a transfer from the airport, as this is where speedboats to nearby resorts arrive and depart. You'll need to book your accommodation and the transfer in advance – it's not generally possible to take transfers to resorts without planning to stay there, though some resorts allow visitors to come for dinner or go diving for the day, though again, this must be organised in advance.

Safari boats and private yachts usually moor between Male island and Viligili, or in the lagoon west of Hulhumale. Safari-boat operators will normally pick up new passengers from the airport or Male and ferry them directly to the boat.

ⓘ Getting Around

TO/FROM THE AIRPORT

Dhonis shuttle between the airport and Male all day and most of the night, departing promptly every 10 minutes. At the airport, dhonis leave from the jetties just north of the arrivals hall. In Male they arrive and depart from the landing at the east end of Boduthakurufaanu Magu. The crossing costs Rf10 per person, or US$1 if you don't have any local cash.

BICYCLE

A bicycle or scooter is a good way to get around, but there's nowhere to rent one. Your guesthouse might be able to arrange something, but if you make a local friend, be prepared to be given a high adrenaline ride through the city. Helmets are generally not worn.

TAXI

The numerous taxis in the city offer a few minutes of cool, air-conditioned comfort and a driver who can usually find any address in Male. Many streets are one way and others may be blocked by construction work or stationary vehicles, so taxis will often take roundabout routes.

Fares are Rf20 for any distance, rising to Rf25 after midnight. Some drivers may charge Rf10 extra for luggage. You don't have to tip. There are various taxi companies, but don't worry about the names – just call ☑ 332 3132, 332 5757 or 332 2454.

AROUND MALE

Hulhumale

Hulhumale is essentially an extension of Male proper on the far side of the airport island, where 1.8 sq km of reef has been built up to create a manmade island – the first phase of an ambitious project to relieve the pressure caused by population growth on Male. Sand and coral were dug up from the lagoon and pumped into big heaps on the reef top. Then bulldozers pushed the rubble around to form a quadrilateral of dry land about 2km long and 1km wide, joined by a causeway to the airport island. It's built up to about 2m above sea level to provide a margin of protection against the possibility of sea-level rises.

This utopian project began in 1997 and now most of it (about three quarters of the island's total area) is a fully functioning town, complete with rather Soviet-looking apartment blocks, a school, a pharmacy, an array of shops and a huge mosque – the golden glass dome of which is visible from all over the southern part of North Male Atoll. There's even a surprisingly attractive artificial beach on the eastern side of the island. When the first-phase land is fully developed by 2020 it will accommodate 50,000 people and have waterfront esplanades, light industrial areas, government offices, shopping centres, boulevards of palm trees, a marina and a national stadium. The basic layout has been carefully planned, but the details are still flexible, allowing for some natural, organic growth through multiple private developments. The second phase, for which building is currently underway, involves reclaiming a further 2.4 sq km of land (engulfing all of Farukolhufushi, formerly the Club Faru resort) and bringing the total population potential of Hulhumale to around 100,000 people, equalling that of Male.

To visit Hulhumale from Male, take the ferry (Rf5.50, 20 minutes, every 15 minutes) from the Hulhumale Ferry Terminal. There's also a speedboat service (Rf25, 10 minutes, every 30 minutes) that leaves from the dock where the airport ferry departs. On the island there are several bus services that connect the ferry terminal to the rest of the island, but it's an easy 10-minute walk if there's not one waiting when you arrive.

🛏 Sleeping & Eating

Hulhumale's relatively low cost, more relaxed vibe and beach has made it something of a backpacker hangout, with good value hotels concentrated along the beachfront on the island's eastern side. There are a few decent restaurants and some conservative beach culture to be enjoyed too, though swimming in the shallow water can be hard.

Le Vieux Nice Inn   GUESTHOUSE $
(☑335 7788; www.levieuxniceinn.com; Nirolhu Magu; s/d US$80/90; ❅🛜) One block back from the beach, this friendly place is remarkably popular for its low prices, good restaurant and excellent location in the middle of Hulhumale's chilled-out backpacker zone. Rooms are comfortable and modern, and the welcome is warm. They will pick you up by car from the airport if you give them notice.

Fuana Inn   GUESTHOUSE $$
(☑335 0610; www.fuanainn.mv; Dhigga Magu; s/d incl breakfast US$75/115; ❅🛜) Right on Hulhumale's bustling beach strip with the roar of the ocean breaking on the reef in front of you, this well-established hotel has modern, clean rooms, and all doubles come with balconies looking out over the sea.

Ravin's   INTERNATIONAL $
(Nirolhu Magu; mains Rf50-200; ⊙10am-1am Sat-Thu, 2pm-1am Fri; 🛜) Ravin's is a popular lifeline for foreigners living on Hulhumale and also with a younger, local crowd who appreciate the international cuisine. As well as Indian curries, there's steak, noodles and rice dishes on the menu, as well as decent coffee. It's one block back from the beach.

Around Male

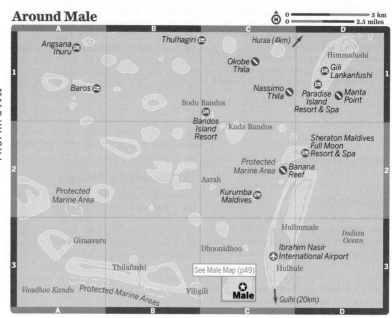

Viligili

Just 1km from the western shore of Male is little Viligili, essentially a suburb of the capital. The short boat ride takes you into a different world, though; far more relaxed than Male, Viligili has something of a Caribbean feel, with brightly painted houses and a laid-back pace. Male residents come here to enjoy some space, play soccer and go swimming. While it's still a great deal more cosmopolitan than most inhabited islands in the Maldives, if you only visit Male and resorts, this is perhaps the best chance you'll have of seeing everyday life. There are several shops, restaurants and places to go for a drink. To get here just catch one of the frequent dhoni ferries from New Harbour on the southwest corner of Male (Rf3.25, 10 minutes, every five minutes).

Hulhule

Better known as the airport island, Hulhule was once densely wooded with very few inhabitants – just a graveyard and a reputation for being haunted. The first airstrip was built here in 1960, and in the early 1980s it had a major upgrade to accommodate long-distance passenger jets. A plan to build a new terminal agreed under President Nasheed was cancelled after his fall from power, and the now rather outdated terminal building will remain in use for the immediate future.

As well as being the country's main international airport, Hulhule also accommodates the seaplane terminal on the lagoon on the east side of the island. Everyone passes through this island on their way in and out of the country, but it's also a serious leisure option from Male due to both the excellent swimming pool and the availability of alcohol at the **Hulhule Island Hotel** (☏ 333 0888; www.hih.com.mv; Hulhule island; s/d/ste incl breakfast US$341/377/450; ✳ ☎ ☒). The hotel runs a free transfer boat 14 times a day, from beside the **President's Jetty** (Jetty No 1) in Male. Day membership, which allows use of the swimming pool, costs US$20.

Other Islands

With so many small islands in the Maldives, some are allocated for particular activities or a specific use. One example is **Funadhoo**, between the airport and Male, which is used for fuel storage – it's a safe distance from inhabited areas, and convenient for both seagoing tankers and smaller boats serving the atolls.

One of the fastest-growing islands in the country, west of Viligili, is **Thilafushi**, also known as 'Rubbish Island'. It's where the capital dumps its garbage. The land is earmarked for industrial development, and its three conspicuous, round towers are part of a cement factory. It's perfectly possible to visit Thilafushi, just take the ferry from the New Harbour (Rfl1, 20 minutes, every one to two hours). While the truly ghastly part is the south side of the island, the north part is a small township of migrant workers tending various industrial plants.

Slightly further north, **Aarah** is a small island that was used as the president's holiday retreat during the Gayoom era and as such was a heavily fortified installation complete with bunkers on the beach. Under President Nasheed the island was used to host the Hay Festival Maldives, an offshoot of the famous British literary festival, as well as to host some big beach parties featuring international DJs for the youth of Male.

Another 3km further north, the island of **Kuda Bandos** was saved from resort development and became the Kuda Bandos Reserve, to be preserved in its natural state for the people's enjoyment. It has a few facilities for day-trippers, but is otherwise undeveloped. Tourists come to Kuda Bandos on island-hopping trips from nearby resorts.

North & South Male Atolls

Best Resorts

➡ One & Only Reethi Rah (p72)

➡ Cocoa Island (p80)

➡ Gili Lankanfushi (p72)

➡ Jumeirah Vittaveli (p79)

➡ Meeru Island Resort (p70)

Best Guesthouses

➡ Cokes Surf Shack (p74)

➡ Kaani Village & Spa (p81)

➡ Crystal Sands (p81)

➡ Arena Beach Hotel (p81)

➡ Palma Guesthouse (p74)

Why Go?

North & South Male Atolls are home to many of the country's most famous and best-established resorts, and all the islands here are within easy reach of the capital city and the Maldives' international airport. South Male Atoll is also home to Maafushi, the single greatest success story of the Maldives recent attempt to encourage independent tourism on inhabited islands, and where there are now dozens of guesthouses, dive operators and even a foreigners' beach.

Both atolls have a wealth of natural draws too: excellent dive sites pepper both sides of Vaadhoo Kandu, the channel that runs between North and South Male Atolls, while Gaafaru Falhu Atoll, north of North Male Atoll, has at least three diveable shipwrecks. Some of the Maldives' best surf breaks are also in North Male Atoll, which is home to a small, seasonal surfer scene, and the beaches are superb almost everywhere.

When to Go

➡ **May-Nov** The best months to surf North & South Male's excellent breaks

➡ **Dec-Mar** High season brings the best weather, with almost unbroken sunshine common for weeks at a time

➡ **Jan-Apr** Divers will experience the best visibility in the water at these times

North Male Atoll

Tourism is well developed in North Male Atoll, and in addition to the many resorts there are several guesthouses on inhabited islands here too. Male itself isn't the atoll capital, as it's considered to be its own administrative district. Instead, the atoll capital is **Thulusdhoo**, on the eastern edge of North Male Atoll, with a population of about 1200. Thulusdhoo is an industrious island, known for manufacturing of *bodu beru* (big drums), for its nascent surfer scene and for its salted-fish warehouse. It is also unique for its Coca-Cola factory, the only one in the world where the drink is made from desalinated water.

The island of **Huraa** (population 750) is well used to tourists visiting from nearby resorts, but it retains its small-island feel. It is now home to several guesthouses, so the tourist presence extends beyond day-trippers. Huraa's dynasty of sultans, founded in 1759 by Sultan Al-Ghaazi Hassan Izzaddeen, built a mosque on the island.

Many tourists visit **Himmafushi** (population 855) on excursions arranged from nearby resorts. The main street has two long rows of shops, where you can pick up some of the least expensive souvenirs in the country. Carved rosewood manta rays, sharks and dolphins are made locally. If you wander into the back streets, you quickly get away from the tourist strip to find a picturesque, well-kept village and an attractive cemetery with coral headstones. A sand spit has joined Himmafushi to the once separate island of Gaamaadhoo, where there used to be a prison. The surf break here, aptly called Jailbreaks, is a great right-hander.

Further north, **Dhiffushi** is an appealing local island, with around 900 inhabitants. Mainly a fishing island, it has lots of greenery, grows tropical fruit, and is home to a couple of guesthouses.

🏃 Activities

North Male Atoll has some superb dive sites. Some are heavily dived, especially in peak seasons, due to the many resorts in the atoll.

★ Helengeli Thila   DIVING
Famous for its prolific marine life, Helengeli Thila, also called Bodu Thila, is a long narrow thila on the eastern edge of the atoll. Reef fish and pelagics (fish that inhabit the upper layers of the open sea) are common,

including sharks, tuna, rays and jacks. Soft corals are spectacular in the cliffs and caves on the west side of the thila at about 25m.

★ Shark Point   DIVING
Also called Saddle, or Kuda Faru, Shark Point is in a Protected Marine Area and is subject to strong currents. Lots of white-tip and grey-tip reef sharks can be seen in the channel between a thila and the reef, along with fusiliers, jackfish, stingrays and some impressive caves.

★ Manta Point   DIVING
The best time to see the mantas for which Manta Point is famous is from May to November. Coral outcrops at about 8m are a 'cleaning station', where cleaner wrasse feed on parasites from the mantas' wings. Cliffs, coral tables, turtles, sharks and numerous reef fish are other attractions, as are the nearby Lankan Caves.

Blue Canyon   DIVING
The alternative, less-picturesque name of Blue Canyon is Kuda Thila, which means 'small thila'. A canyon, 25m to 30m deep and lined with soft, blue corals, runs beside the thila. The numerous overhangs make for an exciting dive for experienced divers.

Bodu Hithi Thila   DIVING
Bodu Hithi Thila is a prime manta-spotting site from December to March, with a good number of sharks and many reef fish. The soft corals on the sides of the thila are in excellent condition. If currents are moderate, this site is suitable for intermediate divers, and the shallow waters atop the thila offer superb snorkelling.

Rasfari   DIVING
The outer-reef slope of Rasfari drops down to a depth of more than 40m, but a couple of thilas rise up to about 25m. Grey-tip reef sharks love it here – you might see 20 or 30 of them, as well as white-tip sharks, barracuda, eagle rays and trevally. It's a Protected Marine Area.

Colosseum   DIVING
A curving cliff near a channel entrance forms the Colosseum, where pelagics do the performing: sharks and barracuda are often seen here. Experienced divers do this as a drift dive, going right into the channel past ledges and caves, with soft corals and the occasional turtle. Even beginners can do this one in good conditions.

Aquarium   DIVING

As the name suggests, Aquarium (a coral rock formation about 15m down) features a large variety of reef fish. A sandy bottom at 25m can have small sharks and rays, and you might also see giant wrasse and schools of snapper. It's an easy dive and is suitable for snorkelling.

Kani Corner   DIVING

Across the kandu from the Aquarium, Kani Corner is the start of a long drift dive through a narrow channel with steep sides, past caves and overhangs decorated with soft corals. Lots of large marine life can be seen, including sharks, barracuda, Napoleon wrasse and tuna. Beware of fast currents.

HP Reef   DIVING

HP Reef sits beside a narrow channel where currents provide nourishment for incredibly rich growths of soft, blue corals, and support a large variety of reef fish and pelagics. The formations include large blocks, spectacular caves and a 25m vertical, swim-through chimney. It is a Protected Marine Area.

Okobe Thila   DIVING

Also called Barracuda Giri, the attraction of Okobe Thila is the variety of spectacular reef fish that inhabit the shallow caves and crannies, including lionfish, scorpionfish, batfish, sweetlips, moray eels, sharks and big Napoleon wrasse.

Nassimo Thila   DIVING

The demanding dive at Nassimo Thila follows the north side of a fine thila, also known as Paradise Rock, which has superb gorgonians and sea fans on coral blocks, cliffs and overhangs. Numerous large fish frequent this site.

Banana Reef   DIVING

The Protected Marine Area of Banana Reef has a bit of everything: dramatic cliffs, caves and overhangs; brilliant coral growths; big predators such as sharks, barracuda and grouper; and prolific reef fish, including jackfish, morays, Napoleon wrasse and blue-striped snapper. It was one of the first dive sites in the country to become internationally known. The reef top is excellent for snorkelling.

🛏 Sleeping

The concentration of resorts and guesthouses in North Male Atoll means that while you might not feel entirely remote, with views of Male and Thilafushi in the distance from some islands, you do enjoy close proximity to the airport. All sleeping options here can be reached by speedboat from the airport in well under an hour, which is a godsend after a long-haul flight.

Resorts

Asdu Sun Island   DIVING RESORT **$**

(☑ 664 5051; www.asdu.com; full board r US$140; @) Perhaps the least self-conscious resort in the country, laid-back Asdu Sun Island is about as far away from the country's famous luxury resorts as can be imagined. As such it's a great spot for divers with few needs beyond a pristine house reef, cheap diving and somewhere to enjoy a beer come sundown.

All the staff on the island are members of owner Ahmed's family, whose quarters are not hidden away out of sight as is the norm in the Maldives, but instead enjoy equal status on the island to those of the guest rooms. Chickens run around freely and reception's own computer is yours to use for checking your email. It's a great place to feel you're meeting locals, while enjoying some of the perks of life on a resort island.

The tiny island is thickly forested and has a stunning white beach around much of it. Many guests come from Italy, but there's a

---

GASFINOLHU: A VISION OF THE FUTURE?

Tiny Gasfinolhu island, just south of North Male Atoll's capital Thulusdhoo, has taken the Maldives' famous pledge to be carbon neutral by 2020 to heart, and in 2015 will become the country's first carbon-neutral resort island. It has managed this through the installation of 6500 square metres of solar panels, allowing it to run on 100% solar power, and it produces almost two times the amount needed to meet peak demand. While the island retains diesel generators to step in during excessive periods of overcast skies and bad weather, it hopes to have to use them very sparingly. Plans for the future include a zero waste management system and re-use of chilled water in the island's air conditioning as well, both important innovations in the Maldives' notoriously environmentally unsustainable resorts.

wide range of nationalities here, all drawn by the cheap and excellent diving. Accommodation is in aging two- and three-unit white-painted concrete huts, all terribly simple and rather worn, free of air-con, TV, hot water and glass windows, but clean. Food is not a highlight, however, with simple pasta and fish served up for all meals; meaning that dining can get boring here rather quickly. If you're looking for a cheap diving holiday with access to alcohol, though, this remains an excellent choice.

Eriyadu Island Resort   DIVING RESORT $
(☑ 664 4487; www.eriyadumaldives.com; half board r from US$342; ✱@⬚) Eriyadu is pleasantly remote, which is a major incentive for divers who come here for the uncrowded waters that surround the resort. It's also a wonderfully mellow place where you're left to your own devices. The oval-shaped island suffers from bad erosion, but the beaches are still attractive, with a beautiful sandbank sometimes created by the changing current.

The island is full of repeat visitors – the vast majority of whom are German. Children aren't really encouraged, as there are no facilities tailored to them, and this leads to a very quiet and undisturbed atmosphere. There's a good reef, great for snorkelling, with turtles and dolphins regular visitors just metres from the beach. There's no pool but there is a spa, and diving is good value.

The rooms are divided into two categories. Most are in two-room units on the beach, each with its own sea-facing patio, though views can be blocked by the island's thick foliage. The six cheaper rooms are in a two-storey block set back from the beach. Rooms have polished timber floors, TVs and minibars, but feel rather old. The island is quite heavily developed, but the buildings are interspersed with lots of shady trees and shrubbery. The sand-floor restaurant serves most meals in buffet style, with a varied selection of European dishes, curries and seafood. The usual water-sports and excursions are available, as is some low-key evening entertainment, but this economical resort is mainly for diving, snorkelling and relaxing on the beach.

Kurumba Maldives   ACTIVITIES RESORT $$
(☑ 664 2324; www.kurumba.com; r incl breakfast from US$376; ✱@⬚⬚) Established in 1972, Kurumba Maldives was the first resort in the country. It is a high-quality place that continues to be extremely popular, combining a huge range of facilities, ease of access from the airport, family friendliness and quality accommodation.

Some may feel the overly manicured gardens and relentlessly modern architecture make the resort feel a little sterile; others, however, will like its grand country-club style – golf buggies rule the roads here and the resort is big enough for this to be justifiable. Kurumba is the closest resort to Male, and as such it regularly caters for business conferences and conventions as well as day-trippers from the capital, who come for the renowned restaurants. There are eight restaurants to choose from (more than any other resort island in the country), including those serving up Indian, Italian, Chinese and Japanese.

The rooms come in a huge range of categories, the pool villas being especially impressive, each with its own pool in a private back garden. There are no water villas here, and few villas have direct beach access, but it's never too far to the water. There's no end to the facilities available, from a huge and well-equipped dive school to a water-sports centre, tennis courts, babysitters, a gorgeous spa, two gyms and two pools. Kurumba is a place for scale and grandeur and not for hiding away on a desert island, and it remains a hugely popular choice for both couples and families.

Sheraton Maldives
Full Moon Resort & Spa   LUXURY RESORT $$
(☑ 664 2010; www.starwoodhotels.com; r incl breakfast from US$572; ✱@⬚⬚) Magnificently laid out with real style and class, this resort has the ambiance of an upscale country club rather than a remote tropical island. This is in part due to its proximity to the capital, but everything here is aimed at the sophisticate, from the understated public areas to the luxurious spa, housed on its own island.

While lavish, Sheraton Maldives offers affordable luxury in its 176 refurbished rooms, including its smart water villas and beachfront deluxe rooms, all of which feature thatched roofs, shuttered windows, plunge pools and private gardens or terraces. For dining, there's a choice between a Thai restaurant; the al fresco Sand Coast, which serves up international cuisine; and the beachfront Sea Salt, where steaks and seafood are the order of the day. Feast, the main

North Male Atoll

0 ——————— 10 km
0 ——————— 6 miles

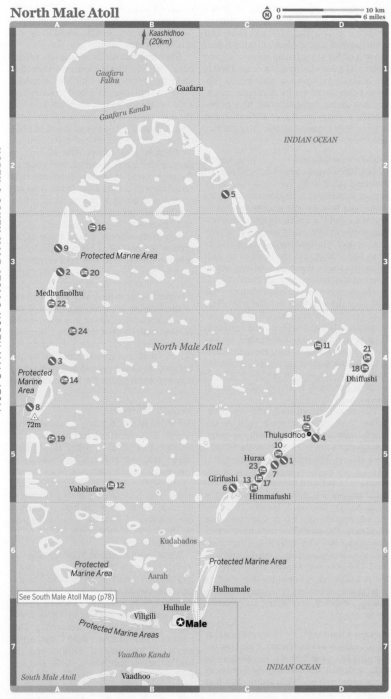

Kaashidhoo
(20km)

*Gaafaru
Falhu*

Gaafaru

Gaafaru Kandu

INDIAN OCEAN

5

16

9

Protected Marine Area

2 20

Medhufinolhu
22

24

11

21

18
Dhiffushi

3

*Protected
Marine
Area*

14

8
72m

15

Thulusdhoo 4

19

10

Huraa

23 7 1

Girifushi 13 17

6

Himmafushi

Vabbinfaru 12

North Male Atoll

Kudabados

Protected Marine Area

*Protected
Marine Area*

Aarah

Hulhumale

See South Male Atoll Map (p78)

Hulhule

Viligili Hulhule

✪ **Male**

Protected Marine Areas

Vaadhoo Kandu

South Male Atoll Vaadhoo

INDIAN OCEAN

restaurant, also serves high-quality buffets three times a day.

A full range of facilities is squeezed onto this small island, including tennis courts, a gym and an inviting swimming pool that has its own waterfall. There are no motorised water-sports, and the lagoon isn't suitable for snorkelling, but sailing, windsurfing and snorkelling trips are offered. There's a full and well-run dive centre, and big-game fishing is also available.

Vivanta by Taj Coral Reef   LUXURY RESORT $$
(☑664 1948; www.tajhotels.com; r incl breakfast from US$675; ❋@⏰❋❋) Totally remodelled in 2009, heart-shaped Taj Vivanta is a glamorous resort that still manages to feel laidback and unpretentious. Although cheaper than its sister resort Taj Exotica, it's not a large step down in service and quality, with all 62 rooms being very plush, including 32 water villas with large terraces and direct access to snorkelling in the lagoon.

Rooms feel thoroughly modern and smart, if a bit anonymous and Ikea-like in their art choices. However, there are great touches such as iPod decks, DVD players and outside showers, though no private plunge pools, save in the top category room.

The resort centres on the large Latitude restaurant, which has a great beachside position and serves up three buffet meals per day. Nearby, there is a pizza station and a teppanyaki bar next to the large infinity pool. The beach isn't the best here, somewhat narrow, rocky in part and held in place by wired rocks, though the sand is wonderfully soft elsewhere.

Other facilities include Jiva Spa, which focuses on Indian massage, Ayurvedic therapies and other treatments and pampering from the subcontinent. You'll find a water-sports centre and a dive school, and snorkelling around the island is excellent (and equipment is free). A reliable number of manta rays turn up at 5pm every day to be fed, an incredible spectacle and one that visitors from nearby resorts sometimes come over to see. Overall, Taj Vivanta is a recommended choice for small, smart, luxury without any fuss.

Makunudu Island   ROMANTIC RESORT $$
(☑664 6464; www.makunudu.com; half board r from US$500; ❋@⏰) Makunudu Island is a favourite of many romantics who return again and again for its utter simplicity, gorgeous beaches, thick vegetation and a sur-

---

North Male Atoll

◆ Activities, Courses & Tours

rounding reef so big that it's hard for speedboats unfamiliar with the island to find their way into the dock. But while the no-frills and utterly simple approach charms many, it's also looking rather aged these days.

Just 2.4 hectares in area, the tiny island almost looks like it might sink under the sheer weight of lush vegetation on it – and the low-key rooms are hard to spot at first, with individual thatched-roof bungalows hidden amid the jungle-like foliage. All rooms face the beach and feature natural finishes, varnished timber, textured white walls and open-air bathrooms, and have all the expected facilities except the deliberately excluded TV. The service and food are both excellent. Breakfast and lunch are buffets, while most dinners are a choice of thoughtfully prepared set menus, served in the delightful open-sided restaurant. Communal beach barbecues are a weekly event.

There are excellent dive sites in the area, the house reef is great for snorkelling, and the Dive Ocean dive school is very experienced at running dives from the island. Windsurfing and sailing are free, as are shorter excursions. This unaffected place won't appeal to travellers wanting pampering, water villas or cutting-edge design, but

BUDDHISM IN THE MALDIVES

It's an uncomfortable truth for many Maldivians, for whom Islam is at the core of their national identity, but it's an irrefutable historic fact that Buddhism actually flourished all over the country before its conversion Islam by a North African Hafiz in 1153.

The islands' pre-Islamic past remains shrouded in mystery, but most historians now believe Buddhism to have been introduced from Sri Lanka in the late 3rd century. Indeed, Buddha statues have been found all over the Maldives, alongside *hawittas*, or stupas – large mounds believed to be related to old Buddhist monuments, located seemingly randomly on islands throughout the Maldives.

Various digs in the 19th and 20th centuries created an excellent national collection of Buddhist relics, which were stored in the National Museum in Male, and included many priceless artifacts such as coral stone Buddha statues and priceless engraved tablets. However, in 2012 an Islamist mob broke into the museum and destroyed nearly the entire collection, deeming them idolatry, meaning that much of the Maldives' rich Buddhist past is now lost forever.

if a small, exclusive, natural-style resort appeals, Makunudu is one of the best choices in the Maldives.

Meeru Island Resort ALL-INCLUSIVE RESORT $$
(☑ 664 3157; www.meeru.com; full board r from US$635; ❄@❅❆) Meeru Island Resort is a long, verdant stretch of land with a dazzling white beach. The resort is enormous, the third-largest in the country, and offers almost every conceivable activity. Indeed, so large is the resort that for convenience there are two receptions and two buffet restaurants, to avoid guests overexerting themselves on the way to dinner.

Rooms come in a startling number of categories, from prefab timber-clad self-contained units that are very cosy to the 87 water villas. The latter range from rustic-style older rooms in bright colours with open-air bathrooms and Jacuzzis to newer, sleeker but perhaps less charming water villas, all in dark wood and with extra luxuries such as espresso machines and direct water access.

All nonmotorised water-sports are included here. There are two excellent spas, the newest of which is entirely over water, and two swimming pools. Other amenities include a nine-hole golf course, two tennis courts, a gym and a golf driving range. Even more unusual is the extraordinary blue-whale skeleton on display in the middle of the island, and a small and rather neglected museum of Maldivian history and traditions above the barnlike main reception.

The house reef can only be reached by boat and these leave every two hours to take snorkellers and divers off to the outer reef, where the aquatic life is fantastic. All the usual water-sports are offered as well as fishing trips, a diving school and a vast lagoon perfect for learning sailing and windsurfing.

Overall, Meeru gets great reviews from guests. It caters to a wide variety of interests and budget levels – it's a big resort but it's not crowded and has retained its personal, friendly feel.

Angsana Ihuru RESORT $$
(☑ 664 3502; www.angsana.com; r incl breakfast from US$595; ❄@❅) With its canopy of palm trees and surrounding gorgeous white beach, Angsana conforms exactly to the tropical-island stereotype and often features in photographs publicising the Maldives. The house reef forms a near-perfect circle around the island, making it brilliant for snorkelling and shore dives, while the relatively low prices here make this a much more affordable way to enjoy the Maldives.

The 45 rooms circle the island, each with direct access to a slice of beach. Rooms are decorated in bright colours, with black furniture, lime-green fabrics and simple outdoor bathrooms. They do rather lack charm, and are definitely rather closely packed together, however. The sand floor restaurant serves buffet meals, though most guests prefer to eat dinner on the deck overlooking the sea. The Thai spa consists of eight treatment rooms, almost all doubles, perfect for romantic pampering.

All nonmotorised water-sports are free, including all snorkelling equipment. While there is some decent shore diving to be done, the best dive sites are some distance away on the edges of the atoll. Boats take divers out each morning and afternoon. One benefit of staying here is the boat that goes to next door sister property Banyan Tree every two hours, meaning that Angsana guests can enjoy the facilities there as well.

Bandos Island Resort

ACTIVITIES RESORT **$$**

(☑664 0088; www.bandosmaldives.com; r incl breakfast US$375; ❉@☎☒♨) One of the largest resorts in the country, Bandos has developed and expanded enormously since it opened as the second resort in the Maldives in 1972. The island is highly developed and re-sembles a well-manicured town centre rather than a typical tropical island. Many love it for that reason, though those looking for true es-cape and isolation may be disappointed.

Bandos has it all, from a conference centre, several restaurants and disco to tennis courts, billiard room, sauna, gym, and beauty salon. The child-care centre is free during the day, and babysitters are affordable in the evening, so in general the resort is one of the most child-friendly in the country.

Fine if rather narrow beaches surround the island, and the house reef is handy for snor-kelling and diving. Lots of fish and a small wreck can be seen here. The dive centre does trips to about 40 dive sites in the area, and even has a decompression chamber. Rooms are modern, with red-tiled roofs, white-tiled floors, and minibar, though they're far from luxurious. The water villas, which include services such as a private butler, are a lot more expensive.

Bandos is great for families and those who like big resorts where there's potential to meet lots of new people and to have a huge range of activities available.

Thulhagiri

RUSTIC RESORT **$$**

(☑664 5930; www.thulhagiri.com.mv; half board r from US$566; ❉☎☒) Small, intimate and low-key, Thulhagiri is as laid-back as it is pretty. Its wide, sloping white beaches and thick palm vegetation greet you as you arrive at its small jetty, beyond which two rows of water villas jut out over the turquoise lagoon. The resort itself is rustic, with an open-air recep-tion and a lily pond among the dense foliage.

The resort is popular with divers, for whom the Sub Aqua Dive Centre offers a full program of courses and activities. There's a good water-sports centre with catamarans and waterskiing available. The small, rather murky swimming pool is the only real evi-dence that this is among the cheaper of North Male Atoll's resorts.

Rooms are in a rustic style, featuring thatched roofs and wooden interiors, and all feel rather dated. The older 17 water villas have four-poster beds, colourful fabrics and coffee-making facilities – they're decent, but not especially great value at their high-season price, while the 17 newer water villas are far smarter and enjoy a more contemporary feel.

There's also the Coconut Spa, offering a full range of treatments. Wi-fi is extra and availa-ble at a hotspot around the bar only. All meals are buffets, and they're passable for a resort in this range. Thulhagiri represents a decent choice for its price range and its small size gives it a more exclusive feel than some of the bigger budget places.

Chaaya Island Dhonveli

RESORT **$$**

(☑664 0055; www.cinnamonhotels.com; half board r US$512; ❉☎☒) This well-run if rather crowded resort boasts a great pool, some lovely beaches, its own surf break and tennis courts. There are six categories of room ca-tering for everyone from honeymooners to keen divers to groups of surfers who come here in big numbers from June to Septem-ber for nearby Pasta Point.

The charming-looking newer water villas are painted blue, and have thatched roofs and Indian-style carved wood frames, al-though they are more impressive outside than in, where furnishings are rather garish. The older water villas are a bit pokey and similarly garish. Better value are the cheaper rooms on the island itself, which are simple but attractive.

While it has some great beaches, the is-land is quite sparse in places, and beach ero-sion is a real problem, with some unsightly sandbags in sight. The beach on the north side of the island is great for swimming and sunbathing, and is safe for children. All meals are buffet style and feature a fair se-lection of good food. All in all, there's a lot going for Dhonveli, as it offers a good stand-ard of service and facilities for the price.

Paradise Island Resort & Spa

ACTIVITIES RESORT **$$**

(☑664 0011; www.villahotels.com; half board r from US$385; ❉@☎☒) Paradise Island is huge and offers some great deals for people seeking a wide range of facilities and services at a bargain price. The beaches are gorgeous, the lagoon an incredible colour even by local standards and the whole place is well run and friendly. It's a great choice if you like endless activities options and plenty going on.

The atmosphere, though, is hardly intimate: you're crowded onto one of the country's biggest island resorts. If you want seclusion and true escape, perhaps move on.

Rooms in Paradise, it turns out, are distinctly simple, with white tiles, white walls, air-con and satellite TV. They are absolutely fine, but unlikely to be places you'll want to spend much of your time. By contrast, the 62 high end rooms in the Haven development, a sort of resort within a resort, come in four categories. They are very sleek, stylish and rather minimalist, the higher categories coming with enormous slate pools and all having large sun terraces with direct access to the water. Though given Haven's prices are comparable to other more intimate, less mass-market resorts, its appeal is rather limited.

Packages with meals at the resort are definitely worth it: you get a decent buffet for every meal and the other three restaurants are nothing to shout about, so you won't find yourself wanting to eat elsewhere that much. Guests staying at the Haven have two restaurants for their exclusive use. The island is well landscaped and has good beaches and a swimming pool. Some rooms are a long way from the restaurant, and many don't have much of a view. The Dive Oceanus dive centre is very friendly and offers boat dives to the many excellent dive sites nearby.

★ **One & Only Reethi Rah**   LUXURY RESORT $$$
(☑ 664 8800; www.oneandonlyresorts.com; r incl breakfast from US$2250; ❊@❂☀⁂) One & Only Reethi Rah is still king of the Maldivian resorts. There may be resorts that cost more, but none have surpassed this extraordinary place, which is all about glamour and style, and shamelessly so. If you aren't comfortable with almost mind-boggling pampering and luxury, this probably isn't the place for you.

Rooms are some of the most enormous in the country, with high ceilings and beautifully furnished Asian interiors. Some have their own pools, and those that don't enjoy direct access to the lagoon or beach. Though you would never guess it, the island is largely man-made and landscaped for optimum beach space, which means there's an unusual number of perfect crescent beaches around the island (if you arrive by seaplane the island's atypical geography is clearly apparent). From its original 15.8 hectares, the island now stands at an incredible (for the Maldives, at least) 44 hectares, which gives the island a spread-out feel, meaning plenty

of privacy, empty beaches and guaranteed tranquillity.

The island is too large to be covered comfortably on foot, and so guests get around by bicycle, though club cars can be called from reception as well. Other unique features include a canal that was built for the sea to flow through the island (a unique example of this in the Maldives), a sumptuous black slate lap pool built out over the ocean and a reception like a Balinese palace. Vegetation is thick and the spotless white-sand beaches truly alluring.

There are three restaurants on the island, a huge ESPA-run spa that focuses on Asian treatments, including Balinese and Thai massage, two tennis courts and a pro-tennis trainer, a superb diving school, a kids club and a full water-sports program.

★ **Gili Lankanfushi**   LUXURY RESORT $$$
(☑ 664 0304; www.gili-lankanfushi.com; water villas incl breakfast US$2110; ❊@❂☀) Astonishingly impressive Gili Lankanfushi is essentially Swiss Family Robinson meets Condé Nast Traveller, and few visitors come away anything but amazed. All villas (for there are no mere rooms here) are over water and as open to the elements as possible (it's only the bedroom that is air-conditioned; the rest of the villa is essentially open-air).

Villas range from the 'standard' Villa Suite, which has three rooms as well as a sea garden, a sun deck and a bed on the roof for stargazing, to the incredible Private Reserve, a free-standing lagoon complex sleeping nine people in the lap of luxury, a short boat ride from the main island. All the buildings are made from natural materials – most woods are imported from sustainable forests elsewhere in Asia – and the attention to detail is incredible, with luxurious treats hidden away under natural fibres in what is one of the Maldives' most environmentally conscious resorts.

The island itself is very pretty, criss-crossed with sand paths, along which guests can cycle to the main communal areas: the infinity pool overlooking the beach, the charming bar and the beachside restaurant, where elaborate buffets and à la carte menus are equally impressive. Foodies will appreciate the wine cellar, a sumptuous subterranean space for private degustation dinners and wine tasting around a huge driftwood table, although the three further restaurants on the island are also excellent and helmed by international chefs creating sumptuous dishes. Every room comes with a 'Man Friday' – a butler whose job it is to bring you anything you need; and indeed this is not a good place for those who don't like to be fussed over; staff appear to magically know your name and seem genuinely determined to ensure you have nothing to worry about but relaxing.

The island is very convenient for the airport, with the journey taking just ten minutes by speedboat, and yet you still feel wonderfully remote at this intelligently luxurious place.

★**Huvafen Fushi**   LUXURY RESORT **$$$**
(☑ 664 4222; www.huvafenfushi.peraquum.com; r from US$2286; ✳ @ 🛜 🕸 🐾) Huvafen Fushi set a new standard for stylish, sophisticated luxury when it opened a decade ago and has inspired countless imitators elsewhere in the Maldives and beyond. Understated and more than a little fabulous, Huvafen Fushi is all about unfussy luxury and hassle-free glamour, making the most of its gorgeous beaches and reef, its superb restaurants and world class rooms.

The villas are thoroughly modern, with clean lines, lots of space and all featuring their own plunge pools, 40-inch plasma-screen TVs, Bose surround systems, iPod plug-in points, espresso machines and remote-control everything. The water villas that have been so widely copied remain some of the most impressive in the country, each with its own enclosed deck overlooking the sea, with access to the lagoon down a staircase.

Despite this, the atmosphere within the resort is informal and relaxed, with no reception and most things being arranged by the *thakuru* (butler) in-room. There's an impressive array of dining options: Celsius for international, Salt for fish and seafood, Raw for innovative uncooked meals and Fogliani's for pizza on the beach, while there's also Vinum, one of the largest wine cellars in the Maldives, and the funky sand-floored UMBar by the enormous infinity pool. The gorgeous Lime Spa has an amazing underwater treatment room, so you can be massaged while schools of fish swim by the windows. There's also a gym, diving and water-sports centres, plus three individually designed dhonis moored in the lagoon that guests can book to stay on for a night or two during their visit.

While the island is on the small side, the entire place feels eerily empty even at full capacity, such is the way in which the resort has been laid out. This is a great place for a luxurious honeymoon or a romantic break with a funky feel.

Four Seasons Kuda Huraa   LUXURY RESORT **$$$**
(☑ 664 4888; www.fourseasons.com/maldiveskh; r incl breakfast from US$1200; ✳ @ 🛜 🕸 🐾) The smaller of the two Four Seasons properties in the Maldives, Four Seasons Kuda Huraa is also the more intimate and laid-back. The style here is that of a Maldivian village, though you wont find many Maldivians living in this amount of luxury. The beaches on the island are lovely and there's an enormous curved infinity pool to boot.

The charming rooms range from beach bungalows with quaint brick walls and high thatched roofs to glamorous water villas on the far side of the resort. The furnishings combine tropical luxury with modern design and are sleek and attractive. All categories of rooms have private plunge pools, save the water villas.

The spa is on a smaller island a short boat ride across the lagoon. The trip is done on a mini-dhoni that goes back and forth whenever guests want to get there. A kids club and a teens club are both free and make this a great option for a family holiday. All nonmotorised water-sports are free, and the gym is excellent.

The island itself is long and very attractive, and the nearby inhabited island of Huraa is a short hop away by boat, and is popular with guests for its many craft workshops, where souvenirs can be bought. This is a glamorous and stylish place with friendly staff and a laid-back approach to luxury. It has a different feel to its grander sister island Landaa Giraavaru, and consequently is often combined with it on a two-centre holiday.

Coco Bodu Hithi   LUXURY RESORT **$$$**
(☑ 334 5555; www.cocoboduhithi.com; r incl breakfast from US$1295; ✳ @ 🛜 🕸 🐾) Coco Bodu Hithi is a large resort, but one that nevertheless manages to impress with its excellent rooms and wide variety of activities, even if it's hardly an isolated or particularly quiet spot. The island boasts superb beaches and one of the best swimming pools in the Maldives.

The rooms come in several different categories. The island villas are sublimely stylish, with a big bathtub central to the room and lots of designer-fabulous touches. The top categories are the Escape villas and residences, a mini resort-within-a-resort found on their own private over-water pier. These are gorgeously sleek, with huge windows onto the sea, private lap pools and enormous bathrooms stuffed with Molton Brown goodies. Escape guests also have their own buggy chauffeur service to take them anywhere on the island.

The rest of the island ticks every box – there are five restaurants, an impressive wine collection, a water-sports centre offering everything from wakeboarding to windsurfing, a top-notch dive school with easy access to a host of excellent sites and a large and beautiful spa that offers every treatment you could reasonably wish for.

Baros   LUXURY RESORT $$$

(☑664 2672; www.baros.com; r incl breakfast from US$1435; ✳@☎) Understated, sophisticated class jumps out at you from the moment you arrive and see Baros' impressive Lighthouse, a fine-dining restaurant and cocktail bar, which has a shapely circus-tent roof and the feel of an exclusive yacht club. This is the centrepiece of the resort, and the calling card for a place that offers classic relaxation and superb service.

Other dining can be had at the far less formal Cayenne Grill overlooking the reef, where you can have your food cooked any way you choose by the fleet of chefs, or the all-day Lime Restaurant, where buffet breakfasts and à la carte lunch and dinner are served. All guests are on a bed-and-breakfast basis, allowing them to enjoy the variety of eating opportunities throughout their stay (although this does add up quickly).

The atmosphere is intimate and quiet, with children under six not allowed. There's 'gentle' jazz and Maldivian music three times a week, and that's about the scope of the nightlife. As well as diving, snorkelling and swimming, there's a spa popular with couples. The three room categories on the island are all beautiful. Even the standard 'deluxe villa' is a refined 89-sq-metre structure with a sumptuous outdoor shower and garden, while the water bungalows are excellent.

Baros is one of many upmarket resorts that has made a conscious decision not to have a swimming pool. It's an excellent resort and has rightly earned a loyal following. This is a great choice for a luxurious and romantic getaway.

Banyan Tree Vabbinfaru   LUXURY RESORT $$$

(☑664 3147; www.banyantree.com; full board r from US$1305; ✳@☎) Banyan Tree's only Maldives resort boasts beautiful wide beaches on a lovely circular island far enough from Male to feel like a true desert island experience. The island offers a refreshing take on the top-end experience, a combination of romantic destination, escape and ecotourism project that is extremely quiet and popular with couples.

While certainly aimed at the luxury market, Banyan Tree is not at the heady heights of some of its competitors who charge at least twice as much for a room. In fact, given that all packages are either full board or all inclusive, this works out as relatively good value for money.

There's good snorkelling on the house reef and good diving a short distance away on the atoll edge, as well as a gym and a water-sports centre. Banyan Tree was one of the first resorts to have a marine laboratory on the island, and guests are able to help out in various capacities – including planting their own coral in the coral garden and monitoring the sharks and turtles kept under observation in cages just off the island shore.

The restaurant and bar are both casually elegant, open-sided spaces with sand floors and quality furniture, and the buffet meals cater to all tastes, though lack of choice in dining options might annoy some. For special meals, in-villa dining and sandbank dining are both available, which appeals to the many honeymooners who come here. A spa with Thai-trained therapists offers a full range of exotic treatments, while a recent renovation means that all 48 villas have plunge pools, although there is no main pool or water villas. Angsana Ihuru, Banyan Tree's 'little sister' resort, is just across a small channel next door – a boat goes back and forth every two hours, allowing guests at each resort to enjoy the other's facilities.

Guesthouses

★ Cokes Surf Shack   GUESTHOUSE $

(☑760 2232; www.cokessurfshack.com; Thulusdhoo; s/d from US$50/100; ✳☎) The most raved-about surf destination in the Maldives, this five-room place right on the beach is perfectly located for two of the country's best surfing spots (best between March and September), one of which, the eponymous Cokes, can literally be seen from the guesthouse. The rooms are simple but comfortable, and there's good quality Maldivian home cooking to be had in both of the dining areas.

Palma Guesthouse   GUESTHOUSE $

(☑794 0123; www.maldives-guesthouse.com; Huraa; s/d incl breakfast US$113/170; ✳☎) The project of a Franco-Maldivian couple, this charming, modern and comfortable house operates with Gallic flair and dubs itself a *chamber d'hôte* (homestay), rather than anything as formal as a guesthouse. Rooms all have good bathrooms with hot water, and guests are actively invited to participate in preparing the meals, giving the place a real community feel.

As well as full board, the price includes an activity each day, ranging from fishing to snorkelling. However, the beach on Huraa is small and public, and there's not much more on the island.

Happy Life Safari Lodge GUESTHOUSE $
(☑977 4151; www.guesthouses-in-maldives.com; Dhiffushi; all inclusive s/d US$142/232; ❈ @) On one of North Male Atoll's most pleasant inhabited islands, this friendly guesthouse has four comfortable rooms, all of which have open-air bathrooms and enjoy (if you crane your neck) sea views. The beach is a short walk away, and it's private, meaning you can swim without offending local sensibilities. Meals are good,

There's an impressive list of activities available, from yoga and snorkelling to sand bank visits and night fishing.

🅸 Getting There & Away

Nearly all resorts in North Male Atoll collect their guests from the airport by launch, as even the furthest island is less than an hour away. All the inhabited islands are connected by ferry from Male's Viligili Ferry Terminal. Ferries run by **Maldives Transport and Contracting Company** (☑799 8821; www.mtcc.com.mv) go in both directions every day except Fridays.

Kaashidhoo

Though in the Kaafu (Male) administrative district, the island of Kaashidhoo is way out by itself, in a channel north of North Male Atoll. The island has a clinic, a secondary school and over 1900 people, which makes it one of the most populous in Kaafu. Some of the ruins here are believed to be remains of an old Buddhist temple. Local crops include watermelon, lemon, banana, cucumber and zucchini, but the island is best known for its *raa* – the 'palm toddy' made from the sap of a palm tree, drunk fresh or slightly fermented.

Local boats going to or from the northern atolls sometimes shelter in the lagoon in Kaashidhoo in bad weather. Dive boats on longer trips might stop to dive Kaashidhoo

East Faru, a good place to see large pelagic marine life.

Gaafaru Falhu

This small atoll has just one island, also called Gaafaru, with a population of 1100. The channel to the north of the atoll, Kaashidhoo Kuda Kandu, has long been a shipping lane, and several vessels have veered off course and ended up on the hidden reefs of Gaafaru Falhu. There are three diveable wrecks – SS *Seagull* (1879), *Erlangen* (1894) and *Lady Christine* (1974). None is anywhere near intact, but the remains all have good coral growth and plentiful fish. Dive trips are possible from Helengeli and Eriyadu, but most visitors are from live-aboard dive boats.

South Male Atoll

Crossing the Vaadhoo Kandu, the choppy channel between North and South Male Atolls, you'll quickly notice that South Male Atoll has a very different feel from its busy northern neighbour. This is partly due to the lack of people – there are only three inhabited islands here, all of which are on the eastern edge of the atoll and have small populations – and partly to do with the fact that the uninhabited islands are spread out and so you really feel that you're removed from the hustle and bustle of Male and its surrounding islands.

The biggest island in South Male Atoll is charming and friendly **Maafushi** (population 1200), which is the centre of the Maldives' independent travel scene. The island has undergone seismic change in the past few years, and now has dozens of guesthouses on it. Indeed, during high season there are as many foreigners as locals on the island, making it the Maldives' most cosmopolitan and progressive inhabited island. There is a foreigner beach here, meaning it's possible to swim in a bikini, and there is a very competitive diving and excursions market to boot. As you can reach Maafushi in just a couple of hours by public ferry from Male, it's quite possible to just turn up here and shop around – competition is fierce and prices are (by local standards) low.

Nearby **Guraidhoo**, more populous than the bigger Maafushi with around 1800 people, is the atoll's largest town. Its lagoon has a good anchorage and it's a busy port used by both fishing dhonis and passing safari boats. Sultans from Male sought refuge here during rebellions from as early as the 17th century, while today it's popular with budget travellers who stay at the cheap guesthouses, and with visitors from nearby resorts (it's actually possible to walk across the lagoon to a neighbouring resort at low tide!).

The island of **Gulhi**, north of Maafushi, is not large but is inhabited by around 750 people. Fishing is the main activity, and there's also a small shipyard, and a couple of guesthouses.

🏃 Activities

Some of the best dive sites are around the Vaadhoo Kandu, which funnels a huge volume of water between the North and South Male Atolls. Various smaller kandus channel water between the atoll and the surrounding sea, and also provide great diving. Due to the high number of independent travellers on Maafushi, most resorts in South Male Atoll are used to having day visitors who pay to use the facilities for the day. Most guesthouses can organise this.

Velassaru Caves   DIVING
The rugged Velassaru Caves and overhangs, on the steep wall of the Vaadhoo Kandu, have very attractive coral growth. You may see sharks, turtles and rays on the bottom at around 30m. This dive is not for beginners, but if the current isn't too strong there's excellent snorkelling on the reef edge.

NONEXCLUSIVE SURFING

With so much in the Maldives being exclusive, the decision of the government in 2014 to end the policy of exclusivity for surf breaks was welcomed by locals and surfers around the world alike. Until recently, surf breaks near to resort islands were deemed to be property of the hotels, meaning that only guests of each property were able to surf these waves, even when they were some distance from the island proper. This created tensions between locals (many of whom love to surf) and hotel managers, with the government initially siding with the resorts. However, following years of debate and campaigning, the government decision has now been overturned, and so provided you can get there, you're now free to surf at any break in the country.

Vaadhoo Caves   DIVING
Vaadhoo Caves consists of a row of small caves, plus a bigger one with a swim-through tunnel, as well as excellent soft corals, gorgonians, jackfish and the odd eagle ray. If the current is strong, this is a demanding dive; if not, it's great for snorkelling.

Embudhoo Express   DIVING
Embudhoo Express is a 2km drift dive through the Embudhoo Kandu, which is a Protected Marine Area. With the current running in, rays, Napoleon wrasse and sharks often congregate around the entrance. The current carries divers along a wall with overhangs and a big cave. The speed of the current makes for a demanding dive.

Kuda Giri   DIVING
The attraction of Kuda Giri is the hulk of a small freight ship, deliberately sunk here to create an artificial reef. Sponges and cup corals are growing on the wreck, and it provides a home for large schools of fish. Sheltered from strong currents, this is a good site for beginners and for night dives.

Vaagali Caves   DIVING
Vaagali Caves is an exciting and not too demanding dive. It's in a less exposed location and has many caves on its north side, at around 15m, filled with sponges and soft corals. There's also good coral regrowth and lots of fish on the top of the reef.

Guraidhoo Kandu   DIVING
A central reef splits Guraidhoo Kandu into two channels, with many possibilities for divers, even those with less experience. There are numerous reef fish, larger pelagics near the entrance and mantas when the current is running out. The kandu is a Protected Marine Area.

🛏 Sleeping

South Male Atoll is easily reached by speedboat transfer from the airport, as well as once- or twice-daily public ferries.

Resorts
Embudu Village   BUDGET RESORT **$**
(📲 664 4776; www.embudu.com; full board s/d from US$176/296; ❄ @ 🛜) Embudu Village is a popular budget resort with a focus on divers and couples. It's as relaxed and unpretentious as its sand-floor reception suggests. This is one of the cheapest resorts in the country, and while it's not particularly charming or rustic, it does have lots going for it.

The island itself has some gorgeous beaches, is thickly vegetated and has a very accessible house reef. All accommodation is on a full-board basis, with buffet meals of average quality. The rooms are basic and fan-cooled with no water, but are still very acceptable for the price. There are also 16 deluxe over-water bungalows, though these are bare and functional and may well disappoint if you're after romance.

Diverland runs the popular diving program here, with over 90 different sites in the nearby area. Diving is excellent value and there are discounts for multidive packages. Annoyingly wi-fi is charged by the hour (US$8 per hour). This is not currently a place to come if you're reliant on being online. However, if you're not looking for luxuries but an unpretentious beach and diving holiday, Embudu Village is a good choice.

Biyadhoo
DIVING RESORT $

(☑ 333 6611; www.biyadhoo.com; full board s/d US$270/320; ✳ @ 🛜) Attractive Biyadhoo has thick foliage, high palms and lovely beaches in parts. It attracts a crowd of loyal divers, many of whom are repeat visitors and love the good deals available here. It's also a popular day trip destination for independent travellers staying on Maafushi who want some alcohol and a change of scene.

All 96 rooms are standards, housed in 16-room blocks. All have air-con and a minibar, but the rooms are pretty tired, so don't expect water villa-levels of glamour. Request a room on the west side of the island for beach proximity – beaches on the east side have been badly affected by erosion and as such are not good for sunbathing, often visibly covered in sandbags. While the main beach on the west side is wide and flat, it can feel crowded.

The in-house dive operation charges guests at the end of their stay for the best overall package based on the number of dives they did, so there's no need to book anything in advance. Most people here are on full-board deals, with buffets served up for each meal in the resort's one restaurant. Other facilities include a football pitch, badminton and volleyball facilities, and a spa. The resort has a friendly and relaxed feel and won't disappoint anyone looking for a good diving base.

★ Rihiveli Beach Resort
RUSTIC RESORT $$

(☑ 664 3731; www.rihiveli-maldives.com; full board r US$560; 🛜) One of the Maldives less main-stream resorts, Rihiveli has almost nothing in common with the massmarket creations aimed at package tourists, and remains true to the spirit of its French founder, who set the place up in the 1980s as a refuge. This was the first resort to use the now ubiquitous 'no news, no shoes' phrase, and you'll quickly understand why.

Accommodation consists of just 48 sea-facing bungalows, all built in a rustic style from coral stone and with traditional thatched roofs. They have all the basics for comfort such as hot water, but nothing considered superfluous, such as air-con, fridges, phones or a TV. This is the secret of its success and also the reason Rihiveli will never be overrun with package tourists.

The open-air bar has a sand floor and shady trees overhead, while the restaurant is built over the lagoon and has a lovely view as well as excellent food. A conch shell is blown to call guests to meals, and everyone is invited to take tea with the staff daily at 5.30pm: yes, this is not your typical Maldivian resort! The usual water-sports and tennis are all included in the room price, as is a daily excursion, so there's no chance of boredom here. You can wade across the lagoon to two uninhabited islands where the resort organises regular barbecue lunches. Frequent boat trips to other reefs make up for the lack of snorkelling sites next to the resort. The main diving destinations are around nearby Hathikolhu Kandu, and there's a small wreck to explore. Wi-fi is available at the lobby for free, but elsewhere it's just you and nature, so there's no need to take your iPhone to the beach.

With its relaxed ambience, French style and natural appeal, Rihiveli is a unique and special resort for those who appreciate the simple things and want a totally laid-back and unfussy beach and activities holiday.

Anantara Dhigu & Anantara Veli
LUXURY RESORT $$

(☑ 664 4100; www.anantara.com; r incl breakfast from US$790; ✳ @ 🛜 ☒ ⛵) This impressive and beautifully set Thai-owned resort is draped over three connected islands that share a turquoise lagoon. All are officially their own resorts, and while in reality they're all centrally managed, we've listed the more exclusive Naladhu separately, as it's out of bounds to guests staying at the other two resorts – not that Dhigu or Veli could ever be considered budget destinations.

South Male Atoll

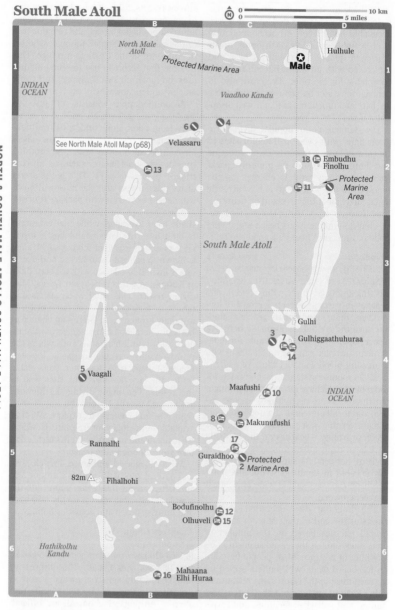

Dhigu is the main resort, where guests arrive and where the majority of the facilities, such as diving school and water-sports centre, are housed. It's a relatively crowded island featuring beach villas and large, very glamorous water villas decorated in classic Asian styles and with spacious sun decks. It has a big pool by the beach, a kids club, and a gorgeous over-water spa.

Crossing the lagoon to next-door Veli by boat, there's more of the same. Veli, where all the accommodation is over water, nev-

South Male Atoll

ertheless has the lowest-priced rooms at the resort, though even in the bottom category they're a good size – 62 sq metres each. Veli feels slightly over-developed in places, with seemingly endless over-water pathways to yet more water villas – but it also has some wonderful rooms, particularly the popular Ocean Pool Bungalows.

Veli has its own large pool and spa, and is connected by a walkway to Naladhu. There are a variety of restaurants here – seven in total across the three islands, including an excellent Thai restaurant on a walkway between Naladhu and Veli. This means that you're unlikely to get bored with the food, or with the huge amount of activities available. Overall both of these resorts offer excellent high-end service and rooms at a relatively affordable price.

Olhuveli Beach & Spa   ACTIVITIES RESORT $$
(664 2788; www.olhuvelimaldives.com; r incl breakfast from US$520;) Olhuveli is a big, midrange resort that somehow manages to feel very intimate. This is largely due to the relatively large size of the island, which accommodates its 129 rooms without feeling crowded, but also due to the clever use of space. The beaches on both sides of the island are very attractive, and Olhuveli understandably has many repeat visitors.

The rooms are spread along beaches in free-standing two-level blocks, one room below and one above. They are tastefully done, furnished throughout with dark-wood four-poster beds, and feature balconies or patios that lead out to the beach. There are also two rings of swish but rather identikit water bungalows stretching over the lagoon.

Snorkelling is excellent off the end of the jetty, at the edge of the reef, where turtles are common. The dive school runs drift dives in

nearby channels, as well as wreck and night dives. Food is served at the main restaurant buffet, but there are also alternatives such as pan-Asian restaurant Four Spices, the poolside Island Pizza and the beachfront Lagoon Restaurant. Overall, Olhuveli offers excellent value. It's a great compromise between budget prices and high standards and between romance and activities.

★ Jumeirah Vittaveli   LUXURY RESORT $$$
(664 2020; www.jumeirah.com; r incl breakfast from $1530;) Meaning 'vastness of space' in Dhivehi, Jumeirah Vittaveli is actually half created from reclaimed land, though you'd never guess that from looking at it. It's a beautiful place, with gorgeous beaches and plentiful thick vegetation (the island was an established resort called Bolifushi for a long time before Jumeirah redeveloped it). But its real draw is its rooms.

Even the starting category, the Beach Villa, is a palatial 184 sq metres, and all rooms have their own private swimming pools as standard, up to and including the 800-sq-metre Presidential Suite, which is astoundingly luxurious. The most notable rooms are the Ocean Suites, six of which stand independent of each over the reef, and can only be reached by dhoni. These are popular with those seeking total privacy, though arguably the Beach Villas on the main island are more charming. As well as being spacious, rooms are tall, with wonderful beamed ceilings, marble floors and distinctive thatched roofs, while decor combines timeless tradition with modern touches such as flat-screen TVs, iPod docks and rain showers.

The island enjoys gorgeous stretches of beach, while the public areas are also impressive, all crafted in gorgeous timbers and sublimely decorated. Facilities on the island

THE MAAFUSHI PHENOMENON

The most concentrated independent tourism in the Maldives can be found on the island of Maafushi, an hour and a half's journey from Male by public ferry. Its combination of good beaches, proximity to the capital and local entrepreneurial spirit have seen some 30 guesthouses and hotels spring up in the past five years, and in high season it seems that almost everyone on the island is working in the tourism sector.

Despite this, the island remains conservative once you get into the back streets, and while foreigners are no longer a novelty, people walking around scantily clad will not feel very welcome. The conservatism of traditional Maldivian society means that the development of Maafushi has not come without its tensions, though projects such as the 'foreigners beach', which is screened off from the rest of the inhabitants to allow visitors to indulge in scandal-free swimming, have helped to manage the disconnect between local cultural values and visitors' holiday expectations. Other benefits include the desalination plant that tourist money has paid for, which supplies the entire island with plentiful drinking water.

include the magnificent Talise Spa, a gym, a water-sports centre and a very smart diving centre with brand new equipment. The resort has two L-shaped communal pools, one for families, the other restricted to adults, so there's peace and quiet even though children are more than welcome on the island, as the excellent kids club demonstrates. There are three restaurants to choose from: Samsara for Pan-Asian cuisine; Mediterranean Fenesse; and steak and seafood at the candlelit MU Beach Bar & Grill. Altogether this is one of the smartest and luxurious resorts in the country, and is a perfect choice for a romantic break.

★ Cocoa Island by COMO LUXURY RESORT $$$
(☑664 1818; www.comohotels.com/cocoaisland; water villas incl breakfast from US$1400; ✱@🛜⛱) This wonderful place is one of the most unique Maldivian resorts, and since its lavish refit at the hands of the COMO group, Cocoa has consistently impressed. Indeed, this is one of the very few resorts that manages to get everything so right with such little fuss: a combination of perfect beaches, beautiful rooms, wonderful food and superb staff.

First of all, the small island has no rooms on it at all – they're all built over water in a shape that mirrors that of the island itself. And what rooms they are – built in the shape of traditional Maldivian dhoni boats – all clean lines, white cotton and dark wood. Newer two-floor loft villas are furnished with white timbers and are even more stunning. Other great touches include outdoor showers, direct sea access from the rooms, and gorgeous COMO Shambhala bathroom products.

On the island proper there is nothing superfluous. A large infinity pool, cracking beaches the entire way around, a superb restaurant with a large range of dishes, a smart cocktail bar, a sumptuous spa, a gym, and the excellent and friendly dive centre. Everything is luxurious, but nothing is over the top. All in all, a great recommendation for unpretentious and low-key luxury that will keep even the most demanding people happy.

Naladhu Maldives LUXURY RESORT $$$
(☑664 4105; www.naladhu.anantara.com; villa incl breakfast from US$1172; ✱@🛜⛱) Naladhu is the most exclusive of three resorts run by Thai group Anantara on three separate islands around a stunningly beautiful lagoon. You get the best of both worlds here; while you're totally secluded on a private island with just 18 villas on it, you also have the option to use the facilities of the other, far larger resorts.

The concept here is simple: an exclusive refuge for those who want to remain unseen and totally private. The villas are sumptuous, with huge private pools and either beach access in the six beach houses or views to the ocean in the ocean houses. The top category room here is the two-bedroom residence, a totally private mansion for utter seclusion.

The island has its own large pool, a spa and the smart Living Room restaurant on the beach, but if you want to explore different restaurants, swim on different beaches, go diving or use any of the other facilities you'd associate with bigger resorts, you can simply walk across the bridge to Veli, or take a boat to Dhigu. Needless to say, the bridge to Veli is for the exclusive use of Naladhu guests.

Taj Exotica
LUXURY RESORT $$$

(☑664 2200; www.tajhotels.com; r incl breakfast from US$1035; ❄@🛜🌊) Within easy striking distance of the airport, yet still feeling wonderfully secluded and exclusive, this elegant, understated resort is all about quiet luxury and indulgence and is the flagship Maldivian resort of the Indian Taj Group. Its super-stylish public areas and gorgeous rooms make it perfectly suited to romantic beach holidays, making it very popular with honeymooners.

The island here is long and thin, with a beach on the lagoon side and water villas on the atoll edge. All categories of rooms are very smart, many of them with their own plunge pools overlooking the beach. The public areas include a DVD and book library, a well-stocked games room, a gorgeous infinity pool and, at the far end of the island, the Jiva Grande Spa. There's a gym and free yoga classes each morning.

Taj Exotica was one of the original pioneers of fine à la carte dining in the Maldives and it's safe to say you'll eat excellently here, with everything ordered and individually cooked from a sumptuous and expensive menu. This is one place where full board would come in handy – the meals here are far from budget. There's also a fine dining restaurant, which is built out over the lagoon and is open in the evenings. Overall this small but beautifully realised island is a real treat for honeymooners or couples looking for a perfect high-style escape.

Guesthouses

⭐**Kaani Village & Spa**
HOTEL $

(☑911 3626; www.kaanivillage.com; Maafushi; r incl breakfast US$112; ❄🛜🌊) This sleekly put together place is impressive, and unique mainly for its great courtyard pool, which allows guests to swim without offending local sensibilities, something no other guesthouse on Maafushi can do. The rooms, over two stories facing the pool, are stylish, comfortable and modern with good bathrooms. There's even a small spa here too: it's almost a resort!

Arena Beach Hotel
HOTEL $

(☑793 3231; www.arenabeachhotel.com; Maafushi; r incl breakfast from US$150; ❄🛜) Brand new in 2014, this (relatively) high-rise place has an enviable location within the screened-off confines of the foreigners' beach, where you're free to frolic in a bikini. The 19 rooms all have balconies (many enjoying great views), safes, minibars and flatscreen TVs.

Staff are friendly and there's a decidedly laid-back vibe to the beach restaurant outside.

Crystal Sands
HOTEL $

(☑779 0660; www.crystalsands.mv; Maafushi; r from US$125; ❄🛜) This three-storey building is right opposite the port where you arrive on Maafushi, and it's a sign of how far this island has come in just a few years of tourism. Very much a hotel rather than a guesthouse, the Crystal Sands has 18 large, bright and impressively designed rooms, complete with rain showers and walk-out balconies.

The hotel also has one of Maafushi's better restaurants on its ground floor, the Symphony Lagoon, which has a big international menu. There's also a great roof terrace for sunbathing, with a view of the beach.

Summer Villa
GUESTHOUSE $

(☑795 4445; www.summervillamaldives.com; Maafushi; s/d incl breakfast US$45/90; ❄🛜) This popular guesthouse is situated a couple of blocks back from the port and is a great choice away from the tourist strip. Run by an enthusiastic team of young locals, Summer Villa organises lots of activities and has a fun and friendly communal vibe. The six rooms are smart and comfortable, and meals are served in the sandy garden.

White Shell Beach Inn
GUESTHOUSE $

(☑989 8778; www.thewhiteshell.com; Maafushi; r incl breakfast from US$85; ❄🛜) Right on the beach, the White Shell offers two types of room, the cheapest of which have no hot water or TV. It's a bit overpriced for what it is (although the rooms are decent), but it's the best option if you want to be able to lounge about in a skimpy outfit all day and not worry about offending the locals.

Rip Tide Vacation Inn
GUESTHOUSE $

(☑777 6272; www.guesthouses-in-maldives.com; Guraidhoo; s/d incl breakfast US$68/75; ❄🛜) The first guesthouse established on quiet Guraidhoo is this seven-room place on the beach facing a resort across a shallow lagoon. The rooms are comfortable with large bathrooms and satellite TVs, and there's a pleasant sand-floored restaurant. It's good value.

ⓘ Getting There & Away

Nearly all resorts in South Male Atoll collect their guests from the airport by launch, as even the furthest island is less than an hour away. All the inhabited islands can be reached by ferry from Male's Viligili Ferry Terminal. Ferries go in both directions every day except Friday.

Ari Atoll

Best Resorts

➡ W Retreat & Spa (p87)

➡ Mirihi (p88)

➡ Conrad Maldives Rangali Island (p89)

➡ Constance Halaveli Maldives (p88)

Best Dive Sites

➡ Hammerhead Point (p83)

➡ Dhidhdhoo Beyru (p83)

➡ Manta Reef (p83)

➡ Fish Head (p83)

Why Go?

Centred on a vast, sumptuous and inviting oval lagoon dotted with reefs, Ari Atoll sits to the west of the capital and is famed for its superb diving and stellar beaches. While the atoll is one natural entity, it's large enough to have been split into two districts – North and South Ari Atoll.

The nutrient-rich water that flows out through channels attracts large creatures from the open sea and divers from all over the world – South Ari remains one of the best places in the world to see whale sharks, the world's largest fish, which are spotted year-round on the outer reef, as well as hammerhead sharks in the atoll's northern parts.

Ari Atoll hosts some of the most famous and exclusive resorts in the country, but its exceptional diving means there are also a host of cheaper diving resorts and a vibrant, growing guesthouse scene on some of the inhabited islands.

When to Go

➡ **May-Dec** The best time to dive or snorkel with the amazing whale sharks.

➡ **Jan-Mar** High season coincides with European winter and the best weather in Ari Atoll; expect blue skies and high temperatures.

➡ **Dec-Apr** This is prime hammerhead shark spotting season in northern Ari Atoll.

Ari Atoll

The geographic entity of Ari Atoll is about 80km from north to south, 30km wide and contains 18 inhabited islands out of a total of 81. The most populous island is **Mahibadhoo**, the capital of South Ari, with around 2000 people. There are now several guesthouse on Mahibadhoo, and it's a good place to experience life in a large Maldivian town.

Maamigili, also in the south of the atoll, has over 1600 people, many of whom work in nearby resorts. There's an airstrip (the only one in Ari Atoll) here with several daily flights to and from Male.

Other inhabited islands, typically with a population of a few hundred, are dotted around the edges of the atoll. Quite a few islands have ruins or artefacts of ancient Buddhist and Hindu settlements.

🏃 Activities

All of the resorts have diving operations and Ari is a top pick for those who love marine life, particularly for its hammerheads and whale sharks.

★ Hammerhead Point   DIVING

Also known as Rasdhoo Madivaru, Hammerhead Point is a more demanding dive on an outer reef where hammerhead sharks, mantas and other large pelagics are frequent visitors. Outside this reef the depth drops rapidly to over 200m and the water is exceptionally clear. Hammerhead dives usually start before dawn, descending by around 6am to have the best chance of spotting these incredible creatures.

★ Dhidhdhoo Beyru   DIVING

From May to September, whale sharks cruise almost continually along the 10km-long Dhidhdhoo Beyru on the southwestern edge of the atoll, which extends from Ariyadhoo Kandu north to the tip of Dhigurah island. However, even out of season there are consistent whale shark sightings here, which increase during a full moon when the currents become faster.

★ Manta Reef   DIVING

Also called Madivaru, Manta Reef is at the end of a channel where powerful currents carry plankton out of the atoll during the northeast monsoon (December to April) – fast food for manta rays. Mantas also come to be cleaned. Reef fish include Napoleon wrasse, snapper and parrotfish, while pe-

lagics such as turtles, tuna and sharks visit the outer reef slope. It's for advanced divers only, and is great for snorkellers in the right conditions.

There has been concern in recent years that the overuse of this famous dive site is leading to a declining number of mantas coming here. Do ask your dive centre about this and follow their instructions very carefully to avoid contributing to further degradation.

Fish Head   DIVING

Also called Mushimasmingali Thila, Fish Head is one of the world's most famous dive sites. Its steep sides are spectacular, with multilevel ledges, overhangs and caves supporting many sea fans and black corals; its top is heavily encrusted with anemones. Beware of stonefish. The prolific fish life at this Protected Marine Area includes fusiliers, large Napoleons, trevally and schools of hungry barracuda. The main attractions, however, are the numerous grey-tip reef sharks, which can be seen up close. Strong currents can make this a demanding dive, and extreme care should be taken not to damage the superb but heavily used site.

Maaya Thila   DIVING

Maaya Thila is a classic round thila known for the white-tip reef sharks that circle it. Caves and overhangs around the thila have lots of gorgonians, soft corals and schools of reef fish. It's a Protected Marine Area.

Halaveli Wreck   DIVING

The well-known Halaveli Wreck was created in 1991 when a 38m cargo ship was deliberately sunk. It's famous for the friendly stingrays enticed here by regular feeding – keep your fingers away from their mouths.

Fesdu Wreck   DIVING

Fesdu wreck is a 30m trawler with a good covering of corals at a depth of 18m to 30m. Moray eels and grouper live inside the hull, which is easily entered and has good growths of soft corals and sponges. Divers can also check the adjacent thila, which has hard and soft corals as well as lots of fish.

Orimas Thila   DIVING

Overhangs, caves, crevices, canyons and coral heads make Orimas Thila an exciting dive. Marine life includes good growths of soft corals, sea fans, anemones and clown fish. The top of the thila is only 3m down, and can be easily enjoyed by snorkellers if the conditions are calm. It's a Protected Marine Area.

Ari Atoll

Thoddoo

INDIAN OCEAN

Thoddoo Kandu

Male (45km)

Rasdhoo Atoll

27

18

Rasdhoo

6

Ukulhas

23

25

Mathiveri

12

Budufolhudhoo

North Ari Atoll

22

8

Protected Marine Area

Feridhoo

5

16

3

29

14

Maalhos

10

Protected Marine Area

Himandhoo

Protected Marine Area

4

Hangnaameedhoo

Kalhuhadhihuraa

11

19

Omadhoo

Kudurudhoo

26

17

Mahibadhoo

Mandhoo

20

28

15

24

Rangalifinolhu

9

13

67m

Dhangethi

1

South Ari Atoll

7

Protected Marine Area

21

Dhigurah

Fenfushi

Dhidhdhoo

2

Villa International Airport Maamigili

Maamigili

Ariadhoo Kandu

Ari Atoll

ARI ATOLL SLEEPING

Panetone
DIVING

The north side of Kalhuhadhihuraa Faru is subject to strong currents, so the caves and overhangs of Panetone are thick with soft coral growth. As well as the many reef fish, there are giant trevally, sharks, barracuda and turtles. From December to April, mantas feed around the outside of the channel; March to November are the best months to see sharks. There's excellent snorkelling in light currents.

Kudarah Thila
DIVING

Kudarah Thila is a very demanding but exciting dive – if there is a current running, this is strictly for experienced divers. There are gorgonians, whip corals, black corals and a whole field of sea fans swaying in the current, surrounded by sharks and trevally from the open sea. In the gaps between large coral blocks, bluestriped snapper, tallfin, batfish, goby and other unusual small fish can be seen. It's a Protected Marine Area.

Broken Rock
DIVING

In the mouth of the Dhigurashu Kandu, Broken Rock is bisected by a canyon up to 10m deep and only 1m to 3m wide. Swimming through the 50m canyon is unforgettable, but extreme care is needed not to damage the coral formations on either side. Rock formations around the thila are decorated with sea fans and superb corals, and are inhabited by abundant marine life.

🛏 Sleeping

While some resorts nearer to Male operate speedboat transfers to and from the international airport, the majority of resorts use seaplane transfers due to the distances involved. These take anything from 20 to 45 minutes, and are more expensive than speedboat transfers. Bear in mind that seaplanes do not fly at night. If you arrive after 4pm at Male airport, you'll have to stopover in Male until the next morning for your seaplane transfer.

Resorts

Chaaya Reef Ellaidhoo DIVING RESORT $
(📞 666 0669; www.cinnamonhotels.com; r incl breakfast from US$330; ✴ @ 🛜 ⚊) Divers look no further: Ellaidhoo is the most hard-core diving destination in the Maldives, with over 100 dive sites within a half-day trip. It has what many consider to be the country's finest house reef (quite an accolade given the competition!), with a 750m wall, lots of caves, corals, rich marine life and even a small shipwreck.

Indeed, it's hard to choose a better base for divers, and it seems like pretty much everyone here is diving and snorkelling focused, although there's plenty for nondivers too. The smart villa-style accommodation and large two-storey water villas are good deals for this price range, having been fully refurbished a few years ago. They're bright and well maintained, though all fairly simple, as you'd expect in a diving resort. Dining is by buffet and most guests are on all inclusive or full board packages. The island isn't the most picturesque in the country by a long shot, with a fairly small beach, but it offers enough of an all-round holiday to attract nondivers and divers alike.

RECOMPRESSION CHAMBERS

Also known as hyperbaric chambers, these emergency treatment units are for people suffering from painful and highly dangerous decompression sickness (also known as 'the bends'), which can affect divers who rise too quickly to the surface after a dive. There is currently one chamber on Bandos in North Male Atoll, and a second on Kuramathi in North Ari Atoll. In the rare case of decompression sickness occurring, divers can be put back under pressure in order to reabsorb the nitrogen bubbles in the blood stream, and rid themselves of the painful condition. For this reason, it's a legal requirement to do a decompression stop in the water at the end of each dive.

Vilamendhoo ACTIVITIES RESORT $
(☑ 644 4487; www.vilamendhooisland.com; full board r from US$315; ✳ @ 🛜 ≋) Vilamendhoo offers a solid midmarket experience to visitors who usually come on all-inclusive deals. The beaches are narrow around most of the island, but there's a big sandy area at one end, or both ends, depending on the season. The house reef is particularly good for snorkelling, and marked channels make it easy to reach the reef edge.

The rooms are divided into four categories; all are spacious, clean and comfortable, with thatched roofs as a concession to natural style. There are two buffets where most all-inclusive guests eat, but also the choice of several other à la carte restaurants open to all (which cost extra). Overall the food is not a highlight, but the main bar is the heart of the resort, and the guests on all-inclusive packages make sure it keeps busy. There are over 40 accessible dive sites in the area, including some of the very best in the Maldives. For nondivers there are numerous excursions, a tennis court, spa, windsurfing and water sports.

Veligandu Island
Resort & Spa ACTIVITIES RESORT $$
(☑ 666 0519; www.veliganduisland.com; full board r & water villas from US$700; ✳ @ 🛜 ≋ 🛏) Fringed with white beaches and featuring a huge 80m sandbank at one end, Veligandu is a great midrange option with good accommodation for its price. Rooms are attractive and stylish, and nearly all of them are over water. The island is rightly famous for its great beaches and is located on a beautiful lagoon.

The Jacuzzi Beach Villas are the starting category and are nestled among the trees on the beach, while the smarter Jacuzzi Water Villas feature outdoor Jacuzzis and semi-open-air bathrooms, and steps down into the lagoon. The main Dhonveli restaurant serves up buffets three times a day, while the à la carte Madivaru restaurant is open in the evenings for a quieter, more romantic dinner.

There are a couple of excellent dive sites nearby, with hammerhead shark sightings very common. The Ocean-Pro dive base charges reasonably. The edge of the house reef is not very accessible and is not great for snorkelling, so most diving and snorkelling is done by boat at a wide range of nearby sites. Overall this is a popular and smart midrange resort with superb beaches and comfortable over-water accommodation.

Kuramathi Island Resort ACTIVITIES RESORT $$
(☑ 666 0527; www.kuramathi.com; full board r from US$735; ✳ @ 🛜 ≋ 🛏) Kuramathi is one of the biggest resorts in the country, with 290 rooms. The island itself is huge by Maldivian standards, 1.8km long, meaning that it has the luxury of thick vegetation and plenty of undeveloped areas, making it ideal for long walks along the perfect beaches. This is a solid upper midrange resort with a huge variety of activities.

The rooms are all contemporary and furnished in an elegant and understated style with four-poster beds, plenty of wooden furniture and stylish outdoor bathrooms. The nine different categories run from the 45-sq-metre beach villas to the honeymoon pool villas, which measure 310 sq metres and include their own 10m lap pools.

For dining there's a suitably enormous choice including the Reef seafood restaurant, Thai at Siam Garden, a pizzeria and Indian food at Tandoor Mahal. The island's list of activities is enormous – it has a huge spa, several swimming pools, a gym, a dive school, a water-sports centre and the excellent Bageecha children's club. There's also a dedicated Eco Centre, which runs projects such as a hydroponic garden (from which the restaurants' salads come) and has a resident marine biologist who tells visitors about the things they've seen while diving or snorkelling.

LUX* Maldives LUXURY RESORT $$
(☑ 668 0901; www.luxresorts.com; r incl breakfast from US$517; ✳ @ 🛜 ≋ 🛏) This long island is

one of the bigger resorts in Maldives, but manages to feel intimate and easily manageable on foot through good design. It also has beautiful beaches and impressive architecture; the over-water rooms complement an already stunning island where most of the rooms are right on the beach.

Rooms range from beach pavilions, which at 65 sq metres are a good size, and go up to the giant 360 sq metre LUX* villa. There is a large set of water villas on each side of the island, both quite some distance from the island itself, which can either make you feel like you have a long walk to the main restaurant, or that you're lucky enough to enjoy some seclusion.

Water villas do not have plunge pools, but the cheaper beach pool villas do, which makes them good value for money. The rest of the island has seven restaurants, multiple bars, a spa, a PADI five-star dive centre, a full water-sports centre and the usual host of excursions.

The lagoon is wide on all sides, and a good place to learn windsurfing or catamaran sailing. There's no snorkelling to be had from the shore: but you can take one of the free boat trips to the reef edge, which depart every afternoon. The island has always been popular with divers, especially for the whale sharks that cruise the outer edge of the atoll here from May to November, and the mantas on the west side of the atoll from December to May, and many guests are here to enjoy the high standard of dive sites on offer combined with good accommodation and high-quality dining.

Madoogali   ACTIVITIES RESORT $$
(☑ 332 7443; www.madoogalimaldives.com; r incl breakfast from US$460; ✳ @) Madoogali is richly verdant, has gorgeous beaches all the way around its circular shore and is set on a lovely lagoon. The resort itself is rather aged these days, but its coral-walled architecture with thatched roofs and wooden interiors are still comfortable and this is a great place for tranquillity and fuss-free escape.

There are no fancy features such as water villas or private pools here (in fact, there's not even a communal swimming pool), just the beaches all round, a dive centre and an excellent house reef for snorkelling. The food is of a very high standard for a midrange resort, however, and gets good reports from travellers, while the Mu Spa offers facials and massages for reasonable rates. As Madoogali is the only resort in this part of the atoll, there is easy access to lots of little-used dive sites, which makes this a popular diving destination.

★ **W Retreat & Spa**   LUXURY RESORT $$$
(☑ 666 2222; www.wretreatmaldives.com; r incl breakfast from US$1200; ✳ @ ⟡ ✳) W Retreat & Spa is sleek and imaginative, a boutique luxury island loaded with more casual cool than any other in the country. W manages to get it right on all levels – staff are informal

ARI ATOLL SLEEPING

THE GENTLE GIANTS OF MALDIVES

Ari Atoll is the best place in Maldives to spot the whale shark (*Rhincodon typus*), the world's largest fish, and indeed one of the largest animals of any species found on earth. These gentle, plankton-eating giants have been spotted in sizes of over 12m long, and are something of a holy grail for divers and snorkellers in these waters. Whale sharks tend to swim on the outer edge of the atoll and can be spotted with relative ease, with many of the resorts and guesthouses near the atoll edge, particularly in South Ari Atoll, focusing on whale sharks encounters as part of their diving and snorkelling trips. While whale sharks live on plankton and small fish that they filter from the water with their giant mouths, their sheer size means that divers need to exercise caution around them. Note that snorkelling is generally thought to disturb whale sharks less than diving.

The Maldives Whale Shark Research Programme (MWSRP; www.maldiveswhaleshark-research.org) is an excellent UK charity that has been monitoring the whale sharks here for a decade now. Based on the inhabited island of Dhigurah in South Male Atoll, its research has established that Maldives has a permanent juvenile whale shark population and has recorded over 200 individuals who return constantly to these waters, though there remains an enormous amount that is still unknown about whale shark behaviour, and so this continued research is vital. The MWSRP also offers one of the few volunteering opportunities in the country, allowing anyone who can raise the money (£1500 per two weeks) to join their team and work monitoring the sharks and collating the information.

and friendly, the reception area is so efficient you'll rarely see anyone even needing to be there and the resort itself is stunning.

To start with, tiny Fesdhoo island is simply gorgeous, with superb white sand beaches and a great house reef packed with turtles, rays and reef sharks. On the island itself are the standard rooms – and even in the starting categories they're wonderful – each with its own private plunge pool and, perhaps their most charming feature, a thatched-roof 'viewing deck' above the room, complete with daybeds. Higher categories are over water, culminating in four vast suites that would satisfy even the most demanding Saudi prince. All rooms are staggeringly cool, with clean lines, Bose surround-sound systems and huge private terraces.

The activities and facilities are just as good – from free nonmotorised water sports and an excellent diving school to a superb spa that looks a world away from any other in the Maldives. There's also has a nightclub (one of the few in the country and definitely the best looking), 15 Below, which is open three times a week and comes with a dangerously wide-ranging vodka collection. Add to this three excellent restaurants, three glamorous bars, a vast swimming pool and even a private desert island for guests to use, and it's easy to see why this is the choice of the discerning, wealthy and cool.

Constance Halaveli

Maldives   LUXURY RESORT **$$$**
(☑ 666 7000; www.halaveli.com; r incl breakfast from US$1600; ✲ @ ☎ ✖ 🏊) This supremely luxurious resort is one of Ari Atoll's most popular honeymoon spots, and one that is still looking superb following its full renovation a few years ago. The small island has gorgeous white sand beaches all around it, but its most obvious feature is the chain of water villas larger than the island itself, protruding over the lagoon.

This is a romantic luxury resort, with lavish accommodation largely in 57 huge water villas, each of which comes with a large plunge pool in black slate, wood and marble flooring and traditional thatched roofs. There are also a number of beach villas on the island itself, which range in size and facilities. The island suffers from bad erosion, though, and as such stone wavebreaks have been placed around the edges, which can rather detract from the idyll in parts.

There are three restaurants; the main buffet restaurant is supplemented by JING, an over-water restaurant serving up Asian-European fusion, and the Beach Grill, which does simple grilled dishes from an à la carte menu. You'll also find a sumptuous spa, dive school, gym, tennis court, water sports centre and kids club. Overall this is a great choice for adult luxury and quiet romance.

Nika Island   RUSTIC RESORT **$$$**

(☑ 666 0515; www.nikaisland.com.mv; full board r from US$835; ✲ @ ☎) 🌿 Nika Island's innovative approach to sustainable and back-to-nature tourism has influenced resorts throughout the country. It's also notable for being the only resort in Maldives where each villa has its own private beach, giving guests privacy and seclusion on stunning white sand beaches that you can't easily find elsewhere.

Individual villas are spacious and imaginatively designed in a seashell shape, with thatched roofs and hand-crafted timber furniture, although they can be rather dark inside. As well as its own beach, each villa also has a private garden. Indeed, the concept is also genuinely ecofriendly, with no pool and no air-conditioning outside the bedrooms – just the sea and natural ventilation through wooden louvre windows. Water villas are a more recent addition and are innovatively designed over three split levels.

All guests are on full board packages here, and the sand-floored main restaurant serves up a lavish breakfast and lunch buffet and then does à la carte in the evening. Dive costs here are on the high side, but groups are small and the attention is personal. Overall this is a luxurious place to relax in privacy and style, with none of the fuss of the top end luxury resorts, and with lots of charming staff and personal touches.

Mirihi   LUXURY RESORT **$$$**

(☑ 668 0500; www.mirihi.com; r incl breakfast from US$972; ✲ @ ☎) Tiny Mirihi is named after the yellow flower that grows around the island, and its philosophy is about simplicity and nature. The wonderful beach that rings the thick vegetation in the centre of the island and the fantastic house reef beyond are both first class. Following a full refurbishment, Mirihi reopened in 2014 looking better than ever before.

While Mirihi is tiny, 30 of its rooms are built over the water, so the island itself doesn't feel too crowded. The newly renovated beach villas, of which there are just six, have polished timber finishes, white linen furnishings, rich orange and yellow accents and every amenity, including iPod docks and espresso machines. The water villas are essentially the same, with the addition of water views and very private sun decks, while the top category room is the Two Bedroom Overwater Suite, which is good for families.

The main restaurant Dhonveli serves a good quality buffet for meals, while fine dining can be had at Muraka on a jetty over the water, where grills and seafood are served. Elsewhere Mirihi manages to pack in a gym, a small spa, and activities such as windsurfing and kayaking. Divers come here for access to sites all over South Ari Atoll, and this is one of the most popular ways to spend the day. The island's yacht, the *Mirihi Thari,* goes out frequently for whale shark spotting on the atoll edge – an unforgettable experience.

Overall Mirihi is remarkable for making the most of a small island without overdeveloping it. It's equally attractive as a stylish luxury resort, a rustic romantic retreat or a top-end dive island.

Conrad Maldives Rangali Island   LUXURY RESORT $$$
(666 0629; conradhotels3.hilton.com; r incl breakfast from US$1550;) Sumptuous barefoot luxury is the name of the game at the Hilton Group's long-standing Maldivian resort. Famous throughout the Maldives for its undersea restaurant and its unique two-island set up, Conrad Maldives is an excellent choice for couples and families wanting to escape in style, while still having a huge choice of activities, cuisine and beaches.

The property immediately looks unique: it is housed on two islands that are connected by walkway across a broad lagoon, a great touch that gives you both a large choice of beaches (all superb) and plenty of space. The heart of the resort, with the main lobby, restaurants, bars, water sports, dive centres and 100 beach villas, is on Rangalifinolhu; on the second island, Rangali, which is only for adults, there are two further restaurants plus a bar, a separate reception area, and 50 water villas.

The rooms are varied and attractively conceived in all 11 categories; even the standard beach villas check in at a spacious 150 sq metres. All rooms have outdoor terraces and outdoor bathrooms as well as sea views from the bath. The spectacular water villas all enjoy their own private terraces, gorgeous wooden interiors and, in the more luxurious ones, glass floors.

With seven restaurants running the whole gamut of cuisines from Maldivian to Japanese and European, you have plenty of choice. Most impressive is the Ithaa Undersea Restaurant, where diners eat in a glass-domed restaurant underwater, an experience almost unlike any other in the country. Diving, water sports, excursions, and a fantastic kids club are all also on offer, as are three spas (including one exclusively for children!). But the real attraction at the Conrad is the unobtrusive, efficient and friendly service and the wonderful beaches.

Centara Grand Island Resort & Spa Maldives   ACTIVITIES RESORT $$$
(668 8000; www.centarahotelsresorts.com; all-inclusive r US$1600;) This upscale place is a very good all-round resort from the Thai Centara Group. Its 112 suites and villas offer a choice for everyone from couples to families and it's particularly child-friendly, with an ethos of welcoming families that extends far beyond the kids club and daily children's activities on offer.

Gorgeous beaches can be found all around the island, while rooms are stylishly modern in decor with grand country-club style and anonymously smart furniture. The two-storey water villas are particularly great, with their two sun decks and thatched roofs overlooking the lagoon.

The resort has all the amenities you'd expect at this price: a good pool, three restaurants (Thai and Italian à la carte places supplement the varied buffet where most guests eat), a dive school, a water-sports centre, a gym, a great spa and plenty of excursions. This is a top choice for a smart, family holiday where everyone will have plenty of options for how to spend their days.

Lily Beach Resort   ALL-INCLUSIVE RESORT $$$
(666 0013; www.lilybeachmaldives.com; all-inclusive r from US$890;) Lily Beach Resort has a unique concept: that of an upmarket all-inclusive resort. This was a first for the Maldives and it has proved exceptionally popular in a destination where extras can quickly add up to rival the amount you paid for your accommodation. If you're looking for an upscale yet affordable activities holiday, this is a great option.

Here guests pay for few or no extras, as everything is included in the 'platinum plan' – from unlimited cocktails (with brand-name spirits) to free snorkelling and even free cigarettes. It's a recipe that has worked well,

ARI ATOLL SLEEPING

and as with any all-inclusive resort, it attracts people looking for a good time who are going to use the facilities and enjoy the supplies of food and alcohol to the max.

The smart rooms come in five categories, ranging from 68-sq-metre beach villas to the 182-sq-metre sunset water suite. The style is modern, sleek and perhaps rather anonymous, but rooms are spacious and comfortable. As well as the main Lily Maa open-air restaurant on the lagoon, there's a fine dining à la carte restaurant, Tamarind, which serves Chinese and Indian cuisine and at which all guests are entitled to have one meal per week. As with most all-inclusive places, the numerous bars are the centre of resort life, and the three bars here are busy all day long.

Guesthouses

★ Mathiveri Inn   GUESTHOUSE $
(⌨ 797 3501; www.mathiveriinn.com; Mathiveri; half board r US$90; ❄ 🛜) Offering some excellent packages, most of which include full or half board, excursions and diving, this friendly place gives you the chance to stay on an inhabited island and to get to know the local area through diving, island visits and even day trips to nearby resorts. Accommodation is in one of eight rooms, three of which are deluxes.

★ Casa Mia   GUESTHOUSE $
(⌨ 799 6626; www.casamiamaldives.com; Mathiveri; full board r from US$250; ❄ @ 🛜 ❄ 🛏) This sleek upmarket place is about as good as Maldivian guesthouses get. Indeed, the feel is far more that of a boutique hotel, with 10 stylish and spacious rooms surrounding a swimming pool, on its own private beach at one end of lovely Mathiveri Island.

Its unique selling point is the availability of alcohol from a safari boat moored just off the shore, a legal way of drinking without having to stay at a resort. This is an excellent base for diving too, with most guests coming here for that, but also for enjoying a comfortable beach holiday in a friendly, local environment.

★ Goby Lodge   GUESTHOUSE $
(⌨ 778 7073; www.gobylodge.com; Mahibadhoo; full board s/d US$95/125; ❄ 🛜) One of the few guesthouses on South Ari's capital, Manhibadhoo, Goby Lodge is a great option if you'd like to immerse yourself in local life. While the four rooms here are relatively simple and basic, the welcome and access to island life you get from the friendly owner is superb.

Food is good (ask for the Maldivian breakfast), and the diving is excellent and good value, too; the owner can arrange certification for learners as well as normal diving and a host of island excursions and activities.

The Amazing Noovilu   GUESTHOUSE $
(⌨ 782 0949; www.theamazingnoovilu.com; Mahibadhoo; r from US$125; ❄ 🛜) With just two simple rooms, this tiny guesthouse nevertheless gets rave reviews for its service and full program of activities and excursions. Host Mazin ensures that everyone who stays here gets a thoroughly local experience, and it's easy to feel like part of the family after just a few days.

Kuri Inn   GUESTHOUSE $
(⌨ 741 6965; www.kuriinn.net; Omadhoo; r incl breakfast US$95; ❄ 🛜) This sweet four-room guesthouse, on the laid-back fishing island of Omadhoo, is a good alternative to staying next door on South Ari's capital, Mahibadhoo. Each simple but comfortable room has its own bathroom, and the house has its own common areas where guests can relax and socialise.

The enthusiastic young team keep the activities coming – snorkelling, island hopping, beach barbecues, big-game fishing and water sports are organised daily. Highly recommended for a slice of real island life.

❶ Getting There & Away

Nearly all resorts in Ari Atoll fly in their guests direct, using seaplane charters. A small airport on the island of **Maamigili** is served by several FlyMe (www.flyme.mv) flights a day from Male airport, which can work out cheaper than seaplane transfers and is a popular way to reach some resorts nearby.

For independent travellers, there are ferry connections from Male's Viligili Ferry Terminal to the South Ari capital of Mahibadhoo (Rf53, 4¼ hours), which continue to Maamigili (Rf53, seven hours). These leave Male at 9am on Saturday, Monday and Wednesday and return from Maamigili (8am) and Mahibadhoo (10.30am) on Sunday, Tuesday and Thursday.

There's also another inter-atoll ferry service connecting Male to Ukulhas (Rf53, 4½ hours) in North Ari, which leaves Male at 9am on Sunday, Tuesday and Thursday, returning from Ukulhas at 10am on Saturday, Monday and Wednesday.

❶ Getting Around

The 18 inhabited islands of Ari Atoll are connected to each other by a number of daily ferries that run daily except on Fridays. See Maldives Transport and Contracting Company website (www.mtcc.com.mv) for up-to-date schedules.

Northern Atolls

Best Places to Stay

➡ Four Seasons Landaa Giraavaru (p99)

➡ Cheval Blanc Randheli (p96)

➡ Soneva Fushi (p101)

➡ Anantara Kihavah Villas (p100)

Best Places to Dive

➡ Hanifaru Huraa (p98)

➡ Kuredhoo Express (p102)

➡ Fushifaru Thila (p103)

➡ Kakani Thila (p99)

Why Go?

The least-developed region of the Maldives, the northern atolls remain scarcely known to foreigners, and that makes them a great place to experience traditional Maldivian life. Maldivian history owes much to this part of the country – national hero Mohammed Thakurufaanu, the man who drove the Portuguese out of the Maldives in the 16th century, was born on the island of Utheemu in Haa Alifu Atoll. The island is today a place of pilgrimage for Maldivians, who come to see his small wooden palace.

There's also huge diving potential throughout the region; there are wrecks along the western fringe of the atolls, many only now being properly explored and documented, while Baa Atoll has been declared a Unesco World Biosphere Reserve, such are its pristine waters and the value of its diverse marine life. With just a handful of resorts and guesthouses, you'll feel like you have the Northern Atolls to yourself.

When to Go

➡ **Jan-Mar** Peak season coincides with the best weather in the North, as well as European winter.

➡ **Jun-Oct** Manta Ray spotting season brings keen divers and snorkellers to swim with these incredible creatures.

➡ **May-Sep** The low season doesn't mean the weather is any worse, and room prices are the lowest they get.

Haa Alifu

Haa Alifu Atoll contains the island of **Utheemu** (population 900), by far the most historically interesting island in the Northern Atolls. The birthplace of Sultan Mohammed Thakurufaanu (who, with his brothers, overthrew Portuguese rule in 1573), the island is centred around a memorial to this Maldivian hero, complete with a small museum and library. There's a gorgeous beach here, though currently no guesthouse, so visitors come on day trips from nearby islands and resorts.

Elsewhere in the atoll is the capital island **Dhidhdhoo** (population 2500), which offers good anchorage for passing yachts, and **Hoarafushi**, the next largest island (population 2200), noted for its music and dancing.

Kelaa (population 1200) was the northern British base during WWII, mirroring Gan at the other end of the country. The mosque here dates from the end of the 17th century.

At the very top of Haa Alifu, **Uligamu** (population 270) is the 'clear-in' port for private yachts arriving in Maldivian waters. It has health and immigration officers, so yachts are able to complete all entry formalities there.

◉ Sights

The main sights in Haa Alifu can be found on small but historically significant Utheemu, which arguably boasts the most important buildings in Maldives outside Male.

★**Utheemu Ganduvaru**   PALACE
(Utheemu; Rf25; ☺9am-6pm Sun-Thu) This small palace was the childhood home of Malidivian national hero Mohammed Thakurufaanu, who, alongside with his brothers, overthrew Portuguese rule in 1573. Visitors are escorted around the complex of buildings by a member of staff from the museum and are able to see the fascinating 500-year-old wooden interiors, including swing beds (used to keep cool in the heat), lamps that burn coco palm oil, elaborate wooden carvings and a large palm-thatch shed used as a sleeping room for guests.

Kandhuvalu Mosque   MOSQUE
(Utheemu) The date of construction for this stone and wood mosque is unknown, although Mohammed Thakurufaanu is known to have prayed here in his youth, meaning that there's been a mosque here since at least the mid-16th century. It's a tiny place with a beautiful teak interior that can be glimpsed from the entrance. Sadly, entry is not possible for non-Muslims. Thakurufaanu's father is buried in the cemetery here.

🛏 Sleeping

If you're arriving in Maldives after a long-haul flight, bear in mind that selecting a resort in the far north of the country will add on at least two hours to your journey each way – often more, depending on flight timings. This can come as a shock to travellers, and is the main cause of complaint from those who come here, so be prepared.

**Hideaway Beach
Resort & Spa**   LUXURY RESORT **$$**
(☑650 1515; www.island-hideaway.com; r incl breakfast from US$792; ❄@🛜🏊🎣) Hideaway is certainly true to its name – located about as remotely as you can imagine in the Maldives' most northerly atoll. But while some resorts might blanch at the idea of being so far removed from Male and the busy international airport, Island Hideaway has effortlessly capitalised on it, attracting those seeking true escape.

Set on a gorgeous crescent-shaped island with beaches 1.5km long on both sides, Hideaway is breathtaking to look at and thickly vegetated. Following a full renovation in 2014, the resort is looking superb, but is also significantly bigger, having more than doubled its number of villas. This hasn't resulted in overcrowding, however, as the majority of these new structures are water villas, which stretch off over the lagoon. These are extremely impressive and spacious structures, each coming with its own 18-sq-metre plunge pool and boasting total privacy. The rooms on the island itself share a rustic style with Maldivian decor and contemporary fittings. All have huge outdoor bathrooms and many have infinity pools. They're enclosed by thick vegetation for privacy and most enjoy their own direct beach access.

The pristine reefs around the island provide superb snorkelling and the untouched sites further afield make diving with the Meridis Diving School another great reason to come here. The resort is totally child-friendly, has a great kids club, and many of the villas are designed to accommodate entire families, so space isn't a problem. Finally, if you're travelling by yacht, Island Hideaway has its own Walcon Marine Marina, with 30 berths for yachts up to 80m. Look no further for total seclusion.

JA Manafaru   LUXURY RESORT $$$
(☑650 0456; www.jaresortshotels.com; r incl breakfast from US$930; ✱ @ ☎ ⊠ ⛵) The most northerly resort in the country, JA Manafaru enjoys splendid isolation and is an exclusive island, previously run as part of the Waldorf Astoria chain. The island itself is gorgeous, with thick vegetation, dazzling turquoise waters and some of the softest sand in the country on its incredible white-sand beach that runs the entire way around the island.

The rooms are stylish, albeit in an anonymous international design, with the starting category alone an enormous 150 sq metres, going up to the 600-sq-metre Two Bedroom Royal Island Suite. Each room on the island has its own private plunge pool and the look is minimal but stylish, with Asian touches such as dark wood fittings and rattan chairs.

The island also has two pools, an enormous spa in huge gardens, several excellent restaurants, a kids club with its own infinity pool and mini-loungers, a good gym, an excellent diving school, a full water-sports centre and even a wine cellar with a choice of some 3500 bottles of wine, which are paired by a sommelier with degustation meals. The resort also owns two nearby desert islands, which are perfect for picnics. Overall this is a great choice for those wanting a glamorous but understated break on a luxuriously appointed island with dazzling beaches and few other people around.

❶ Getting There & Away

There is no airport in Haa Alifu, but the main airport of the northern Maldives, Hanimaadhoo, is just a short distance away in Haa Dhaalu. Most resorts arrange for their guests to take scheduled Maldivian flights to Hanimaadhoo and collect them by launch.

Haa Dhaalu

Haa Dhaalu is an administrative district spread over 16 inhabited islands and made up of South Thiladhunmathee Atoll and the far smaller Maamakunudhoo Atoll. The capital island is **Kulhuduffushi** (population 10,500). It's the most important island in the northern Maldives and has a hospital, secondary school and plenty of shops, although no airport. The traditional industries here are rope making and shark fishing, though a national ban introduced in 2009 by the Maldivian government has forced local fishermen to hunt for other fish.

The regional airport is on **Hanimaadhoo** (population 1800). **Maldivian** (www.maldivian.aero) has multiple daily flights to and from Male, and there's a popular guesthouse here, one of the few to exist in this scantly developed atoll.

Elsewhere in Haa Dhaalu, there's a stone circle that is thought to be the base of a Buddhist stupa on the island of **Kumundhoo**, and *hawitta* (artificial mound) remains can still be seen on **Vaikaradhoo**.

The area around Haa Dhaalu suffers severe storms, and quite a few vessels have gone down in these waters. Maamakunudhoo Atoll is the graveyard of several ships, including the English ships *Persia Merchant,* wrecked here in 1658, and the *Hayston,* which ran onto a reef in 1819. In each instance, survivors were rescued by local people and treated with kindness, a source of great local pride.

🛏 Sleeping

There are no resorts in Haa Dhaalu Atoll, but there's an excellent guesthouse on Hanimaadhoo.

★**Asseyri Tourist Inn**   GUESTHOUSE $
(☑988 2222; www.asseyri.travel/inn; Hanimaadhoo; s/d incl breakfast from US$85/110; ✱ ☎) ◢ This simple six-room guesthouse is a charming place, set in a gorgeous tropical garden, and perfect for a diving and excursions holiday. Rooms are large, with low-slung beds and quirky wooden interiors cheered up by bright splashes of colour. There's a good restaurant here too and it's worth taking out a full-board package.

Around 70% of the building materials used for the lodge are recycled, and at reception locally made soap and coconut oil are sold, bringing money into the local community. The owners have created a screened-off private beach where it's possible to swim without offending local sensibilities, although it's not the best-maintained in the country. Most guests busy themselves with the various excursions offered, including snorkelling, fishing, sand bank trips, bike hire and island hopping. This is a great choice if being a part of the local community is more important to you than luxurious seclusion.

❶ Getting There & Away

The main **airport** in the northern Maldives is on Hanimaadhoo in Haa Dhaalu. There are five flights a day between Hanimaadhoo and Male

Northern Atolls

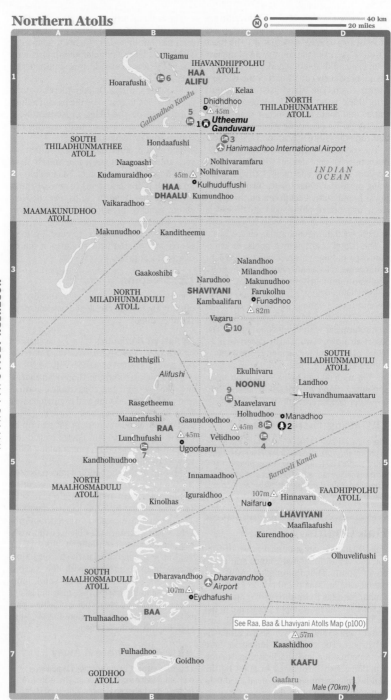

N

0 — 40 km
0 — 20 miles

Uligamu

IHAVANDHIPPOLHU
ATOLL

HAA
ALIFU

Hoarafushi

🛏6

Kelaa

NORTH
THILADHUNMATHEE
ATOLL

Gallandhoo Kandu

Dhidhdhoo

△45m

5

1 🏯 Utheemu
Ganduvaru

SOUTH
THILADHUNMATHEE
ATOLL

Hondaafushi

🛏3
🛕 Hanimaadhoo International Airport

Naagoashi

Nolhivaramfaru

INDIAN
OCEAN

Kudamuraidhoo

△45m

Nolhivaram

HAA
DHAALU

●Kulhuduffushi

Kumundhoo

Vaikaradhoo

MAAMAKUNUDHOO
ATOLL

Makunudhoo

Kanditheemu

Nalandhoo
Milandhoo

Gaakoshibi

Narudhoo

Makunudhoo

SHAVIYANI

Farukolhu
●Funadhoo

NORTH
MILADHUNMADULU
ATOLL

Kambaalifaru

△82m

Vagaru

🛏10

SOUTH
MILADHUNMADULU
ATOLL

Eththigili

Alifushi

Ekulhivaru

NOONU

Landhoo

←Huvandhumaavattaru

Rasgetheemu

9

Maavelavaru

Maanenfushi

Gaaundoodhoo

RAA

△45m

Lundhufushi

Holhudhoo
8🛏

●Manadhoo
♀2

Velidhoo

🛏
7

●Ugoofaaru

4

Kandholhudhoo

Innamaadhoo

Baraveli Kandu

NORTH
MAALHOSMADULU
ATOLL

Kinolhas

Iguraidhoo

107m△ Hinnavaru

Naifaru●

FAADHIPPOLHU
ATOLL

LHAVIYANI

Maafilaafushi

Kurendhoo

Olhuvelifushi

SOUTH
MAALHOSMADULU
ATOLL

Dharavandhoo

🛕Dharavandhoo
Airport

107m△

●Eydhafushi

BAA

Thulhaadhoo

See Raa, Baa & Lhaviyani Atolls Map (p100)

△57m

Kaashidhoo

Fulhadhoo

Goidhoo

KAAFU

GOIDHOO
ATOLL

Gaafaru

Male (70km)

(one hour, US$390 return) on Maldivian (www. maldivian.aero). Ferries connect the inhabited islands in Haa Dhaalu and also run to islands in Haa Alifu and Shaviyani. The main hubs are the capital Kulhuduffushi and the airport island Hanimaadhoo. See www.mtcc.com.mv for timetables.

Shaviyani

Untouched by tourism until recently, Shaviyani Atoll contains 16 inhabited islands and is most famous today as a major breeding ground for turtles, which lay their eggs very successfully on its pristine beaches.

Since 2009, the atoll's capital has been the island of **Milandhoo** (population 2145), an island that was uninhabited until 1997, when it was quickly settled to relocate the population of the nearby Makunudhoo, whose water supply had become contaminated. Much of the island has been cleared for plantain growing, the island's main industry.

The former atoll capital is **Funadhoo** (population 2900), a pretty island with the ruins of an ancient mosque and 13th-century tombstones. **Narudhoo** (population 473) is a tiny island with a natural freshwater lake on it – one of just a few places in the whole country where water collects above ground.

The main mosque on the island of **Kanditheemu** (population 1300) incorporates the oldest known example of the Maldives' unique Thaana script – it's an inscription on a doorframe, which notes that the roof was constructed in 1588.

🛏 Sleeping

Viceroy Maldives   LUXURY RESORT **$$$**
(📋 654 5000; www.viceroyhotelsandresorts.com/ en/maldives; r incl breakfast from US$1090; ❄ @ 🛜 🏊 🛥) This recently opened resort boasts gorgeous beaches and a fantastic lagoon. The island's shape is mirrored by the imposing water villas that extend off to one side, which are some of the more imposing and architecturally interesting in the country.

Indeed, it's clear from the moment you arrive that no expense has been spared; the 60 villas are enormous and each features its own plunge pool, as well as being well decorated, and each either over water or directly on the beach. The duplex villas are perfect for families wanting to be together under one roof.

Public areas are similarly impressive, with three dining venues, including the Middle Eastern Treehouse, buffets at Vista and international fusion at Anguru by the

---

gorgeous infinity pool. There's also an overwater spa, dive school, water sports centre, gym and kids club. This is a superb new addition to the country's top end resorts, and well worth the extra journey time.

❶ Getting There & Away

One of the Maldives' least accessible atolls, Shaviyani has no airport and so the only way to get there is by seaplane charter.

Noonu

Noonu Atoll contains 13 inhabited islands. The capital island, **Manadhoo** (population 1580), is less populous than **Holhudhoo** (population 2040) and **Velidhoo** (2150).

On the island of **Landhoo** (population 880) are the remnants of a *hawitta* supposedly left by the fabled Redin, a people who figure in Maldivian folklore. The *hawitta* is a 6m-high mound known locally as *maa badhige* (great cooking place). Thor Heyerdahl writes extensively about the tall, fair-haired Redin in his book *The Maldive Mystery*. He believes them to have been the first inhabitants of the Maldives, as long ago as 2000 BC.

Right now Noonu has just three resorts, and while another resort is being built, it's still very quiet up here. The 2011 decision to create the **Edu Faru National Marine Park** here, the first of its kind in Maldives, has also put the atoll on the map. This is the first place in the country to be given full national park status, and it's a significant step for marine conservation in the Maldives. The park will cover the Edu Faru Archipelago of nine uninhabited islands on the eastern side of the

THE LEGEND OF THAKURUFAANU

As the man who led a successful revolution against foreign domination, and then as the leader of the newly liberated nation, Mohammed Thakurufaanu (sultan from 1573 to 1585) is the Maldives' national hero. Respectfully referred to as Bodu Thakurufaanu (*bodu* meaning 'big' or 'great'), he is to the Maldives what George Washington is to the USA. The story of his raid on the Portuguese headquarters in Male is part of Maldivian folklore, and known to every Maldivian child.

In his home island of Utheemu Thakurufaanu's family was known and respected as sailors, traders and *kateebs* (island chiefs). The family gained the trust of Viyazoaru, the Portuguese ruler of the four northern atolls, and was given the responsibility of disseminating orders, collecting taxes and carrying tribute to the Portuguese base in Sri Lanka. Unbeknown to Viyazoaru, Thakurufaanu and his brothers used their position to foster anti-Portuguese sentiment, recruit sympathisers and gain intelligence. It also afforded them the opportunity to visit southern India, where Thakurufaanu obtained a pledge from the rajah of Cannanore to assist in overthrowing the Portuguese rulers of the Maldives.

Back on Utheemu, Thakurufaanu and his brothers built a boat with which to conduct an attack on Male. This sailing vessel, named *Kalhuoffummi,* has its own legendary status – it was said to be not only fast and beautiful, but to have almost magical qualities that enabled it to elude the Portuguese on guerrilla raids and reconnaissance missions.

For the final assault, they sailed south through the atolls by night, stopping by day to gather provisions and supporters. Approaching Male, they concealed themselves on a nearby island. They stole into the capital at night to make contact with supporters there and to assess the Portuguese defences. They were assisted in this by the local imam, who subtly changed the times of the morning prayer calls, tricking the Portuguese into sleeping late and giving Thakurufaanu extra time to escape after his night-time reconnaissance visits.

In the ensuing battle the Maldivians, with help from a detachment of Cannanore soldiers, defeated and killed some 300 Portuguese. The Thakurufaanu brothers then set about re-establishing a Maldivian administration under Islamic law. Soon after, Bodu Thakurufaanu became the new sultan, with the title of Al Sultan-ul Ghazi Mohammed Thakurufaanu Al Auzam Siree Savahitha Maharadhun, first Sultan of the third dynasty of the Kingdom of the Maldives.

atoll, meaning nothing can be built in this pristine environment, and only certain boats may enter its waters. Progress has been slow, however, and the boundaries of the park were still being established in 2015. The resorts in Noonu Atoll have virtually exclusive access to the dive sites within the park at present, which makes them a popular choice with divers.

🛏 Sleeping

Sun Siam

Iru Fushi Maldives ACTIVITIES RESORT **$$**
(📞 656 0591; www.thesunsiyam.com; r incl breakfast from US$565; ❋ @ 🛜 ⛱ 🐾) This enormous resort is impressive, smart and well run. There is a superb white-sand beach all the way around the long island, making it easy to find a perfect spot in solitude, despite the large number of visitors to the island. There's no superfluous luxury here, but it's a very solid, smart place that is tastefully designed and rigorously staffed.

Especially popular with Chinese and Russian holidaymakers, the resort has 221 rooms, including two enormous sets of water villas. Other villas range from beach villas with charming thatched roofs to the self-contained three-bedroom 'Celebrity Retreat' with its own private pool. Decor throughout is in a minimalist tropical-Asian style, with lots of black wood and rattan furniture. The list of amenities here is huge: six high-quality restaurants, two pools (one for families, one child-free), free tennis and badminton, a dive centre, a water-sports centre, a golf simulator, a huge spa, a good gym and even a karaoke room (popular with the Chinese guests). The free kids club is superb and has its own pool and infants nursery room.

Cheval Blanc Randheli LUXURY RESORT **$$$**
(📞 656 1515; www.randheli.chevalblanc.com; r incl breakfast from US$4025; ❋ @ 🛜 ⛱ 🐾) Easily the most talked about new resort in Mal-

dives for a decade, this ultra top-end hotel is the Maldives product of the French LVMH group (that's short for Louis Vuitton Moët Hennessy, you know – and actually, if you didn't, this might not be quite the place for you). It's a dazzling retreat of utter extravagance and see-and-be-seen fabulousness.

The setting is stunning, and it's not at all apparent that the four small islands that make up the resort beyond the main, natural island Randheli are all man made. The beaches everywhere are as excellent as you'd expect them to be if you designed them yourself, while the public areas are defiantly modern, with little concession to Maldive tradition; instead the Jean-Michel Gathy designed buildings soar high, have lots of glass and brushed concrete in them and generally conform to the tastes of its demanding clientele, such as the Duke & Duchess of Cambridge, who stayed here in 2014.

The rooms are sumptuous, as they should be with the highest rack rates in the entire country, and there are 45 in total, fifteen of which are on the main island, fifteen of which are expansive water villas built off two of the small islands and fourteen of which are unique over-water rooms on stilts with their own private gardens. All categories boast a private 12m long pool and private beach (or terrace with sea access), huge living rooms, outdoor dining pergolas, outdoor showers and every other possible convenience. They're stunning in their elegant minimalism and all designed for total privacy. The top category room, the four bedroom Owner's Villa, is on its own private island, and features such must-have facilities as its own staff detail, a private spa and a private fleet of dhonis.

Of course every imaginable activity is available, including a spa on its own private island, tennis courts on another and a personal Majordome assigned to each guest to take on onerous tasks such as unpacking suitcases. Cheval Blanc is famous for its food too, though: it may be the home to a US$100 burger, but qualms about money aside (after all, that's not really a big issue if you're staying here) it's also home to Le 1947 French restaurant, Iberian and Japanese at The Diptyque, seafood and Italian at The Deelani and an all-day poolside brasserie at The White.

Velaa Private Island LUXURY RESORT $$$
(☑ 656 5000; www.velaaprivateisland.com; r from US$2956; ❇ @ ☎ ⛱) Opening in 2013, within its first year Velaa has become a byword for personal attention and ultimate luxury,

and all this without being a part of an international hotel chain like many of its ultra top end competitors. Instead this impressive island is the personal creation of a Czech couple who turned their private island fantasy into a business.

The island is a stunner; a perfect circle with beach all the way around, perched above a wide circular reef. There are 43 rooms, which range from the one bedroom Beach Pool Villa to the four bedroom Private Residence. All have enormous private pools, and are decorated in an exotically pan-Asian style with lots of dark wood furniture and beautifully crafted bathrooms.

The island also boasts the white Tavaru Tower, apparently the Maldives' highest restaurant (a whopping 22m – Everest by local standards), where a teppanyaki restaurant provides the centrepiece to Velaa's interesting design. There's also a Clarin's spa, tennis courts, a small golf course and two further restaurants, each helmed by Michelin-starred chefs. The entire place is wonderfully secluded and service is an absolute highlight. The flipside to the more showy international brands in Maldives, Velaa offers exactly the same standards of accommodation and service with a more understated approach, which will appeal to luxury travellers who nevertheless appreciate a down-to-earth atmosphere.

❶ Getting There & Away

Resorts in Noonu are served by seaplane charters from Male. Independent travellers can also use these services by arrangement. Alternatively there's a weekly overnight ferry between Male's Fish Market Harbour and Velidhoo (Rf 200, 10 hours). The ferry leaves Male on Wednesday night and returns from Velidhoo on Saturday night. This is a very local experience, with no seating and people sleeping on the floor.

Raa

Raa Atoll is popular with divers who normally come here on diving safari boats, as this corner of the Maldives is still virtually pristine, with just a couple of resorts. The capital island **Ugoofaaru** (population 1250) has one of the largest fishing fleets in the country, while the island of **Alifushi** (population 2300) is famously home of the finest traditional dhoni builders in the Maldives.

According to local legend, the now uninhabited island of **Rasgetheemu** is where

Koimala Kaloa and his princess wife landed after being exiled from Sri Lanka before moving to Male to found a ruling dynasty. Another important visitor to the atoll was the Arab seafarer Ibn Battuta, who landed at **Kinolhas** in 1343 and then moved on to Male.

The channel between Baa and Raa, locally known as Hani Kandu, is also named Moresby Channel after the Royal Navy officer Robert Moresby, who was responsible for the original marine survey of the Maldives made from 1834 to 1836. There's good diving on both sides of Hani Kandu, as it funnels water between the atolls, bringing pelagic fish and promoting coral growth. Mantas abound in October and November.

🛌 Sleeping

Adaaran Select Meedhupparu   RESORT $$

(☑658 7700; www.adaaran.com/selectmeedhupparu; full board r from US$472; ❉@🛜🖥) Meedhupparu has gorgeous white beaches sloping down to a perfect turquoise lagoon. While once colonised by the Italian market, Meedhupparu today is the biggest Maldivian resort in the Adaaran chain's group of properties and it attracts mostly Indian, Russian and Italian visitors.

The resort is large and features several distinct types of accommodation, including an Ayurvedic Village made up of 24 houses and an area known as the 'Water Villas', which functions as a resort-within-a-resort and includes an exclusive Balinese spa and a garden full of Sri Lankan flowers. Water sports and diving are big attractions here. The remote location of the resort means that divers never have to share sites with other groups, and some 30 dive sites are regularly visited.

Loama Resort Maldives
at Maamigili   LUXURY RESORT $$$

(☑658 8100; www.loamahotelsandresorts.com; r incl breakfast from US$898; ❉@🛜🖥🛉) The second resort in Raa Atoll opened in 2014 and is a charming place which, while still firmly a luxurious experience, makes the most of its Maldivian location, with the design and approach of the property focussed on Maldivian traditions, arts, crafts and patterns – whether this means coral stone walls, traditional lacquer boxes or *kunaa* (reed) mats hung as ornaments.

The teardrop-shaped island of Maamigili is gorgeous, with superb beaches that peak into a wonderful sandspit alongside a row of sleek water villas that make up the majority of the accommodation. All are charmingly decorated in a rich Maldivian style and all

feature outdoor pools or bathtubs. There are three restaurants that offer up Japanese, Mediterranean and gastronomic menus, and the island also boasts a gorgeous main pool, a big spa and an excellent diving school.

ℹ️ Getting There & Away

Resort guests travelling to Raa Atoll use seaplane transfers from Male airport that bring them directly to each resort. Otherwise the only way to get here is by slow and infrequent ferries from Male. Local ferries 203 and 204 connect the 15 inhabited islands in Raa Atoll daily except Fridays.

Baa

Baa Atoll's inhabitants are spread over 13 islands as well as over a variety of resorts. The atoll is famous for its lacquer work and the fine woven cotton sarong, called a *feyli,* though today it's a big centre of tourism, and contains some of the country's most exclusive resorts. In 2011, the entire atoll was designated a Unesco World Biosphere Reserve for its superb biological diversity. The designation was mainly due to the extraordinary wealth of marine life at Hanifaru Huraa, where whale sharks and manta rays both breed.

Eydhafushi, the atoll capital (population 2800), is also the *feyli* centre. The second-largest island in the atoll and the main centre for the production of lacquered boxes and jars is **Thulhaadhoo** (population 2500).

🏊 Activities

Baa Atoll offers superb diving in pristine waters, just as you'd expect in the Maldives' first Unesco World Biosphere Reserve.

⭐ Hanifaru Huraa   DIVING

The centrepiece to the Baa Atoll Unesco World Biosphere Reserve, Hanifaru Huraa is a vital feeding and breeding ground for manta rays and whale sharks, meaning that you have an excellent chance of seeing these sea giants on diving trips here. The best time to see mantas is from June to October, while whale sharks can be seen here year-round.

Milaidhoo Reef   DIVING

Strong currents flowing through the Kamadhoo Kandu provide an environment for soft corals, which thrive on Milaidhoo Reef, on the north side of an uninhabited island. The reef top, at 2m, is great for snorkelling, and it drops straight down to about 35m. This cliff has numerous caves and overhangs with sea fans and sponges.

Kakani Thila
DIVING

The north side of Kakani Thila, at 25m to 30m, has coral formations in excellent condition, and colourful soft corals fill the overhangs. It's also home to lots of fish, including Napoleons, jackfish and Oriental sweetlips.

Dhigali Haa
DIVING

The small Dhigali Haa, though well inside the atoll, attracts pelagic species such as barracuda and grey-tip reef sharks. Other fish you'll likely see include jacks, batfish and trevally. It's also a good place to see nudibranchs, yellow and orange soft corals and anemones.

Madi Finolhu
DIVING

The sandy Madi Finolhu has large coral blocks on which black corals grow. Stingrays can be seen on the sand, and mantas also pass through. This is a good beginners' dive (20m).

Muthafushi Thila
DIVING

Overhangs at Muthafushi Thila are home to soft corals and anemones. Many hard corals are in good condition and also very colourful, while soft corals can also be seen. There are large schools of blue-striped snapper.

🛌 Sleeping

Reethi Beach Resort
ACTIVITIES RESORT **$**

(☎660 2626; www.reethibeach.com; r incl breakfast from US$260; ❄️@🛜🏊) 🌊 Reethi Beach is a long-running resort with plenty of charm. The island has lots of natural vegetation wide white beaches and an accessible house reef. The thatched-roof buildings are designed to blend with the environment, and also incorporate some Maldivian design elements such as the deep horizontal mouldings used on the old Friday Mosque in Male.

The deluxe villas are more spacious and have better beach frontage, while the water villas are decent but not show-stopping. There are five restaurants on the island, as well as swimming pool, gym, squash, badminton and tennis courts. Windsurfing, sailing and other water sports are popular because of the wide lagoon. Kitesurfing is also on offer, as are parasailing, wakeboarding and jet skiing. The Sea-Explorer dive centre is reasonably priced, although qualified divers can also make dives off the house reef. Overall this is a great option combining comfort, good beaches and quality diving.

Coco Palm Dhuni Kolhu
ACTIVITIES RESORT **$$**

(☎660 0011; www.cocopalm.com; r incl breakfast from US$474; ❄️@🛜🏊) Dhuni Kolhu is a favourite with honeymooners and has an enormous number of repeat visitors. The island is a stunner, with a wide beach on one side, thick vegetation and an architecturally interesting space with a tentlike thatched pavilion for reception, restaurant and bar areas. Erosion means sandbags are in evidence in some places, but it's still a gorgeous place.

The beach villa rooms are circular with high, thatched, conical roofs, quality furnishings and open-air bathrooms, while the deluxe rooms have, in addition, plunge pools. A highlight is the food. All meals are buffet in the main restaurant, but they are very good, while the à la carte Thai restaurant is also excellent. Other nice touches include an outdoor cinema, which couples can hire to watch a movie on the beach, a lovely spa and an Ocean-Pro dive centre.

★ Four Seasons Landaa Giraavaru
LUXURY RESORT **$$$**

(☎660 0888; www.fourseasons.com/maldiveslg; r incl breakfast from US$2100; ❄️@🛜🏊🚹) Four Seasons Landaa Giraavaru is an extraordinary place. It's a palace of a hotel in the grand style, whose combination of brilliantly designed, vast rooms, great beaches and service make it one of the absolute top resorts in the country. Its style fuses traditional Maldivian village and international designer minimalism to stunning effect, and it's also superbly friendly and welcoming.

The rooms here are some of the biggest and best in Maldives; our favourites are the

---

> ### HANIFARU UNESCO BIOSPHERE RESERVE
>
> The entirety of Baa Atoll was made a Unesco Biosphere Reserve in 2011, joining the illustrious ranks of places such as the Galapagos Islands, Uluru in Australia and the Pantanal wetlands of Brazil. This honour reflects the pristine nature of the atoll's astonishing biodiversity, in particular its corals and impressive whale shark and manta ray populations, which can be seen with particular frequency in and around Hanifaru Bay, the centrepiece to the biosphere reserve, and one of the most famous diving and snorkelling site in the Maldives. All resorts in Baa Atoll can arrange trips here, and for many this extraordinary place is a reason to choose Baa Atoll above all others.

Raa, Baa & Lhaviyani Atolls

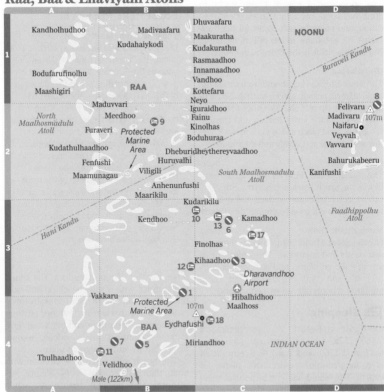

Beach Villas With Pool: freestanding houses surrounded by coral stone brick walls with a private lap pool in the garden, a mezzanine living room gazebo and direct access on to the gorgeous beach. The water villas, built from repurposed coral stone, are also huge, beautifully designed and offer ultimate privacy.

The centre of the resort is its large spa, which offers treatments in over-water rooms, as well as offering many different types of yoga including anti-gravity, not to mention a 'night spa' in the jungle where a couple is given romantic treatments together after dark.

With a choice of three vast pools, four great restaurants, an outstanding kids club, a teenagers club, free water sports and a marine biology lab, it's not a place you can easily be bored. A luxurious diving school runs trips morning and afternoon with a maximum of 12 participants in each group. Twenty dive sites are nearby and whale sharks and mantas are very common in September.

Four Seasons Landaa Giraavaru is perhaps the ultimate Maldivian resort: wonderfully conceived, superbly run and home to a glamorous, truly mixed international crowd.

★ Anantara Kihavah Villas LUXURY RESORT $$$
(☑ 660 1020; www.kihavah-maldives.anantara.com; r incl breakfast from US$2464; ✳ @ 🛜 ⚟ 👬) The island of Kihavahhuruvalhi is round and beautiful, with gorgeous white-sand beaches ringing a thickly vegetated island surrounded by a perfectly circular reef: you couldn't ask for a more perfect-looking Maldivian island. However, the resort's biggest attraction is its 82 stunning villas, all superbly realised homages to ultimate luxury, crammed full of gorgeous Asian furnishings and with stunning outdoor bathrooms.

All accommodation here comes with a private pool, whether on land or over water. This is one place, though, where the beach villas are even better than the more expensive water

Rightly one of the most famous resorts in the country, ecofabulous Soneva Fushi is the place to get back to nature in style. The personal creation of hoteliers Sonu and his wife Eva, it's an incredibly impressive island where rustic private houses are scattered amid the thick vegetation of one of the Maldives' largest resort islands.

Each villa here is like a small (and in many cases not-so-small) house built with natural materials, fitted with designer furnishings and finished in rustic style. All the deluxe and modern features you'd expect of a five-star hotel are included, but most of them are concealed so that no plastic is visible. Villas are well spaced around the edges of the island, affording complete privacy – they're reached by sandy tracks that wind through the lush vegetation, which is kept as natural as possible.

With the choice of five superb restaurants (including the wonderful treehouse-style Fresh in the Garden, where you cross a rope bridge to get to your table above the jungle canopy), the food is a real highlight of the resort. This is a resort that takes its ecocredentials and social responsibility seriously. You can take a tour of the resort's recycling area and see the ingenious ways many things are reused on the island, while across the lagoon on Baa's capital Eydhafushi, the resort has built and continues to fund a school. It's hard not to be impressed.

villas – they enjoy far more seclusion and have perhaps the best bathrooms in Maldives.

The dining options are just as opulent, including the showcase Sea.Fire.Salt.Sky dining complex, made up of four sections, including one (Sea) where you can dine on a gourmet, wine-paired set menu in a glass box underwater while fish swim around you. You're spoiled for choice as elsewhere there's Fire, a top-notch Japanese teppanyaki restaurant (book ahead) and various beach dining options.

The resort has every facility you'd expect at this price – a gorgeous pool, a sumptuous spa, a water-sports centre, a dive school, an outdoor cinema, gym, tennis courts, yoga and cookery lessons and a super kids club. Look no further for a superb luxury option with excellent service and terrific beaches.

★ **Soneva Fushi** LUXURY RESORT $$$
(☑660 0304; www.soneva.com/soneva-fushi; r incl breakfast from US$2242; ❋@☎☒⚙) ⚐

SHIPWRECKED IN PARADISE

Due to their geographical isolation, the Maldives largely became known and explored by the western world through shipwrecked sailors who stumbled across the islands by chance, and succumbed to the treacherous coral atolls.

The most famous of these early explorers was François Pyrard, a French navigator, who found himself and his surviving crew stuck on the island of Fulhadhoo in Baa Atoll after his ship, the *Corbin*, was wrecked in 1602. Spending five years on Fulhadhoo and later on Male as an effective prisoner in the Maldives, Pyrard learned Dhivehi (unlike his fellow crew members) and wrote the first extensive account of Maldivian culture: *The Voyage of François Pyrard of Laval to the East Indies, the Maldives, the Moluccas, and Brazil*. Pyrard eventually managed to escape from Male during a Bengali raid in 1611, and is still remembered as the first European to have acquired an in-depth knowledge of the country.

The Soleni Dive Centre has years of experience diving the sites nearby, while the excellent Six Senses spa, set among the trees, is a place for pure relaxation. More unusual (free) activities include watching an outdoor film at the lovely Cinema Paradiso and observing the stars in the only resort observatory in the Maldives. For back-to-nature meets haute cusine, you'll find nowhere better than Soneva Fushi.

Dusit Thani Maldives　　　LUXURY RESORT $$$
(☑660 8888; www.dusit.com; r incl breakfast from US$1476; ✸@☎⊠⊞) ⊘ Dusit Thani is a large, mass-market, Thai-owned luxury resort. It's rather expensive for what it offers, which matches other top end resorts in facilities but not in charm and intimacy. However, it does boast the largest swimming pool in the country, a tree-top spa and one of the best Thai restaurants we've ever eaten at, so there are many positives too.

The 100 state-of-the-art villas are rather closely packed together around the island, but even the lowest room category, the Beach Villa, is 122 sq metres of gorgeously attired space, complete with fabulous bathroom and direct beach access. All room categories above the

Beach Villa have their own private pools, and they're all a very good size. The water villas are particularly good, huge and fitted out with all manner of stylish extras such as espresso machines and iPod docks. The beaches are good in part, though some are rather rocky.

Dusit Thani's environmental credentials include solar panels, no chlorine in its pools, the production of its own drinking water, and LED lighting in all guest areas – all great initiatives that deserve support. The resort also boasts three restaurants, two bars, tennis courts, a kids club, a water-sports centre, gym, dive school and perhaps its most impressive feature, the Devarana Spa, which has treatment rooms above in the treetops. This is a good resort for families and anyone wanting lots of activities, though perhaps not the best spot for romance.

❶ Getting There & Away

There's a small **airstrip** on the island of Dharavandhoo that has daily scheduled flights to and from Male on Maldivian (www.maldivian.aero) and FlyMe (www.flyme.mv). Resorts in Baa Atoll normally fly their guests in on seaplane charters. In addition, there are seven atoll ferry routes that connect the 13 inhabited islands every day except Friday.

Lhaviyani

Fishing is the main industry of Lhaviyani Atoll, although tourism also employs many people, with several large resorts located here. On the capital island, **Naifaru** (population 4720), the residents have a reputation for making attractive handicrafts from coral and mother-of-pearl, and for concocting local medicines.

✹ Activities

Kuredhoo Express　　　DIVING
Usually done as a long drift dive through the channel next to the Kuredu resort, Kuredhoo Express is a demanding dive in strong currents, but it also offers brilliant snorkelling on the eastern side. Napoleon wrasse, grey-tip reef sharks and trevally frequent the channel entrance, while inside are overhangs dripping with soft corals. Look for morays, turtles and stingrays. It's a Protected Marine Area.

Shipyard　　　DIVING
Another demanding dive, with two wrecks within 50m of each other. Strong currents

around these ships have promoted the rapid growth of soft and hard corals, which now form a habitat for many types of reef fish. Moray eels and sweepers live inside the wrecks, while nurse sharks cruise around the bottom.

Fushifaru Thila   DIVING

When the current is strong, Fushifaru Thila is no place for beginners, but when the currents are slow the top of the thila is superb for snorkelling. The thila, with lovely soft corals, sits in the centre of a broad channel and attracts mantas, eagle rays, sharks, grouper, sweetlips and turtles. Cleaner wrasse abound on the thila, which is a Protected Marine Area.

🛏 Sleeping

Komandoo Island Resort   ROMANTIC RESORT $$
(🖰 662 1010; www.komandoo.com; r incl breakfast from US$683; ❄ @ 🛜) Komandoo is an intensively relaxed spot and the resort ethos is one of pampering and romance. There are no children allowed here, making this a favourite spot for honeymooners and other couples enjoying a romantic break. The round island is ringed by a strikingly beautiful beach, although the sea breaks that surround much of the island obscure the perfection somewhat.

The hexagonal rooms, prefabricated in pine from Finland, come with four-poster beds and they all front directly onto a pure white beach. There are 15 rustic-style water bungalows that are suitably impressive and equipped with solid teak furniture.

The four reefs accessible through two channels from the island have a wide variety of marine life, so are ideal for snorkelling from the beach. The main restaurant and bar buildings have sea views, sand floors and an intimate feel. This is a superb spot for a tranquil, romantic break from the real world.

**Kuredu Island
Resort & Spa**   ACTIVITIES RESORT $$
(🖰 662 0332; www.kuredu.com; half board r from US$480; ❄ @ 🛜 🛥) Kuredu Island Resort is about as close as you can get to a resort city in the Maldives – this truly is the resort that has everything, so look no further if you want a fun, sociable and action-packed holiday destination as well as the usual gleaming beaches and great diving.

You can effectively have whatever kind of holiday you're after here – the sheer number of activities and facilities available is mind-boggling. From a six hole golf course to kite-boarding and a football pitch, Kuredu has it all. There are nine room categories running from the simple but charming Bonthi Garden Bungalows to the beach villas, which face the island's best beach. The buffets in the main restaurant are pretty good, with a fair selection of Asian and international dishes. In addition there are three à la carte restaurants. Other facilities include a gym, tennis courts, a well-used beach volleyball court and the golf course. The spa offers Swedish, Thai and Oriental massages as well as lessons. Excellent dive sites are accessible from Kuredu. All in all, Kuredu is a well-run resort with a lively, sociable atmosphere.

Kanuhura   LUXURY RESORT $$$
(🖰 662 0044; www.kanuhura.com; r/wv incl breakfast from US$989; ❄ @ 🛜 🛥) Kanuhura is a sumptuous, impressive place with magnificent beaches, stunning accommodation and top-notch food. It's classy and stylish without being too formal, it's romantic without being too quiet and it's welcoming to families without allowing kids to run riot. If you want a laid-back, high-end beach holiday with considerable style, this may be for you.

Kanuhura is a big island, about 1km long, with perfect beaches go right around the island without a sandbag or sea wall in sight. The rooms combine classical luxury and elegant simplicity. The beach villas have four-poster beds, a separate dressing area, a lovely indoor-outdoor bathroom, lots of polished timber and a frontage onto the perfect beach. The more expensive suites and water villas are even bigger and feature several rooms, private spas, sun decks and direct sea access.

The resort's public areas, restaurants and spa are focused on the expansive infinity pool near the main jetty. At the other end of the island is the high-end outdoor dining option of the Veli Café – overlooking the resort's very own desert islet of Jehunuhura. A complimentary boat shuttles guests back and forth between the two, and picnics can be ordered to take with you. Otherwise it's a fantasy desert island, perfect for Robinson Crusoe role play.

❶ Getting There & Away

There's no airport in Lhaviyani Atoll, and all resorts use seaplane charters to get guests here. There's a daily ferry connecting the inhabited islands, though, as well as a twice-weekly ferry to and from Male (Rf50, six hours) from Naifaru.

NORTHERN ATOLLS LHAVIYANI

Southern Atolls

Best Resorts

➡ Shangri-La Villingili Resort & Spa (p119)

➡ Six Senses Laamu (p113)

➡ NIYAMA Maldives (p110)

➡ Maalifushi by COMO (p111)

Best Guesthouses

➡ Reveries Diving Village (p113)

➡ Viluxer Retreat (p116)

➡ Casa Barabaru (p105)

➡ Villa Stella (p110)

Why Go?

The southern atolls have been busy over the past few years as new resorts have been built on ever more atolls. With better transport infrastructure than the north of the country – there are five regional airports, all with multiple daily connections to the capital – it's surprising that tourism didn't catch on here sooner.

Outside the resorts, the southern atolls have mostly retained a traditional way of life. The exception is Gan, where the British established military facilities in WWII and maintained an air-force base that operated until 1976.

Development is continuing, with each atoll now hosting at least one resort, and several new guesthouses opening. Safari boats explore dive sites, and surfing trips visit the remotest breaks of Gaafu Dhaalu and Seenu Atolls. Welcome to the pristine islands of the southern Maldives.

When to Go

➡ **Dec-Apr** The best time to see manta rays swimming in the waters of the south.

➡ **Feb-Apr & Aug-Oct** Surf's up in Gaafu Dhaal and Seenu Atolls.

➡ **May-Nov** Great visibility makes this an excellent time to snorkel and dive.

Vaavu

Vaavu is made up of Felidhoo Atoll and the small, uninhabited Vattaru Falhu Atoll. This is the least populous area of the country, with around 2100 inhabitants spread over just five inhabited islands.

The main industry is fishing, and there is also some boat building. The capital island is Felidhoo, which has only about 500 people, but visitors are more likely to go to its neighbouring island, Keyodhoo (population 670), which has a good anchorage for safari boats. At the northern edge of the atoll, Fulidhoo (population 390) is an attractive island known for its boat building. Rakeedhoo (population 360), at the southern tip of the atoll, is used as an anchorage by safari boats taking divers to the nearby channel.

🏃 Activities

With over 25 dive sites in the atoll, and only three resorts in the area, you're unlikely to feel crowded when diving here. Some dive sites are not readily accessible, even from the resorts, and are mostly visited by safari boats. The following sites are rated among the best in the whole of the Maldives, and they all offer superb snorkelling.

★ Fotteyo   DIVING
Fotteyo is a brilliant diving and snorkelling site in and around a channel entrance – it's worth making several dives here. There are numerous small caves, several large caves and various arches and holes, all decorated with colourful soft corals. Rays, reef sharks, grouper, tuna, jackfish, barracuda, turtles and even hammerhead sharks can be seen. Inside, the channel floor is known as 'triggerfish alley'.

Vattaru Kandu   DIVING
A remote channel dive on the southern edge of Vattaru Falhu, Vattaru Kandu is now a designated Protected Marine Area. It is not too demanding unless the currents are running at full speed. The reef next to Vattaru is a fine snorkelling area. Around the entrance are many caves and overhangs with soft corals, sea fans and abundant fish life – barracuda, fusilier and white-tip reef sharks. Turtles are sometimes seen here, as are manta rays from December to April.

Devana Kandu   DIVING
This is a drift dive that's not too demanding, in a channel divided by a narrow thila.

Devana Kandu is a great snorkelling area too. There are several entrances to the channel, which has overhangs, caves, reef sharks and eagle rays. The southern side has soft corals and lots of reef fish. Further in, the passages join up and there is a broad area of hard corals, the deeper parts being less affected by bleaching.

Rakeedhoo Kandu   DIVING
Rakeedhoo Kandu is a challenging dive in a deep channel – the east and west sides are usually done as separate drift dives. Broad coral shelves cover overhangs and caves, which have sea fans and black corals. Turtles, Napoleon wrasse, sharks and schools of trevally are often seen, and the snorkelling on the reef top is brilliant.

🛏 Sleeping

Casa Barabaru   GUESTHOUSE $
(📞790 4997; www.barabaru.com; Thinadhoo; r from US$99; ❄ @) This Italian-run guesthouse on the charming island of Thinadhoo is a great place for an island holiday. Accommodation is in two comfortable rooms with rustic wooden fittings and modern bathrooms, and the sea is just 50m away. Due to the Italian owners, it's particularly popular with independent Italian travellers (but some English is spoken).

It's also popular with travellers wishing to fish – night fishing and deep-sea fishing are all available. Good meals and an enthusiastic team are the main highlights of a trip here, as are the nearby great beaches, which can be visited easily on day trips.

❶ Getting There & Away

Vaavu is easily reached by ferry from Male's Viligili Terminal. Ferries (Rf22, two hours) to the northerly island of Fulidhoo leave Male at 10am on Sunday, Tuesday and Thursday, stopping off at Maafushi on the way, and return from Fulidhoo at 11am on Saturday, Monday and Wednesday. From Fulidhoo, it's possible to connect to the other inhabited islands in the atoll daily except Friday. See www.mtcc.com.mv for timetables.

Meemu

Meemu Atoll has eight inhabited islands and three resorts. The capital island is Muli (population 850), a small and traditional island with little to attract visitors. Nearby Mulah and more southerly Kolhufushi are both more populous with about 1450 and

Southern Atolls

See Vaavu, Meemu, Faafu & Dhaalua Atolls Map (p108)

See Laamu, Thaa, Gaafu Alifu & Gnaviyani Map (p112)

See Addu Atoll Map (p118)

1225 people respectively. Both these islands grow yams, which are an important food staple on fertile islands. Elsewhere the main industry in Meemu is fishing.

As well as several superb dive sites, Meemu has some excellent surf breaks on its eastern edge, including Veyvah Point, Boahuraa Point and Mulee Point, which are gradually being explored by more adventurous surfers. Guesthouses have yet to take off in the atoll, however, so most of these sites are visited by boat.

🏃 Activities

★ Shark's Tongue   DIVING
Shark's Tongue is east of Boli Mulah, in the mouth of the Mulah Kandu. White-tips sleep on the sandy plateau, and grey-tip reef sharks hang around a cleaning station at 20m. In strong currents, black-tip, grey and silver-tip sharks cruise through the coral blocks, making this a fascinating dive spot.

Giant Clam   DIVING
Giant Clam is an easy dive around two sheltered giris, where several giant clams are seen between 8m and 15m, even by snorkellers. Numerous caves and overhangs are rich with anemones and home to lobsters, grouper and glassfish. Colourful butterflyfish and clown triggerfish are easily spotted, but look hard for well-camouflaged stonefish and scorpionfish.

🛏 Sleeping

Chaaya Lagoon
Hakuraa Huraa   ACTIVITIES RESORT $$
(✆ 672 0014; www.cinnamonhotels.com; r incl breakfast from US$576; ✳@🤶) Chaaya Lagoon Hakuraa Huraa is a well-designed resort combining romance and water sports. With nearly all its unusual villas over water (they have tented white roofs and are quite unlike the typical water villas you'll see in other places), some stunning beaches and plenty of activities, this is a great place to combine activity and indolence, although you don't get a great sense of privacy in the rooms as they're quite closely packed together. The water villas are a solid attraction though, and there's an enormous number of them, running along the entire length of one side of the island.

The lagoon is not good for snorkelling, though snorkelling gear and twice-daily trips are included in the package. The dive school is good value and offers what so few

centres in the Maldives can these days –
access to truly pristine dive sites. With so
many little-visited dive sites in the area,
diving might be the best reason to stay at
Hakuraa Huraa, though the quality food
and friendly staff are others.

❶ Getting There & Away

Three daily ferry routes connect all the inhabited islands in the atoll and there are inter-atoll
ferry connections to Male from Muli every other
day (Rf150, four hours). Resorts use seaplane
charters.

Faafu

Faafu Atoll has about 4000 people living
on its five inhabited islands. The capital island, **Magoodhoo** (population 680), is a
small fishing village with a very traditional
community. There are just two resorts in the
atoll, and as one is a private island for the super rich (called the Rania Experience), nearly
everyone coming here stays at Filitheyo.

◎ Sights & Activities

Nilandhoo   ISLAND
On the southern edge of the atoll, Niland-
hoo (population 1500) has the second-oldest
mosque in the country, **Aasaari Miskiiy**,
built during the reign of Sultan Mohammed Ibn Abdullah (r 1153–66). It is made of
dressed stone and the interior is decorated
with carved woodwork. It's possible that
the stones were recycled from the ruins of
earlier, pre-Islamic structures.

Filitheyo Reef   DIVING
Filitheyo Reef, the kandu south of Filitheyo
resort, is now a Protected Marine Area and
has several diving possibilities. Only accessible by boat, the house reef on the southeast corner of the resort descends in big
steps, where great clouds of fish congregate.
Swarms of batfish and several Napoleons
are resident, while grey-tip reef sharks, rays
and trevally are frequent visitors.

Two Brothers   DIVING
The Two Brothers are two thilas located in
a narrow channel. The big 'brother' (north)
tops out at 3m and is covered with soft corals and sponges, and attracts snorkellers.
Many turtles live here. Big pelagics cruise
around both 'brothers' and there are lots
of nudibranchs, pipefish, gobies and other
small marine species.

🛏 Sleeping

Filitheyo Island Resort   ROMANTIC RESORT **$$**
(☑ 674 0025; www.aaaresorts.com.mv; half board
r from US$495; ❄ @ ♜ ≋) Filitheyo is a lush,
triangular island with superb white-sand
beaches. The public buildings are spacious,
open-sided Balinese-style pavilions with
palm-thatch roofs and natural touches,
and the whole place feels chic but laid-
back and informal. It's a solid midrange
option with many guests on all-inclusive
packages who come for relaxation.

Most rooms are comfortable timber
bungalows facing the beach, nested among
the palm trees and equipped with amen-
ities, including open-air bathrooms and
personal sun decks. Deluxe villas provide
extra space and style, while the water vil-
las have sea views and private balconies.
Resort facilities include a gym, small spa,
infinity pool, reading room and shops.
There's an interesting program of excur-
sions and fishing trips at this isolated and
little-visited atoll.

Beaches are pretty all around, but the
lagoon is shallow on the south side, and
not suitable for swimming on the east side.
The north side has it all – soft sand, good
swimming and an accessible house reef
that's great for snorkelling. Qualified di-
vers can do unguided dives off the house
reef too.

❶ Getting There & Away

Ferry route 404 connects the five inhabited
islands in the atoll daily, while inter-atoll ferry
407 connects Nilandhoo to Meedhoo in Dhaalu,
to the south, every day except Friday (Rf20, 30
minutes).

Dhaalu

Dhaalu Atoll is home to around 6500 peo-
ple, who live on its seven inhabited islands.
The biggest island is the capital, **Kudahu-
vadhoo** (population 1550), which is a busy
fishing centre, but also has an ancient and
mysterious mound. The mound is now just
sand, but originally this was the foundation
of a structure made of fine stonework. The
building stones were later removed to build
part of the island's mosque. Heyerdahl said
the rear wall of this mosque had some of the
finest masonry he had ever seen, surpassing
even that of the famous Inca wall in Cuzco,
Peru. He was amazed to find a masterpiece
of stone-shaping art on such an isolated

Vaavu, Meemu, Faafu & Dhaalu Atolls

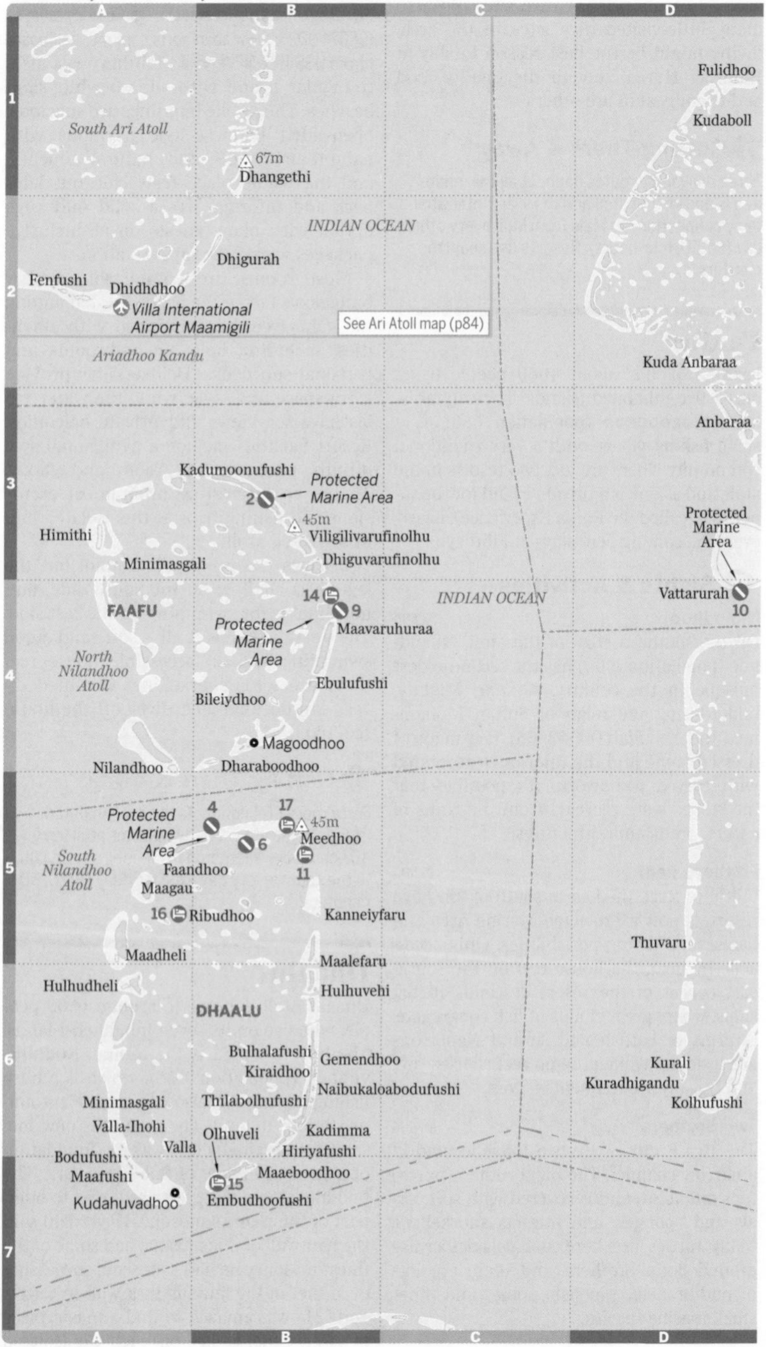

South Ari Atoll

Fulidhoo

Kudaboll

△ 67m
Dhangethi

INDIAN OCEAN

Dhigurah

Fenfushi

Dhidhdhoo

Villa International
Airport Maamigili

See Ari Atoll map (p84)

Kuda Anbaraa

Ariadhoo Kandu

Anbaraa

Kadumoonufushi

2 ⊘ Protected
Marine Area

Himithi

△ 45m
Viligilivarufinolhu

Dhiguvarufinolhu

Protected
Marine
Area

Minimasgali

FAAFU

14 ⊟
⊘ 9

INDIAN OCEAN

Vattarurah
10 ⊘

North
Nilandhoo
Atoll

Protected
Marine
Area

Maavaruhuraa

Ebulufushi

Bileiydhoo

Magoodhoo ●

Nilandhoo

Dharaboodhoo

Protected
Marine Area

4 ⊘

17
⊟ △ 45m
Meedhoo

South
Nilandhoo
Atoll

⊘ 6

Faandhoo

Maagau

11 ⊟

16 ⊟ Ribudhoo

Kanneiyfaru

Thuvaru

Maadheli

Maalefaru

Hulhudheli

Hulhuvehi

DHAALU

Bulhalafushi

Kiraidhoo

Gemendhoo

Naibukaloaboodufushi

Kurali

Kuradhigandu

Kolhufushi

Minimasgali

Thilabolhufushi

Valla-Ihohi

Olhuveli

Kadimma

Valla

Hiriyafushi

Bodufushi

Maafushi

Maaeboodhoo

Kudahuvadhoo ●

⊟ 15
Embudhoofushi

island, although the Maldivians had a reputation in the Islamic world for finely carved tombstones.

In the north of the atoll are the so-called jewellers' islands. **Ribudhoo** (population 700) has long been known for its silversmiths and goldsmiths, who are believed to have learnt the craft from a royal jeweller banished here by a sultan centuries ago. Another possibility is that they developed their skills on gold taken from a shipwreck in the 1700s. The nearby island of **Hulhudheli** (population 740) is a community of traditional silversmiths. Many of the craftspeople here now make jewellery, beads and carvings from black corals and mother-of-pearl.

🏃 Activities

Fushi Kandu　　　　　　　　　　DIVING

A channel on the northern edge of the atoll, Fushi Kandu is a Protected Marine Area. Steps on the east side have eagle rays and white-tip reef sharks. Thilas inside the channel are covered with hard and soft corals, and are frequented by turtles, Napoleon wrasse and schooling snappers. Look for yellowmouth morays and scorpionfish in the crevices.

Macro Spot　　　　　　　　　　　DIVING

Macro Spot, a sheltered, shallow giri, makes a suitable site for snorkellers, novices and macrophotographers. Overhangs and nooks shelter lobsters, cowries, glassfish, blennies and gobies.

🛏 Sleeping

Villa Stella
GUESTHOUSE $

(📞778 4769; www.guesthouses-in-maldives.com; s/d full board $100/200; ❄@) One of the very first guesthouses in the Maldives, Villa Stella is a great place to enjoy life on an inhabited island and explore several spots around this largely tourist-free atoll. Even though Villa Stella is used to catering to Italians, English is spoken, although there's a definite Italian feel to the meals served.

The six rooms here all have private bathrooms and share a living room with satellite TV and a communal kitchen. The staff members keep all visitors busy with daily excursions to a nearby uninhabited island where there's a superb beach. Snorkelling and fishing trips are also arranged, and Ribudhoo island is a very friendly place to walk around and get to know the locals.

Angsana Velavaru
MIDRANGE RESORT $$

(📞676 0028; www.angsana.com; r incl breakfast from US$660; ❄@🛜) Angsana's second Maldivian property is one that boasts classy accommodation with a strong Asian feel and is most notable for its 'InOcean' water villas, stand-alone structures a kilometre out from the main island, connected by boats across the lagoon. This is an upper-midrange place that attracts an international crowd looking for affordable relaxation.

The island itself is a real stunner – it has wide sandy beaches where turtles once nested (Velavaru means 'turtle island') – and while the wide lagoon is no good for snorkelling, there are free snorkelling trips to other islands every day. The deluxe beachfront villas with pools are impressive, though the 'InOcean' villas are an acquired taste: while they're dazzling, with every possible feature, including vast swimming pools, terraces, day beds and outdoor bathrooms, surely we can't be alone in wondering why you'd want to be so far from the main island? The food is good here, and a US$70 full board option per person is a good way to save money, though drinking water is extra even on this plan. There's a choice of three restaurants, as well as in villa dining. Other facilities include a small gym, spa, watersports centre and a marine biology lab.

Vilu Reef
ACTIVITIES RESORT $$

(📞676 0011; www.vilureefmaldives.com; r incl breakfast from US$528; ❄@🛜🏊) Vilu Reef is small but perennially popular resort notable for its huge palms and great beaches, which are especially good on the lagoon side and which run almost all the way around the island and include a beautiful sand spit. The island is thick with trees and bushes and, despite being quite crowded, has been developed with considerable care.

The accommodation style is traditional on the outside (white walls, thatched roofs) but veers more towards modern convenience inside. The rooms range from the attractive but simple beach villas to the far more sumptuous water villas, which mirror the shape of the island forming a huge oval. They are all equipped with mod cons and decent outdoor bathrooms.

On one side, a wide beach faces a lagoon that's perfect for sailing and sheltered swimming, while on the other side a good but narrower beach runs alongside a house reef that offers excellent snorkelling. Divers are well catered for by the reasonably priced diving school, which runs a full range of courses. The resort has a buffet main restaurant and a smarter à la carte place, although dining options in the buffet are limited. Vilu Reef combines friendly informality with some class and style – and it's suited to people looking for well-priced diving without having to go to a very basic resort.

NIYAMA Maldives
LUXURY RESORT $$$

(📞676 2676; www.niyama.peraquum.com; r incl breakfast from US$1160; ❄@🛜🏊🚹) Meaning 'bon voyage' in Dhivehi, NIYAMA is indeed an excellent way to ensure you have a good trip to Maldives. This Per Aquum resort, spread between two islands, is an extremely impressive fusion of gorgeous beaches, ultra high-end accommodation and superb service, with plenty of quirky and interesting touches, including Maldives' only deli and a unique new tree house restaurant.

The two islands, the latter of which only opened in 2015, are divided into two concepts: chill and play. The main island, Olhuveli, is chill, while the other, Embudhufushi, is devoted to play. There are rooms on both, and they're a highlight: all but one category have their own pools, and enjoy direct access to the water. They are lavishly furnished, with huge bathrooms and vast sliding doors leading to spacious gardens, though the beach villas are far more charming than the vast but slightly sterile water villas. The upper categories are simply enormous and have everything from electric guitars to telescopes supplied.

For eating, there's a deli, where you can get excellent sandwiches to go, a blissfully easy way to enjoy lunch without the normal fuss and formality, while for more substantial fare there's the poolside all-day restaurant Epicure, Nest, a tree house restaurant serving pan-Asian food, African cuisine at Tribal, Italian at Blu and fine dining at Edge, an evening-only fine dining restaurant built over the reef for which you need to take a bespoke boat: yes, it's undeniably gimmicky, but the food is fabulous. The Lime Spa is large and glamorous, and there's also a dive centre, gym, water-sports centre, kids club, marine biology lab and a perfect nearby desert island to visit. All in all, Niyama is an exciting and imaginative new addition to Maldives' very top resorts.

❶ Getting There & Away

Seaplane charters serve the resorts in Dhaalu, while two ferry services connect the atoll's seven inhabited islands. Ferry routes 405 and 406 connect the inhabited islands in the atoll three times a week. Tickets cost Rf20.

Thaa

Thaa Atoll consists of 13 inhabited islands and just one, brand new, resort. The capital is **Veymandhoo**, with a population of 1100 people. All the islands are on the edges of the atoll, mostly clustered around the kandus, and they're quite densely settled. **Thimarafushi** (population 2400), near the capital, is the most populous island, and has a recently opened airstrip. Ruins of a 25m-wide mound on the island of **Kibidhoo** show this group of islands has been populated for centuries.

On **Guraidhoo** (population 1800), in another island group, is the grave of Sultan Usman I, who ruled the Maldives for only two months before being banished here. On **Dhiyamigili** (population 750) there are ruins of the palace of Mohammed Imaaduddeen II, a much more successful sultan who ruled from 1704 to 1721 and founded one of the Maldives' longest-ruling dynasties.

The northern island of **Burunee** (population 560) is a centre for carpenters, many of whom work elsewhere, building boats and tourist resorts. The women make coir rope and reed mats. Around the mosque are an old sundial and tombstones that have been dated to the late 18th century.

🛏 Sleeping

⭐ **Maalifushi by COMO**   LUXURY RESORT $$$
(📞 678 0008; www.comohotels.com/maalifushi; r incl breakfast from US$1050; ✳@🔍❄) The first resort in remote Thaa Atoll is the glorious new creation of the COMO group. The highlights are the superb food and the state-of-the-art rooms, which combine to make staying here a real treat. The island itself has great stretches of beach, and also enjoys its own highly atmospheric desert island.

Maalifushi's 59 rooms are as cutting edge as you'd expect them to be with the resort opening in 2014. All are huge, and the palatial water villas are particularly impressive, each with a separate living room/dining area, bedroom, vast terrace and big plunge pools. Indeed, all but six rooms on the island have their own pools, and while the style is rather anonymously international, the look is thoroughly contemporary and tasteful. Food is definitely a highlight though, with the Japanese Tai Restaurant, the all-day Madi and Thila restaurants and in-villa dining all absolutely top-notch. The Como Shambhala Spa is over water and offers a full program of pampering. Tourism in Thaa Atoll could not have got off to a better start.

❶ Getting There & Away

The island of **Thimarafushi** has daily flights to and from Male (US$390, 50 mins) on Maldivian (www.maldivian.aero). Many resort guests fly directly to Maalifushi by seaplane charter, though.

Laamu

Laamu Atoll has about 14,000 people living on its 12 inhabited islands. The island of **Kadhoo** has an airfield that has several daily flights from Male. Kadhoo is linked by causeways to the large capital island of **Fonadhoo** (population 1770) to the south. The causeway also goes north to the island of **Gan** (population 2500), forming one of the longest stretches of road in the country – all of 12km.

There are numerous archaeological sites in Laamu, with evidence of pre-Muslim

Laamu, Thaa, Gaafu Alifu & Gnaviyani

N 0 — 30 km
0 — 15 miles

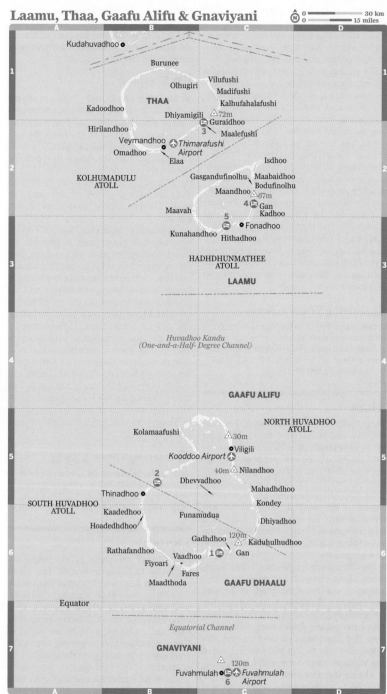

Kudahuvadhoo

Burunee

Vilufushi
Olhugiri
Madifushi
Kalhufahalafushi

THAA

Kadoodhoo
Dhiyamigili △72m
Guraidhoo
3
Maalefushi
Hirilandhoo
Veymandhoo ✈ *Thimarafushi*
Omadhoo *Airport*
Elaa

**KOLHUMADULU
ATOLL**

Isdhoo
Gasgandufinolhu Maabaidhoo
Bodufinolhu
Maandhoo △67m
4 Gan
Kadhoo
Maavah **5**
Fonadhoo
Kunahandhoo Hithadhoo

**HADHDHUNMATHEE
ATOLL**

LAAMU

*Huvadhoo Kandu
(One-and-a-Half- Degree Channel)*

GAAFU ALIFU

**NORTH HUVADHOO
ATOLL**

Kolamaafushi △30m
Viligili
Kooddoo Airport ✈
40m △ Nilandhoo
2
Dhevvadhoo
Mahadhdhoo
Thinadhoo Kondey
Funamudua Dhiyadhoo

**SOUTH HUVADHOO
ATOLL**

Kaadedhoo
Hoadedhdhoo Gadhdhoo 120m
1 △ Kaduhulhudhoo
Rathafandhoo Gan
Fiyoari Vaadhoo
Fares
Maadthoda **GAAFU DHAALU**

Equator

Equatorial Channel

GNAVIYANI

△ 120m
Fuvahmulah ✈ *Fuvahmulah*
6 *Airport*

civilisations on many islands. At the north-eastern tip of the atoll, on **Isdhoo**, a giant, black dome rises above the palms. Who built the ancient artificial mound, known as a *hawitta*, and for what reason, is not really known. Buddha images have been found on the island, and HCP Bell (the British leader of archaeological expeditions) believed such mounds to be the remains of Buddhist stupas, while Heyerdahl speculated that Buddhists had built on even earlier mounds left by the legendary Redin people. The **Friday Mosque** on Isdhoo is around 300 years old. It was probably built on the site of an earlier temple, because it faces directly west, rather than towards Mecca, which is to the northwest.

Bell also found quite a few mounds on Gan, which he also believed to be Buddhist stupas, and he found a fragment of a stone Buddha face, which he estimated was from a statue over 4m high. Almost nothing remains of these structures because the stones have been removed to use in more modern buildings. There are mounds on several other islands in Laamu, including Kadhoo, Maandhoo and Hithadhoo – one is over 5m high.

🛏 Sleeping

Reveries Diving Village   GUESTHOUSE $$
(☑680 8866; www.reveriesmaldives.com; Gan; r incl breakfast from $138; ❀☎☒) The first guesthouse in Laamu is this very smart place, one of the best compromises between the luxury of a resort and the cost of a guesthouse we have yet found. The 20 rooms are some of the smartest guesthouse accommodation in the country, with stylish furniture, minibars, good bathrooms with rain showers, balconies and satellite TV.

As its name suggests, the guesthouse is aimed at divers who take advantage of the incredible diving all over the atoll, much of it still being discovered. However, there are plenty of other activities on offer, including

surfing at six nearby breaks, wakeboarding, fishing and kayaking, so it's hard to be bored. There's a private beach in front of the hotel that is screened off from the rest of the town, meaning you can swim without upsetting local sensibilities. Meals are taken at one of three onsite restaurants and are good, while the young staff members are keen to help out and ensure you enjoy your stay. There's a small gym and even a rooftop spa here too.

Gan, the island the guesthouse on, is the longest in the country and one of its most interesting too, boasting a large lake (by local standards) and a slew of Buddhist ruins. Moreover, as Gan is connected to Kadhoo and Fonadhoo by causeways, it's possible to explore other nearby islands without hiring a boat, making this a great choice if you'd like to see lots of local life.

★**Six Senses Laamu**   LUXURY RESORT $$$
(☑680 0800; www.sixsenses.com; r incl breakfast from US$1200; ❀@☎☒) ✐ Six Senses Laamu is an amazing place, combining thoughtful luxury, rustic simplicity, outstanding culinary options and plenty of activities. The island truly feels like it's in the middle of nowhere: an hour's flight south of Male followed by a 15-minute speedboat ride to the island may add a significant amount of time to your journey, but it's certainly worth it.

The first impression of the island is created by the giant wooden over-water structure where you dock; here you'll find the reception, several dining and drinking options, a library and even an ice-cream parlour and chocolate bar, where delicious free treats are given to guests all day long.

The island itself, beyond the over-water reception area, is ringed by a gorgeous white beach and boasts a gorgeous cyan-blue lagoon where dolphins swim in great numbers all year round. The 97 villas are all either right on the beach or over water, and they're something truly special, made from ecologically sourced wood and evoking a grand, classic style with plenty of hidden luxuries such as iPod docks and Bose entertainment systems. The water villas are particularly impressive with over-water hammocks, all-glass bathtubs and their own treetop decks, while the beach villas are ringed with trees and feel wonderfully private, but still offer direct beach access with your own loungers and expansive outdoor bathrooms.

Elsewhere on the island, there's a brand new pool, several superb restaurants (we particularly love Leaf, which overlooks the beach from the treetops and which you cross a wooden bridge to reach, though sushi at Longditude is also absolutely superb), a yoga and meditation centre, gym, outdoor cinema, wine cellar, gorgeous spa and full diving school and water-sports centre. There's also fantastically well-trained staff whose efficiency and problem-solving abilities are second to none in an industry where customer service can still be very hit and miss, even at the top end of the market. If you can afford it, this resort is a great choice for intelligent luxury and indulgent pampering.

❶ Getting There & Away

There are four daily flights with Maldivian (www.maldivian.aero) from Male to the **airstrip** on Kadhoo ($390 return, 50 minutes), while two ferry routes connect the inhabited islands in the atoll. Route 504 connects Gan to all islands north to Isdhoo, while route 505 connects Fonadhoo to Maavah, calling at each inhabited island on the way. Inter-atoll ferry route 503 connects Kadhoo with Thimarafushi in Thaa Atoll. It leaves Thimarafushi at 11.15am daily, arriving in Kadhoo at 2.45pm, and then returns to Thimarafushi at 3.15pm. It costs Rf50 each way.

Gaafu Alifu

The giant Huvadhoo Atoll, one of the largest coral atolls in the world, is separated from Laamu by the 90km-wide Huvadhoo Kandu. This stretch of water is also called the One-and-a-Half-Degree Channel, because of its latitude, and it's the safest place for ships to pass between the atolls that make up the Maldives.

Because Huvadhoo is so big, the atoll is divided into two administrative districts. The northern district is called Gaafu Alifu, and it has 11 inhabited islands and about 12,000 people. **Viligili**, the capital island, is also the most populated, with about 3000 people. Just south, the island of **Kudhoo** has an ice plant and fish-packing works. The atoll also has some productive agriculture, much of it on **Kondey** (population 440), which is also home to four *hawittas* – evidence of Buddhist settlement. Heyerdahl discovered a limestone carving here, which he believed to be of the Hindu water god Makara. The statue must have been here before the Islamic period and is thought to be over 1000 years old. Its significance, Heyerdahl believed, lay in the fact that it demonstrated that other religions aside from Buddhism permeated the Maldives before Islam took hold in 1153.

In the centre of the atoll, **Dhevvadhoo** (population 1000) is famous for its textile weaving and coir rope making. There are also mosques from the 16th and 17th centuries.

🛏 Sleeping

Jumeirah Dhevanafushi LUXURY RESORT $$$
(🖉 682 8800; www.jumeirah.com; r incl breakfast from $1412; ❋ @ 🛜 ⛱) This is the smaller and (even) more high end of the two Jumeirah resorts in Maldives. It's remote, fabulously luxurious and focused very much on stylish relaxation and private romance. The island is small even by local standards and notable mainly for its bold white modernist architecture, sumptu-

---

BRIDGES OVER TROUBLED WATERS

The Maldives may be famous for having virtually no roads, but there are a few places where this is not strictly speaking true, and where you can even see a fair number of cars in use. Outside the capital and a few larger towns, this is most prevalent where a series of islands have been joined together by bridges over the reef, effectively creating a single island. The two best examples of this can be found in Laamu and Addu Atolls.

In Laamu Atoll, road bridges connect four islands, including Gan, the largest single island in the country (checking in at almost a whopping 8km long!), while in Addu Atoll, you can find the longest stretch of road in the country, at 14km, connecting four islands.

Bridge building is a serious business in the Maldives, with islands linked to others by causeways having enormous economic and social advantages over those that aren't, as infrastructure can be shared. The next project on the cards is connecting the capital Male to the airport island of Hulhule, an ambitious prestige project of the current government that is likely to begin construction very shortly.

ous private villas and its calling card – its Ocean Pearl water villas.

The Ocean Pearls are not attached to the main island, but are freestanding on the lagoon 850m from shore and only accessible by boat. Their main purpose is total privacy, and they achieve their goal. The Ocean Pearl complex has its own restaurant and infinity pool, in case you deem waiting for the dhoni too exhausting. The rooms on the main island are actually more charming however; they start at a palatial 270 sq metres, all have their own wonderful slate plunge pools, Hermes goodies in the bathroom, 24-hour butler service, marble bathtubs that can accommodate a sports team and massive four poster beds.

The style of the resort is thoroughly contemporary, with its unusual white arrival jetty, spa and reception area, which definitely stand out. Despite the resort being small and exclusive, there are three outstanding dining options to choose from as well as an excellent cocktail bar. Look no further for total luxury and pampering in a contemporary and stylish setting.

❶ Getting There & Away

There is an **airstrip** on Kooddoo, with several flights a day to Male (US$430 return, 70 mins) with Maldivian (www.maldivian.aero). There are six frequent ferries connecting most of the inhabited islands in the two atolls, including Kaadedhoo. The network is centred on the Gaafu Dhaalu's capital island Thinadhoo, and to a lesser extent on Gaafu Alifu's capital Viligili.

Gaafu Dhaalu

Geographically isolated from Male, but strategically located on the Indian Ocean trade routes, Gaafu Dhaalu – or Huvadhoo Atoll, to use its geographical name – had independent tendencies dating back many years. It had its own direct trade links with Sri Lanka, and the people spoke a distinct dialect almost incomprehensible to other Maldivians. The island of **Thinadhoo** was a focal point of the 'southern rebellion' against the central rule of Male during the early 1960s, so much so that troops from Male invaded in February 1962 and destroyed all the homes. The people fled to neighbouring islands and Thinadhoo was not resettled until four years later. It now has a population of around 6400, while the

rest of the atoll's inhabitants are scattered among a further nine inhabited islands.

Although there's now a resort here, Gaafu Dhaalu remains a remote part of the country to visit, though it attracts a consistent number of foreign visitors who make boat trips around the southeastern edge of the atoll to surf the uncrowded waves that break around the channel entrances. On the island of **Kaadedhoo**, near Thinadhoo, a small airport has daily flights to Male, and surfing safari boats meet clients there.

On **Gadhdhoo** (population 2750), women make superb examples of the mats known as *thundu kunaa,* which are woven from special reeds found on an adjacent island. Souvenir shops in Male and on some resorts sell these mats – those from Gadhdhoo are the softest and most finely woven.

In the south of the atoll, only about 20km from the equator, the island of **Vaadhoo** has two *hawittas,* and a mosque that dates from the 17th century. The mosque is elaborately decorated inside and has a stone bath outside, as well as ancient tombstones carved with three different kinds of early Maldivian script.

🛏 Sleeping

Ayada Maldives   LUXURY RESORT **$$$**
(☑ 684 4444; www.ayadamaldives.com; r incl breakfast from $1099; ❇ @ 🛜 ⛱ 🚣) The first resort in this pristine corner of the Maldives is a wonderfully realised venture, with fantastic accommodation in large and beautifully designed villas on a perfect island surrounded by superb and largely undiscovered reefs for diving. It's a great choice for anyone into diving and water-sports, with some excellent surf breaks nearby.

There are eight different villa types, sized from around 100 sq metres up to 300 sq metres. They're done out in timber and thatch and enjoy their own pools, sleek and contemporary furnishings with an Asian flavour and lots of luxurious extras such as Nespresso machines, iPod docks and full in-room bars. There are three restaurants on the island, as well as the fabulously indulgent overwater Ile de Joie, where fine wines, cheeses, oysters, caviar and chocolates are all served in a variety of gastronomic combinations. Other facilities include a gorgeous ESPA spa, a hammam and steam room, tennis and badminton courts, a full gym, a water-sports centre and a top-of-the-range dive school. This is a great place to escape the crowds and enjoy your own slice of Indian Ocean paradise in sumptuous but laid-back style.

ⓘ Getting There & Away

There is an airstrip (p115) on Kooddoo in next door Gaafu Alifu, with several flights a day to Male with Maldivian (US$430 return, 70 mins). Flights also run to the airstrip on **Kaadedhoo**. There is also a network of six frequent ferries connecting most of the inhabited islands in the atoll, as well as those in Gaafu Alifu. The network is centred on the capital island Thinadhoo.

Gnaviyani

The interesting island of **Fuvahmulah** (also called Foammulah or Fuamulaku) makes up the administrative district of Gnaviyani, a solitary place stuck in the middle of the Equatorial Channel with a population of around 11,000. About 5km long and 1km wide, it's the biggest single island in the Maldives and one of the most fertile, producing many fruits and vegetables such as mangoes, papayas, oranges and pineapples. The natural vegetation is lush, and there are two freshwater lakes, making it geographically about the most varied place in the country. In recent years the building of

a harbour and an airport here has greatly reduced Fuvahmulah's isolation.

Despite Fuvahmulah's apparent isolation, navigators passing between the Middle East, India and Southeast Asia have long used the Equatorial Channel. Ibn Battuta visited in 1344, stayed for two months and married two women. Two Frenchmen visited in 1529 and admired the old mosque at the west end of the island. In 1922 HCP Bell stopped here briefly, and noted a 7m-high *hawitta*. Heyerdahl found the *hawitta* in poor condition, and discovered remnants of another nearby. He also investigated the nearby mosque, the oldest one on the island, and believed it had been built on the foundations of an earlier structure built by skilled stonemasons. Another old mosque, on the north side of the island, had expertly made stonework in its foundations and in an adjacent stone bath.

ⓘ Sleeping

★**Viluxer Retreat**   GUESTHOUSE $
(🖉686 1711; www.viluxer.com; Naibu Thuththu Hingun; r incl breakfast from US$110; ❄@🛜) This guesthouse is the best choice on Fuvahmulah. It's in the centre of the town, but also right by the sea, and has large, stylish rooms (check out those white leather beds...) and a good restaurant. The staff here are very helpful and it's a great choice for a holiday where you can combine the excellent beaches with local interaction.

ⓘ Getting There & Away

There is a daily flight with **Maldivian** (www.maldivian.aero) to and from Male from Fuvahmulah's **airstrip** ($340 return, 70 minutes). There is also a daily ferry to and from Addu Atoll (1½ hours, Rf50), which leaves from the harbour at Maradhoo in Addu at 9.30am each day (2pm on Friday) and returns from Fuvahmulah at 12.30pm daily (4pm on Fridays).

MYSTERIOUS GAN

Just southwest of Gadhdhoo, the uninhabited island of **Gan** has remnants of what was once the most impressive *hawitta* (stone prayer mound) in the Maldives, originally a pyramid with stepped ramps on all four sides, like many Mexican pyramids. The ruin was 8.5m high and 23m square. Norwegian ethnographer Thor Heyerdahl also found stones here decorated with sun motifs, which he believed were proof of a sun-worshipping society even older than the Buddhist and Hindu settlements. This is the subject of Heyerdhahl's book *The Maldive Mystery*, and while many of Heyerdahl's theories are now rejected by ethnographers and archeologists, there is no doubt that his excavations in the Maldives in the 1980s was a turning point for the official version of Maldivian history, which had until that time simply ignored all evidence of pre-Muslim civilisations on the islands.

Addu Atoll

Heart-shaped Addu Atoll is the southern extreme of Maldives and is home to some of the most colourful corals in the country. There's a splash of late colonial flavour on Gan Island, where there was a British military base until the 1970s, and an independent streak flows through the locals, who even speak a different dialect of Dhivehi to that spoken in Male.

Addu Atoll (often called Addu City these days) is the main economic and administrative centre in the south of the country, and the only place to rival Male in size and importance. Its 18,000 people are spread out over seven islands that are connected to each other by causeways and land reclamation.

The biggest influence on Addu's modern history has been the British bases, first established on Gan during WWII as part of the Indian Ocean defences. In 1956, when the British could no longer use Sri Lanka, they developed a Royal Air Force base on Addu as a strategic Cold War outpost. The base had around 600 personnel permanently stationed here, with up to 3000 during periods of peak activity. The British built a series of causeways connecting Feydhoo, Maradhoo and Hithadhoo islands and employed most of the population on or around the base. In 1976 the British pulled out, leaving an airport, some large industrial buildings, barracks and a lot of unemployed people who spoke good English and had experience working for Westerners. When the tourism industry took off in the late 1970s, many of the men of Addu went to Male to seek work in resorts and tourist shops. They have never lost their head start in the tourism business and to this day, in resorts all over the country, there's a better than even chance that the Maldivian staff will be from Addu.

⊙ Sights

◉ Gan

Gan is atypical of the Maldives: it has a far more colonial feel and a refreshingly different atmosphere from anywhere else in the country. Inhabited since ancient times, Gan was the site where HCP Bell excavated a large 9m-high mound. He believed it to be the ruins of a Buddhist stupa. His expedition made careful measurements of the site, took photos and made precise drawings that are published in his monograph. This was fortunate, as the archaeological sites and almost everything else on Gan were levelled to create the air-force base in 1956.

The British took over the entire island and constructed airport buildings, barracks, jetties, maintenance sheds, and even a golf course. Many of these structures remain, some picturesquely run-down, others used for various purposes. Most of the island's lush native vegetation was cleared, but the British then landscaped with new plants – avenues of casuarinas, clumps of bougainvillea, swaths of lawn and rose gardens. It's much more spacious than most resort islands and it has a slightly weird and eerie atmosphere, but it's very peaceful and relaxed – like an old, abandoned movie set.

There's a low-key **memorial** to those who served on the base, including Indian regiments based here. Big guns, which were part of the WWII defences, now guard the memorial.

◉ Feydhoo, Maradhoo & Hithadhoo

Causeways connect Gan to the atoll capital Hithadhoo via Feydhoo and Maradhoo as well as some other tiny islands. Local teashops serve tea, cakes and 'short eats', and some will have a more substantial fish curry. Remember that these villages are inevitably very conservative, so dress modestly.

Most of the houses have corrugated iron roofs, but are otherwise traditional. Older buildings are made of coral-stone while newer ones are made of concrete blocks. There's usually a courtyard or an open space with a shady tree and a *joli* (net seat in a rectangular frame) or *undholi* (swing seat) providing a cool place to sit in the heat of the day. Notice the big, square chimney blocks – there are wooden racks inside them, where fish are hung to be smoked. Another distinctive feature can be seen at street junctions, where walls and buildings all have rounded corners.

You can easily walk from Gan to Feydhoo, which has several mosques. Boats to Fuvahmulah use the small harbour here.

When the British took over, the villagers from Gan were resettled on Feydhoo, and some of the people from Feydhoo were then moved to the next island, Maradhoo, where they formed a new village. Maradhoo now has a population of 3300 in two villages that have run together – the southern one is called Maradhoo-Feydhoo. Further north, the road follows an isthmus that was once three narrow, uninhabited islands before bringing you to Hithadhoo, the Maldives' largest town outside Male, with a population of 9500.

SOUTHERN ATOLLS ADDU ATOLL

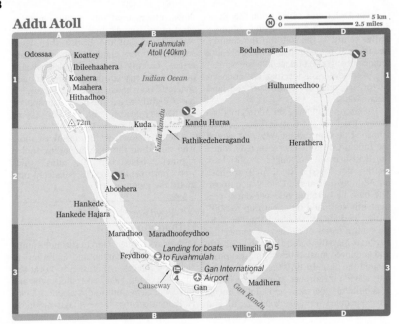

Addu Atoll

◉ Hulhumeedhoo

At the northeast corner of the lagoon, this island has two adjoining villages, Hulhudoo and Meedhoo, both known as Hulhumeedhoo (total population around 6000). Legend says an Arab shipwrecked here in about 872 converted the islanders to Islam 280 years before the people of Male. The cemetery is known for its ancient headstones, many of which are beautifully carved with the archaic Dhives Akuru script. The southern half of Hulhumeedhoo is now the Herathera Resort, which is the second-largest resort in the country, and unusual for being on the same island as Maldivian settlements.

🏃 Activities

A highlight of Addu is the magnificent coral, much of which escaped the widespread bleaching of 1998, which still affects much of the coral elsewhere in the country, despite impressive regrowth. If you've been diving elsewhere in the Maldives and then come here you'll be amazed. On the northern edge of the atoll you can see huge table corals that might be hundreds of years old, and fields of staghorns that have all but disappeared in most parts of the country. It's not all good, though – corals inside the lagoon suffered as badly as anywhere else from coral bleaching.

★ British Loyalty Wreck   DIVING
The *British Loyalty* wreck has a good covering of soft corals, and turtles, trevally and many reef fish inhabit the encrusted decks. This oil tanker was torpedoed in 1944 by the German submarine U-183, which fired through an opening in the antisubmarine nets at the entrance to Gan Kandu. The disabled ship stayed in the atoll until 1946 when it was towed to its present location and used for target practice by another British ship.

The 140m wreck lies in 33m of water with its port side about 16m below the surface.

Maa Kandu   DIVING

The northeastern edge of Maa Kandu has a wide reef top covered with live acrophora corals, big brain corals, long branching staghorns and table corals. White-tip reef sharks, eagle rays and sometimes mantas can be spotted, along with turtles and numerous reef fish. It's also excellent for snorkelling.

Kuda Kandu   DIVING

Near Maa Kandu, Kuda Kandu is a superb site where a huge array of coral thrives between 5m and 15m. Currents can be strong here, so it's not for novices.

Shark Point   DIVING

Off the northeast corner of the atoll, Shark Point, sometimes called the Shark Hotel, is a plateau at about 30m. Grey-tip reef sharks cruise around here, white-tip reef sharks lie on the sand and other sharks can be seen in deeper water further out.

🛏 Sleeping

Be aware that if you plan to stay in the country's far south, you'll need to take a 70-minute flight from Male, which can be exhausting after a long-haul flight. However, the magnificent diving and snorkelling are well worth the extra effort to get here.

Equator Village   DIVING RESORT $

(☑ 689 8721; www.equatorvillage.com; r all inclusive US$224; ✳@⬆⬚) Equator Village is, for our money, one of the best-value diving resorts in the country. The low room rates and the all-inclusive packages they come with make this a great deal. Staying here also gives you the unique opportunity to see something of 'normal life' in the Maldives, as it is connected to several inhabited islands by a causeway.

It's clear this was formerly a British RAF base; neat lines of rooms (former barracks) fan out from the main building, and are surrounded by well-tended gardens that overflow with exotic flowers and plants. The rooms are functional and thoroughly unromantic – this is not a honeymooners' destination – but they're comfortable and great for divers.

The reception, bar and dining areas have been created from the old mess, completely redecorated in very unmilitary pink, white and grey. These open-sided spaces with their cane furniture and ceiling fans look out onto a sizeable swimming pool and

through palm trees to the blue sea beyond. The full-sized billiard table is a handsome inheritance from the Brits, as are the first-class tennis courts. The meals are all buffet with a limited selection. However, most guests are on an all-inclusive package, and can wash it down with beer or house wine. The all inclusive packages include free bike use, an island-hopping excursion with a barbecue, and twice-daily snorkelling trips. However, divers take note: the coral here is flabbergasting – and this should definitely be high on your list of top diving resorts. The dive centre is a small but friendly operation run by Diverland and includes the great dive sites in the area at very reasonable prices.

★**Shangri-La Villingili**
Resort & Spa   LUXURY HOTEL $$$

(☑ 689 7888; www.shangri-la.com/male/villingiliresort; r incl breakfast from US$1065; ✳@ ⬆⬚⬛) ⬤ This enormous but beautifully and thoughtfully conceived island ranks among the absolute top resorts in the Maldives. It's right at the south of the country, but well worth the extra travel time: you're essentially alone here, on a stunning island, with vast water villas, great beaches and a selection of super amenities that will satisfy even the most demanding travellers.

First of all the island is enormous – enough so that the resort has its own nine-hole golf course, which includes Maldives' highest natural point (a dizzying 5m!), a big attraction for some in itself. The island also boasts three freshwater lakes, extremely rare in Maldives, and something that gives the interior of the island more scope for exploration than most.

The accommodation is another highlight; the seven types of villa all come with their own private pool, Middle Eastern- and Indian-influenced decor and every little luxury you could wish for, from Nespresso machines to iPod docks. Particularly great are the utterly enormous water villas, which are at least twice the size of normal ones, even in luxury resorts, and the tree-house-style villas, which are raised off the ground and look and feel like a luxury version of Swiss Family Robinson, complete with a raised infinity pool.

There are three restaurants here; the main restaurant, Dr Ali's, is effectively three restaurants in one, with separate chefs specialising in Indian, Chinese and Arabic flavours. Others include Javvu, which overlooks the beach and serves up Mediterranean cuisine, and the Fashala fine dining restaurant. The resort also has a huge chef's garden, where many different herbs, fruits, and vegetables are grown; there is a scheme to buy produce from the next-door inhabited island.

The rest of the resort is just as impressive, including the incredibly lavish CHI spa, stunning white powder sand beaches, a full gym that includes a sauna and steam room, a superb kids club called the Cool Zone, tennis courts, a dive centre, a water-sports centre and a great reef for snorkelling. You may have to travel a little further to get here, but Shangri-La Maldives really is worth it – a truly amazing slice of the Maldives paired with utter luxury and sophistication.

ⓘ Getting There & Away

Maldivian (www.maldivian.aero) flies from Male to Gan and back four to five times a day. There are also regular flights from Fuvahmulah on FlyMe (www.flyme.mv), which originate in Male. There's a ferry to and from Fuvahmulah (1½ hours, Rf50), which leaves from the harbour at Maradhoo at 9.30am each day (2pm on Friday) and returns at 12.30pm daily (4pm on Fridays).

ⓘ Getting Around

The best way to get around Gan and over the causeway to neighbouring villages is by bicycle. Equator Village includes bike hire in its rates. Taxis shuttle between the islands and around the villages; from Gan to Hithadhoo should cost about Rf100. Taxis wait at the airport and you can order one from Equator Village.

Understand the Maldives

Maldives Today

The Maldives today is undergoing something of an identity crisis. After decades of tightly controlled one-party rule, the country emerged blinking into a new dawn in 2008 with the election of its first democratically elected president, Mohammed Nasheed. The four years that followed saw momentous, progressive changes, which didn't always go down well with the conservative island populations suspicious of change. Following an alleged coup in February 2012, the former dictator's brother-in-law, Abdulla Yameen, became president, and the country's course now seems very unclear.

Best in Print

Beach Babylon (Imogen Edwards-Jones, 2004) An amusing behind the scenes exposé set in a luxurious Maldivian resort.
Dive the Maldives (Sam Harwood & Rob Bryning, 2009) The best guidebook to dive sites, fish and other marine life for the Maldives.

Best on Film

The Island President (Jon Shenk, 2011) Fascinating and revealing documentary about the rise of former President Nasheed and his quest to make the world care about climate change.

Etiquette

On inhabited islands you must conform to local dress codes. This means shoulders and midriffs need to be covered and, for women, the knees too.

During Ramazan it's not acceptable to eat in public during daylight hours, except in resorts.

In the atolls men don't normally shake hands with women, but it's quite acceptable for women to shake hands with other women. Likewise, foreign women shaking hands with local men isn't seen as unusual.

Democratic Dawn

In many ways it was an incredible feat for the conservative, poorly educated Maldives to move so boldly to full democracy in 2008, becoming one of the first true Islamic democracies in the world. It's sadly unsurprising, then, that President Nasheed fell so dramatically from grace in 2012, mostly because his modernising, reformist agenda was at odds with the conservative island chiefs in the regions as well as the country's rich elite, for whom the pre-Nasheed status quo had been very favourable.

Despite only having been president for four years, Mohammed Nasheed left a huge mark on the Maldives. He introduced a national tax system, public healthcare, a state pension, and a national ferry network; he also lifted travel restrictions on foreigners and allowed the building of guesthouses on inhabited islands for the first time. He arguably moved the country forward decades in less that one full presidential term.

A Return to the Past

Following the coup of 2012, the 2013 presidential election saw the presidency go to Abdulla Yameen, the half-brother of former dictator Maumoon Abdul Gayoom, who ruled unchallenged for 30 years before the democratic elections of 2008. The former president, Mohammed Nasheed, was promptly arrested on charges of terrorism and found guilty on 13 March 2015 by the High Court after a series of trials whose constitutional shortcomings were widely condemned by international and local observers.

Parallel to Nasheed's liberal rule, the Maldives also saw the rise of an Islamist influence, previously kept at bay by the country's one-party state. Since Abdulla Yameen's ascension to the presidency, support for Islamist parties has continued to increase, with hundreds of

Maldivian nationals believed to be fighting alongside Islamic State rebels in Syria. In 2014 the country also saw a pro-IS march in Male, something until then totally unheard of in the peaceful and non-radicalised Maldives, which has brought to light the growing influence of wahhabism in the country.

Worryingly, conditions have also worsened for journalists in the Maldives in recent years. Ahmed Rilwan Abdulla, a journalist for the newspaper *Minivan News,* disappeared in 2014 following death threats after he carried out a series of investigations into corrupt politicians, Islamic extremists and Maldivians fighting in Syria. He is missing and assumed to be dead, having last been seen being abducted at knife-point outside his house.

Tourism Industry

Yet despite the political tension and worryingly authoritarian developments, tourism remains the country's biggest business – and it is booming, with well over a million tourists arriving on Maldivian shores in 2014. Hotels at both ends of the spectrum are being built with astonishing speed: new luxury properties at the top end and far cheaper guesthouses on inhabited islands are completed almost monthly.

This is therefore a fascinating time to visit the Maldives, especially if you're lucky enough to visit the capital or any other inhabited islands. The fast pace of change here, whether it be embracing modernity or reinvigorating traditional values, is all part of the charm of discovering this proud and fiercely independent island nation.

AREA: **90,000 SQ KM (ABOVE WATER 298 SQ KM)**

POPULATION: **345,000**

% OF POPULATION LIVING IN MALE: **30%**

GDP PER CAPITA: **US$6,665**

if Maldives were 100 people

65 would work in services
24 would work in secondary industries
11 would work in agriculture

belief systems
(% of population)

Sunni Muslim

population per sq km

MALDIVES   INDIA   UK

 ≈ 130 people

History

The Maldives is historically a small, isolated and peaceful nation, whose main challenge has been constantly trying to contain the desires of its distant neighbours and would-be colonisers. For the most part, its history is incredibly hazy, with little known of the period before the conversion to Islam in 1153. The pre-Muslim era is full of heroic myths and conjecture, based on inconclusive archaeological discoveries. The Maldivian character has clearly been shaped by this tumultuous past: hospitable and friendly but fiercely proud and independent at the same time. It's safe to say that conquering armies haven't got very far trying to persuade the Maldivian people of their benevolence.

Early Days

Some archaeologists, including Thor Heyerdahl, believe that the Maldives was well-known from around 2000 BC, and was a trading junction for several ancient maritime civilisations, including Egyptians, Romans, Mesopotamians and Indus Valley traders. The legendary sun-worshipping people called the Redin may have descended from one of these groups.

Around 500 BC the Redin either left or were absorbed by Buddhists, probably from Sri Lanka, and by Hindus from northwest India. HCP Bell, a British commissioner of the Ceylon Civil Service, led archaeological expeditions to the Maldives in 1920 and 1922. Among other things, he investigated the ruined, dome-shaped structures *(hawittas),* mostly in the southern atolls, which he believed were Buddhist stupas similar to the *dagobas* found in Sri Lanka.

The Maldive Islands: Monograph on the History, Archaeology & Epigraphy is HCP Bell's main work. The Ceylon Government Press published it in 1940, three years after his death. Original copies of the book are rare, though reprints are available from bookshops in Male.

Conversion to Islam

For many years Arab traders stopped at the Maldives en route to the Far East – their first record of the Maldive islands, which they called Dibajat, is from the 2nd century AD. Known as the 'Money Isles', the Maldives provided enormous quantities of cowry shells, an international currency of the early ages. It must have seemed a magical land to discover at the time – forget money growing on trees, in the Maldives it washed up on the shore!

TIMELINE	3rd century BC	AD 1117	1153
	Although historical records are scant, it is believed that Buddhism came to the Maldives during the time of Ashoka the Great, and spread throughout the islands.	The first king of the Theemuge dynasty, and the first king of the Maldives, Sri Mahabarana, is crowned, bringing together under one ruler the many fiefdoms that made up the country at the time.	The Maldives is converted to Islam by Berber scholar Abu Al Barakat Yusuf Al Barbari.

Abu Al Barakat Yusuf Al Barbari, a North African, is credited with converting the Maldivians to Islam in 1153. Though little is really known about what happened, Barakat was a Hafiz, a scholar who knew the entire Quran by heart, and who proselytised in Male for some time before meeting with success. One of the converts was the sultan, followed by the royal family. After conversion the sultan sent missionaries to the atolls to convert them too, and Buddhist temples around the country were destroyed or neglected.

A series of six sultanic dynasties followed, 84 sultans and sultanas in all, although some did not belong to the line of succession. At one stage, when the Portuguese first arrived on the scene, there were actually two ruling dynasties, the Theemuge (or Malei) dynasty and the Hilali.

The Maldive Mystery, by Thor Heyerdahl, the Norwegian explorer of *Kon-Tiki* fame, describes a short expedition in 1982–83 looking for remains of pre-Muslim societies.

The Portuguese

Early in the 16th century the Portuguese, who were already well established in Goa in western India, decided they wanted a greater share of the profitable trade routes of the Indian Ocean. They were given permission by the sultan to build a fort and a factory in Male, but it wasn't long before they wanted more from the Maldives.

In 1558, after a few unsuccessful attempts, Portuguese Captain Andreas Andre led an invasion army and killed Sultan Ali VI. The Maldivians called the captain 'Andiri Andirin' and he ruled Male and much of the country for the next 15 years. According to some Maldivian beliefs, Andre was born in the Maldives and went to Goa as a young man, where he came to serve the Portuguese. Apart from a few months of Malabar domination in Male during the 18th century, this was the only time that another country has occupied the Maldives; some argue that the Portuguese never actually ruled the Maldives at all, but had merely established a trading post.

According to popular belief, the Portuguese were cruel rulers, and ultimately decreed that Maldivians must convert to Christianity or be killed. There was ongoing resistance, especially from Mohammed Thakurufaanu, son of an influential family on Utheemu Island in the northern atoll of Haa Alifu. Thakurufaanu, with the help of his two brothers and some friends, started a series of guerrilla raids, culminating in an attack on Male in which all the Portuguese were slaughtered.

This victory is commemorated annually as National Day on the first day of the third month of the lunar year. There is a memorial centre on the island of Utheemu to Thakurufaanu, the Maldives' greatest hero, who went on to found the next sultanic dynasty, the Utheemu, which ruled for 120 years. Many reforms were introduced, including a new judicial system, a defence force and a coinage to replace the cowry currency.

1194	1333	1337	1573
The Isdhoo Loamaafaanu, a copperplate now believed to show the earliest recorded example of Maldivian script, is made. Among other things it details the execution of Buddhist monks in the south of the Maldives.	Ibn Battuta arrives in the Maldives for a nine-month stay, during which time he marries twice and apparently leaves disappointed by the moral laxity of the locals.	The Friday Mosque in Male is rebuilt by order of Sultan Ahmed Shihabuddin. The previous Friday Mosque, dating from 1153, had become run-down.	The Portuguese are driven out of the Maldives following an attack on the Portuguese garrison led by Mohammed Thakurufaanu. To this day, the event is celebrated as the country's National Day.

Protected Independence

The Portuguese attacked several more times, and the rajahs of Canna-nore in South India (who had helped Thakurufaanu) also attempted to gain control. In the 17th century, the Maldives accepted the protection of the Dutch, who ruled Ceylon at the time. They also had a short-lived defence treaty with the French, and maintained good relations with the British, especially after the British took possession of Ceylon in 1796. These relations enabled the Maldives to be free from external threats while maintaining internal autonomy. In any case, the remoteness of the islands, along with the prevalence of malaria and the lack of good ports, naval stores or productive land, were probably the main reasons that neither the Dutch nor the British established a colonial administration.

In the 1860s Borah merchants from Bombay were invited to Male to establish warehouses and shops, but it wasn't long before they acquired an almost exclusive monopoly on foreign trade. The Maldivians feared the Borahs would soon gain complete control of the islands, so Sultan Mohammed Mueenuddin II signed an agreement with the British in 1887 recognising the Maldives' statehood and formalising its status as a crown protectorate.

The Early 20th Century

In 1932 the Maldives' first constitution was drawn up under Sultan Shamsuddin, marking the dawn of true Maldivian statehood. The sultan was to be elected by a 'council of advisers' made up of the Maldivian elite, rather than being a hereditary position. In 1934 Shamsuddin was deposed and Hasan Nurudin became sultan.

WWII brought great hardship to the Maldives. Maritime trade with Ceylon was severely reduced, leading to shortages of rice and other necessities – many died of illness or malnutrition. A new constitution was introduced in 1942, and Nurudin was persuaded to abdicate the following year. His replacement, the elderly Abdul Majeed Didi, retired to Ceylon, leaving the control of the government in the hands of his prime minister, Mohammed Amin Didi, who nationalised the fish export industry, instituted a broad modernisation program and introduced an unpopular ban on tobacco smoking.

Travels in Asia & Africa 1325–54, by Ibn Battuta, is the account of a great Moorish globetrotter's travels and includes early testimony of life in the Maldives shortly after the arrival of Islam.

When Ceylon gained independence in 1948, the Maldivians signed a defence pact with the British, which gave the latter control over foreign affairs but not the right to interfere internally. In return, the Maldivians agreed to provide facilities for British defence forces, giving the waning British Empire a vital foothold in the Indian Ocean after the loss of India.

In 1953 the sultanate was abolished and a republic was proclaimed with Amin Didi as its first president, but he was overthrown within a

1796	1834	1887	1932
The British expel the Dutch from Ceylon and stake their claim to the Maldives, declaring it a 'British Protected Area'.	Captain Robert Moresby, the British maritime surveyor, begins his celebrated charting of the Maldives' waters, the first time the complex atolls, islands and reefs are mapped.	The Maldives becomes a self-governing British Protectorate after Borah merchants, British citizens from India, become embroiled in local disagreements. The British step in, but Maldivian sultans continue to rule.	The country writes its first constitution, curbing the sultan's powers.

year. The sultanate was returned, with Mohammed Farid Didi elected as the 94th sultan of the Maldives.

British Bases & Southern Secession

While Britain did not overtly interfere in the running of the country, it did secure permission to re-establish its wartime airfield on Gan in the southernmost atoll of the country, Addu. In 1956 the Royal Air Force began developing the base, employing hundreds of Maldivians and resettling local people on neighbouring islands. The British were informally granted a 100-year lease of Gan that required them to pay £2000 a year.

When Ibrahim Nasir was elected prime minister in 1957, he immediately called for a review of the agreement with the British on Gan, demanding that the lease be shortened and the annual payment increased. This was followed by an insurrection against the Maldivian government by the inhabitants of the southern atolls of Addu, Huvadhoo and Gnaviyani, who objected to Nasir's demand that the British cease employing local labour. They decided to cut ties altogether and form an independent state in 1959, electing Abdulla Afif Didi president and believing that their United Suvadive Republic would be recognised by the British.

In 1960 the Maldivian government officially granted the British the use of Gan and other facilities in Addu Atoll for 30 years (effective from December 1956) in return for the payment of £100,000 a year and a grant of £750,000 to finance specific development projects. Brokering a deal with the British on Gan effectively ruled out the UK recognising the breakaway south, and indeed Nasir eventually sent gunboats from Male to quash the rebellion. Afif fled to the Seychelles, then a British colony, while other leaders were banished to various islands in the Maldives.

In 1965 Britain recognised the islands as a sovereign and independent state, and ceased to be responsible for their defence (though it retained the use of Gan and continued to pay rent until 1976). The Maldives was granted full independence from Britain on 26 July 1965 and later became a member of the UN.

The Republic

Following a referendum in 1968, the sultanate was again abolished, Sultan Majeed Didi retired to Sri Lanka and a new republic was inaugurated. Nasir was elected president, although as political parties remained illegal, he didn't face much opposition. In 1972 the Sri Lankan market for dried fish, the Maldives' biggest export, collapsed. The first tourist resorts opened that year, but the money generated didn't benefit many ordinary inhabitants of the country. Prices kept going up and there were revolts, plots and banishments, as Nasir attempted to cling to power. In

The emblem of the Maldives Monetary Authority is the cowry shell, which is very common locally. These shells were used as currency in the ancient world, explaining the Arab sailors' delight when they discovered 'the Money Isles'.

1953	1954	1959	1962
The Maldives declares itself a republic within the British Commonwealth and dissolves the sultanate.	The sultanate is restored as debate rages about how best to replace the institution.	The three southernmost atolls of the Maldives – Addu, Gnaviyani and Huvadhoo – declare their independence from the rest of the country, founding the United Suvadive Republic.	The United Suvadive Republic is forced to give up its independence bid, fostering wide resentment against the British, who many in the southern atolls believe betrayed them.

1978, fearing for his life, Nasir stepped down and skipped across to Singapore, reputedly with US$4 million from the Maldivian national coffers.

A former university lecturer and Maldivian ambassador to the UN, Maumoon Abdul Gayoom, became president in Nasir's place. Hailed as a reformer, Gayoom's style of governance was initially much more open, and he immediately denounced Nasir's regime and banished several of the former president's associates. A 1980 attempted coup against Gayoom, involving mercenaries, was discovered and prevented, but led to more people being banished. Despite Gayoom's reputation as a reformer, he made no move to institute democracy in the Maldives.

Gayoom was re-elected in 1983 and continued to promote education, health and industry, particularly tourism. He gave the tiny country a higher international profile with full membership in the Commonwealth and the South Asian Association for Regional Co-operation (SAARC). The focus of the country's economy remained the development of tourism, which continued throughout the 1980s.

The 1988 Coup

In September 1988, 51-year-old Gayoom began a third term as president, having again won an election where he was the only candidate. Only a month later a group of disaffected Maldivian businessmen attempted a coup, employing about 90 Sri Lankan Tamil mercenaries. Half of these soldiers infiltrated Male as visitors, while the rest landed by boat. The mercenaries took several key installations, but failed to capture the National Security Service (NSS) headquarters.

More than 1600 Indian paratroopers, immediately dispatched by the Indian prime minister, Rajiv Gandhi, ended further gains by the invaders who then fled by boat towards Sri Lanka. They took 27 hostages and left 14 people dead and 40 wounded. No tourists were affected – many didn't even know that a coup had been attempted, isolated as they were in their tourist resorts. The mercenaries were caught by an Indian frigate 100km from the Sri Lankan coast. Most were returned to the Maldives for trial: several were sentenced to death, though they were later reprieved and returned to Sri Lanka.

The coup attempt saw the standards of police and NSS behaviour decline. Many people in police captivity reportedly faced an increased use of torture and the NSS became a widely feared entity.

Growth & Development

In 1993 Gayoom was nominated for a fourth five-year term, confirmed with an overwhelming referendum vote (yet again, there were no free elections). While on paper the country continued to grow economically, thanks to the now massive tourism industry and the stable fishing

The Story of Mohamed Thakurufaanu, by Hussain Salahuddeen, tells the story of the Maldives' greatest hero, who liberated the people from the Portuguese.

1965	1968	1972	1976
The Maldives finally gains full independence from the UK. The country does not opt to join the British Commonwealth, however, and remains outside the organisation until 1982.	The Maldives abolishes the sultanate and declares itself a republic again. Ibrahim Nasir becomes the first president of the country.	Kurumba Island, the Maldives' first holiday resort, just a short distance from Male, opens and a small trickle of intrepid travellers begin to arrive in search of the best beaches in the world.	The British Royal Air Force base at Gan in the southern Maldives closes, causing an economic recession.

industry, much of this wealth was concentrated in the hands of a small group of people, and almost none of it trickled down to the population of the atolls.

At the same time, the Maldives experienced many of the problems of developing countries, notably rapid growth in the main city, the environmental effects of growth, regional disparities, youth unemployment and income inequality.

The 1998 El Niño weather event, which caused coral bleaching throughout the atolls, was detrimental for tourism and signalled that global warming might soon threaten the existence of the Maldives. When Gayoom began a fifth term as president in 1998, the environment and sea-level rises were his priorities.

The 1990s saw rapid development in the Maldives – the whole country became linked up with a modern telecommunications system, and mobile phones and the internet became widely available. By the end of the century 90% of Maldivians had electricity and access to basic healthcare, and secondary school centres had been established in the outer atolls. With Japanese assistance, Male was surrounded by an ingenious sea wall (which was to prove very useful just a few years later when the tsunami struck). In 1997, to accommodate a growing population, work began on a new island near the capital, Hulhumale, built on reclaimed land an extra metre or so above sea level.

Uprising & Inundation

When a 19-year-old inmate at Maafushi Prison in South Male Atoll was beaten to death by guards in September 2003, a public outcry quickly followed. Evan Naseem's family put their son's brutally tortured corpse on display in Male and the capital spontaneously erupted in rioting. The People's Majlis (parliament), also known as the Citizens' Council, was stoned and police stations were burned by the mob. The NSS arrested and beat many rioters. In the same month, President Gayoom was renominated as the sole presidential candidate for the referendum by the Majlis, a body made up in no small part of Gayoom family members and people appointed by the president himself.

Realising that something was up, Gayoom made an example of the torturers who killed Evan Naseem, but stopped short of punishing or removing any senior ministers or Adam Zahir, the NSS chief of staff. Meanwhile, seeing that the hour for popular action had come, the Maldivian Democratic Party (MDP) was founded in Colombo, Sri Lanka, by young democracy activist and former political prisoner Mohammed Nasheed.

Under pressure from colleagues, and in a move to outflank the growing reform movement, Gayoom launched his own reform program in 2004. His proposals included having multiple candidates in the presidential

Norwegian explorer and ethnographer Thor Heyerdahl was fascinated by the Maldives and its pre-Islamic culture. Although he spent many years trying to uncover the secrets of the past, many of his conclusions were later rejected.

HISTORY UPRISING & INUNDATION

1978	1988	1998	2003
President Gayoom comes to power, ushering in three decades of massive development and growth in the tourism industry, but simultaneously seeing the stifling of dissent and the banning of political parties.	A coup d'état attempt by Sri Lankan mercenaries in Male is quickly foiled with Indian assistance.	The El Niño weather system causes water temperatures to rise above 32°C for two weeks, killing vital algae and causing coral bleaching still in evidence almost two decades later.	The beating to death of 19-year old Evan Naseem at Maafushi prison causes public protests in Male and across the country, and the first cracks in the Gayoom regime begin to show.

THE UNEXPECTED PRESIDENT

Mohammed Nasheed was born in Male in 1967, and grew up in a middle-class family in the capital. His academic skills allowed him to finish his education in Sri Lanka, and then later at a private school in England, before taking a degree in Maritime Studies at what is now Liverpool John Moores University. He returned to Maldives in 1989 to begin his career as a marine biologist, but instead quickly found himself in trouble with the increasingly authoritarian regime of Maumood Abdul Gayoom, whose police force arrested and imprisoned Nasheed in 1990 for claiming in a newspaper article that the presidential election the year before had been rigged.

Having been named an Amnesty International Prisoner of Conscience in 1991, Nasheed was rarely left alone by Gayoom's government, who considered him a dangerous firebrand and potential threat to their rule in an otherwise largely placid populace that made little demand for democracy. Nasheed spent the 1990s in and out of jail, totalling over 20 stints in prison, including one single period in solitary confinement that lasted 18 months. Despite his virtual outlaw status, he managed to get elected as an MP in 1999, an incredible achievement at the time for someone outside the political establishment. In 2001, however, Nasheed was exiled to a remote island and then – irony of ironies – expelled from the People's Majlis some time later for non-attendance.

Following his two-and-a-half-year period of internal exile, Nasheed voluntarily left the country for Sri Lanka, where he founded the Maldivian Democratic Party in 2004. Following the popular anger that followed the Evan Naseem killing and the shock of the 2004 tsunami, Nasheed returned to Maldives in 2005, on the eve of the Gayoom government's decision to allow the formation of political parties. Known then to locals by his nickname 'Anni', Nasheed was given a hero's welcome on his return to the Maldives, for the first time giving people unhappy with the long rule of Gayoom an opposition figure around whom to rally.

It's safe to say that Gayoom totally underestimated the appeal of Nasheed, and really believed he could be beaten at the ballot box even without opposition parties being outlawed. Indeed, Nasheed's eventual triumph in the second round of the 2008 presidential election seemed to shock Nasheed's supporters and international observers as much as it did the ruling junta. But if Nasheed's popular appeal was misjudged, Nasheed himself also gravely underestimated the enmity that Gayoom's long-established network of family members, business associates and cronies had for him personally, upsetting as he was their very lucrative Maldivian apple cart. Nasheed's announcement that he wouldn't seek to prosecute any wrongdoers under Gayoom's rule must have been music to the ears of the former Gayoom allies who remained in positions of power in the new democractic Maldives.

Ultimately, these interconnected figures, loyal to the old regime, and resistant to the enormous changes that Nasheed was implementing, spelled the end of this brief but extraordinary era in Maldives' modern history. Following a campaign of protests that were widely regarded as a coup by international observers, Nasheed was replaced by Abdulla Yameen, half-brother to Gayoom. In March 2015, the former president was convicted of questionable terrorism charges, and his future, like his legacy, remains uncertain.

2004	2005	2007	2008
The Indian Ocean tsunami wreaks havoc on the country, wiping out many towns and villages, leading to the abandonment of several islands and creating thousands of internally displaced people.	The People's Majlis, the Maldivian Parliament, votes to allow multiparty elections after a campaign for democracy that saw many activists beaten, imprisoned and harassed by the authorities.	A bomb in Sultan's Park in Male explodes, injuring 12 tourists. Later the same year three men are sentenced to 15 years in jail for terrorism, admitting they were targeting non-Muslims as part of a jihad.	The first democratic election in the Maldives sees Mohammed Nasheed elected to the presidency, beating Maumoon Abdul Gayoom and beginning a new era in Maldivian politics.

election, a two-term limit for the president and the legalisation of political parties.

Just as change appeared to be coming to the country, disaster struck. On December 24 2004 the South Asian tsunami claimed thousands of lives across the continent and caused immense damage. The low-lying Maldives, with no land between them and Indonesia, took a direct hit, over 100 people were killed and dozens of islands and resorts were all but washed away. An estimated 15,000 people were displaced, a huge number in such a tiny country, and some islands were abandoned entirely and remain 'ghost islands' today. The country was exhausted, angry and ready for change.

President Mohammed Waheed Hassan was coincidentally the first person ever shown on the first broadcast of Maldivian TV back in 1978, years before he became a politician.

Democracy Arrives

Gayoom surprised many observers by following through with his reform package and a new constitution was ratified in August 2008, which led to the country's first freely contested elections later that year. As no party won an overall majority in the first round, a run-off election was held on 29 October in which the Maldivian Democratic Party's Mohammed Nasheed, with the other candidates throwing their weight behind him, took 53.65% of the vote, becoming the country's first democratically elected leader.

One of Nasheed's first pronouncements as president was that his administration would not seek to prosecute any member of the former government, and in particular former president Gayoom. The government then embarked on a radical reform and liberalisation agenda with pledges to make the Maldives a carbon-neutral country within a decade, the creation of a fund to buy land for the future of the Maldives in the event that the country would eventually be lost to rising sea levels, a total ban on shark hunting, the privatisation of over 20 cumbersome state-run enterprises, the introduction of a national transportation network, the diversification of the tourism industry by the ending of the long-term policy of separating locals and travellers, and the creation of tax, pension and health-care systems. In just four years the Nasheed government dragged the country into the 21st century and made a name for the Maldives as a progressive Muslim state.

The 2012 Coup & Its Aftermath

All that changed on 7 February 2012, when President Nasheed resigned following a mutiny against his rule by first the police and then the army. As mandated in the constitution, the then vice president, Dr Mohammed Waheed Hassan, assumed the mantle of the presidency, and the country's new government was quickly recognised by all major powers as legitimate.

2009	2010	2012	2012
President Nasheed holds the world's first ever underwater cabinet meeting to highlight the effects of global warming and rising sea levels on the world's lowest-lying country.	A couple having a wedding at the Vilu Reef resort are filmed being insulted by the Maldivian staff, causing a huge embarrassment for the country's tourist industry.	Mohammed Nasheed resigns from the presidency in what is quickly called a coup, following a military mutiny against the government and weeks of protests in Male.	Mohammed Waheed Hassan takes over as president of the Maldives.

For a detailed overview of Maldivian history see www.maldives-story.com.mv.

Over the next few days, however, it transpired that things weren't as cut and dry as they appeared. The former president claimed that he had been pressured at gunpoint to resign, with various businessmen known to be close to his predecessor, Maumoon Abdul Gayoom, being named as ringleaders in what was soon being called a coup d'état by the world's press.

The catalyst for the tide turning against the president was his arrest of the chief justice of the criminal court, Abdulla Mohamed, who President Nasheed claimed was blocking investigation of former Gayoom loyalists and who had ordered the release of Mohammed Jaleel Ahmed. Ahmed, an opposition politician, had been inciting demonstrations against the president by distributing leaflets accusing him of conspiring with Christians and Jews against Islam. Before finally deciding to arrest Abdulla Mohammed, Nasheed had tried to investigate his allegedly corrupt behaviour only to have the civil court ban the Judicial Services Commission from proceeding with its inquiries, effectively making Abdulla Mohammed untouchable. Eventually, Nasheed sent the Maldivian military to make the arrest, which immediately brought criticism both domestically and internationally, including claims that the president had overreached his power.

The arrest triggered protests in Male in late January and early February 2012, culminating in the resignation of the president on 8 February, once both the police and the army changed sides and the game was clearly up. The country then effectively spent 2012 and most of 2013 in limbo, under the rule of Nasheed's former deputy, Mohammed Waheed Hassan, until a fraught presidential election in November 2013 awarded the presidency to Abdulla Yameen, who has held the office since then.

Nasheed remained politically active, despite a slow-moving trial against him for exceeding his powers as president in ordering the arrest of Abdulla Mohammed, but in March 2015, he was convicted of terrorism charges in a trial that was condemned as constitutionally flawed by observers. At the time of writing, the Maldives remains deeply politically divided and its future course is at present far from clear.

2013	2014	2014	2015
Abdulla Yameen, the brother of former president Maumoon Abdul Gayoom, is elected to the presidency.	A fire at Male's water desalination plant leaves the city without drinking water for a week, highlighting the difficulty of life in the middle of the ocean.	Maldivian journalist Ahmed Rilwan Abdulla disappears after reporting on government links to gang violence, corruption and religious extremism.	Mohamed Nasheed is convicted of terrorism charges for the 'abduction' of a judge implicated in corruption while he was president; international observers decry the trial as a sham.

Maldivian Way of Life

Away from the tourist resorts, the Maldivian people live and work on their home islands much as they have done for centuries, and this traditional and hard-working lifestyle is key to understanding this fascinating land. The combination of ancient and modern, Muslim and secular, and conservative and progressive elements in Maldivian society may be contradictory, but getting to know how Maldivians live day-to-day is an enormously rewarding flip side to only meeting Maldivians working in holiday resorts.

National Psyche

Maldivians are devout Muslims. In some countries this might be considered incidental, but the national faith is the cornerstone of Maldivian identity and is defended passionately at all levels of society. Officially 100% of the population are practising Sunni Muslims, and indeed, under the 2008 constitution, it's impossible to be a citizen of the Maldives if you are a non-Muslim. There's no scope for religious dissent, which presents some serious human rights issues, and apostasy for locals is still punishable by death.

This deep religious faith breeds a generally high level of conservatism, but that does not preclude the arrival of over a million non-Muslim tourists to the islands every year, coming to bathe seminaked, drink alcohol and eat pork. It's definitely an incongruous situation, and one that is likely to come under some strain now that the tourist industry is no longer so separate from the local population following the government's decision to allow the building of guesthouses on inhabited islands in 2009. While the new guesthouses and hotels on inhabited islands enforce local standards of dress and behaviour, just the regular presence of foreigners on islands that have historically been isolated from the outside world will inevitably bring change.

Not quite Asia, not quite Africa and not the Middle East, despite the cultural similarities, the Maldives has been slow to join the international community (it only joined the Commonwealth and the South Asian Association for Regional Co-operation in the 1980s). Indeed, a deep island mentality permeates the country, so much so that people's first loyalty is to their own small island before their atoll or even the country as a whole.

The hardship implicit in survival on these remote and relatively barren islands has created a nation of hard workers. The strong work ethic runs throughout the country; historically a lazy Maldivian was a Maldivian who didn't eat.

Another feature of the Maldivian people is their earthy humour and cheerfulness. Joking and laughter is a way of life and you'll notice this

The Maldivian caste system has effectively disappeared today. Traditionally, the very lowest caste was that of the palm-toddy tappers (raa-veri).

without even leaving your resort – take a few minutes to speak to the local staff and you'll see exactly how true this is.

Lifestyle

The most obvious dichotomy in lifestyle in the Maldives is between people in the capital Male and those 'in the atolls' – the term used by everyone to denote 'islanders' or anyone who lives outside the immediate area of chaotic modernity that is Male.

In Male, life is considerably easier and more comfortable than in the rest of the country on most fronts, with the obvious exception of space. Life in Male, one of the most densely populated places on earth, is very crowded and can feel intensely claustrophobic. The past two decades of extraordinary growth have created a massive economy in Male, although many residents of the city complain that while there are plenty of opportunities to earn and live well in the commercial and tourism sectors, there's a great lack of challenging, creative jobs if exporting fish and importing tourists are not your idea of fun. With limited education beyond high school and few careers for those who are ambitious but lack good connections, it's no surprise that many young people in Male dream of going abroad, at least to complete their education and training.

On the islands things are far more simple and laid-back, but people's lives aren't always as easy as those in Male. In the atolls most people live on the extended family homestead (it's unusual to live alone or just as a couple in a way that it wouldn't be in Male), and both men and women assume fairly traditional roles. While men go out to work (in general either as fishermen or on jobs that keep them away from home for long stretches at a time in the tourist or shipping industries), women are the

You can address Maldivians by their first or last name. Since so many men are called Moham-med, Hassan or Ali, the surname is often more appropriate. In some cases an honorary title like Maniku or Didi is used to show respect.

ALL-PURPOSE, ALL-MALDIVIAN DHONI

The truck and bus of the Maldives is the sturdy dhoni, a vessel so ubiquitous that the word will become part of your vocabulary just hours after landing. Built in numerous shapes and sizes, the dhoni has been adapted for use in many different ways. The traditional dhoni is thought to derive from the Arab dhow, but the design has been used and refined for so long in the Maldives that it is truly a local product.

Traditionally, dhonis have a tall, curved prow that stands up like a scimitar cutting through the sea breezes. Most Maldivians say this distinctive prow is purely decorative, but in shallow water a man will stand at the front, spotting the reefs and channels, signalling to the skipper and holding the prow for balance.

The flat stern is purely functional – it's where the skipper stands and steers, casually holding the tiller with his foot or between his legs. The stern platform is also used for fishing, and for one other thing – when a small dhoni makes a long trip, the 'head' is at the back. If nature calls, go right to the stern of the boat, face forward or backwards as your needs and gender dictate, and rely on the skipper, passengers and crew to keep facing the front. Longer distance dhonis that are part of the national ferry system now tend to come with built-in toilets.

The details on a dhoni are a mix of modern and traditional. The rudder is attached with neat rope lashing, but nowadays the rope is always plastic, not coir (coconut fibre). The propeller is protected so it won't snag on mooring lines or get damaged on a shallow reef. The rooftop of the dhoni often functions as a sundeck and a place to relax, though most sun-wary Maldivians prefer to stay in the shade downstairs.

The best dhoni builders are said to come from Raa Atoll, and teams of them can be contracted to come to an island to make a new boat. Twelve workers, six on each side of the boat, can make a 14m hull in about 45 days. The keel is made from imported hardwood, while the hull planks are traditionally from coconut trees. A lot of the work is now done with power tools, but no plans are used.

homemakers, looking after the children, cooking and maintaining the household. Fish are traded for other necessities at the nearest big island. Attending the mosque is the main religious activity, and on smaller islands it's the main social and cultural activity as well.

Life expectancy for a Maldivian is about 63 years for men and 65 years for women.

The most important ritual in a male's life comes when he is circumcised at the age of six or seven. These are big celebrations that last for a week and are far more significant than marriages and birthdays (the latter of which are generally not celebrated). Marriage is important, but it's not the massive celebration it is in most of the rest of Asia.

Rural life for the young can be fairly dull, although, despite appearances, even tiny fishing villages are surprisingly modern and most now have internet access, phones and TV. Nevertheless, many teenagers effectively go to boarding school, as provision for education outside population centres is scant. There are a few preschools or kindergartens, where children start learning the Quran from about the age of three. There are government primary schools on every inhabited island, but some are very small and do not go past grade five. For grades six and seven, children may have to go to a middle school on a larger island. Atoll capitals have an Atoll Education Centre (AEC) with adult education and secondary schooling to grade 10 (16 years old).

Officially, 90% of students finish primary school, and the adult literacy rate is an impressive 98%. English is taught as a second language from grade one and is the usual language of instruction at higher secondary school – most Maldivians with a secondary education will speak decent, if heavily accented and rather old fashioned, English.

The best students can continue to a free-of-charge higher secondary school, which teaches children to the age of 18 – there's one in Male, one in Hithadhoo, in the country's far south, and one in Kulhuduffushi, in the far north. Students coming to Male to study generally take live-in domestic jobs, affecting their study time. Girls are often expected to do a lot of housework.

The Maldives College of Higher Education, also in Male, has faculties of health, education, tourism-hospitality and engineering as well as one for Sharia'a law. Many young Maldivians go abroad for university studies, usually to Sri Lanka, India, Britain, Australia or Fiji, although since 2011 the Maldives National University in Male has been offering full degree courses.

Politics

Maldivian politics has undergone a sea change in the past decade. Having spent the second half of the 20th century under a series of strongmen authoritarian rulers, the tide finally turned and – to the surprise of everyone, not least the activists who had been campaigning for it so bravely, in 2005 former President Maumoon Abdul Gayoom announced that a multiparty system would be created.

This announcement, approved unanimously by the People's Majlis, or parliament, was then followed by the promulgation of a new constitution in 2008. Under the 2008 constitution, which enacted the separation of powers and provided for a bill of rights, the Maldives was made a presidential republic, with the president as both head of state and head of government.

The Maldivian president is directly elected by the people and is limited to two five-year terms in office. The People's Majlis is in Male, and each of the 20 administrative atolls, plus the island of Male, have two representatives each, elected for five-year terms. The president chooses the remaining eight parliamentary representatives, has the power to

The Maldives' biggest international ally is India, which has supported the new government and donated US$100m to the tiny island nation. Cynics point out that this generosity might have been because China is also wooing the Maldives as a friend, with an eye to building a submarine base in the country.

MEDIA IN THE MALDIVES

Until the election of a democratic government in 2008, the media in the Maldives was exceptionally tame and did very little but repeat the government line on the issues of the day. Debate was stifled, religious programming was almost nonexistent and the only possible means of dissent was online, which saw the rise of internet news sites such as the excellent *Minivan News* (www.minivannews.com), still your best first port of call for an overview of Maldivian news and opinion.

Things are rather different today, with a vibrant national debate being carried out in all media. Daily newspapers include *Miadhu* (www.miadhu.com) and *Haveeru* (www.haveeru.com.mv), both of which have excellent online English editions. You'll also see *Jazeera* and *Aufathis* on sale, but neither of these has an English edition online.

TV and radio stations are now crowded with debate and political programming too – the state-owned TV channel TVM often hosts talk shows and discussion panels about the political situation.

appoint or dismiss cabinet ministers, and appoints all judges. All citizens over 21 years of age can vote.

The main political parties operating in the Maldives are the ruling Progressive Party of Maldives, former President Nasheed's Maldivian Democratic Party (MDP) and the Republican Party (Jumhooree Party).

Politics is likely to be a subject you'll hear many people talking about, due to the political turbulence the country has experienced in recent years. Mohameed Nasheed became the country's first democratically elected president in 2008, following the 30-year iron-fisted rule of Maumoon Abdul Gayoom. But in 2012 Nasheed was overthrown in a military coup, and replaced by his vice-president, Mohammed Waheed Hassan. Hassan was then himself replaced by the Gayoom's brother in law Abdulla Yameen following the 2013 presidential election. It's fair to say that the country is pretty polarised politically.

Economy

Fish and ships just about sum up the Maldivian economy beyond the tourist industry. Tourism accounts for 28% of GDP and up to 90% of government tax revenue. Each traveller pays a US$8 'bed tax' per night in the Maldives, and with almost one million visitors usually spending at least a week in the country per year, it adds up to a considerable amount!

As with luxury destinations around the world, the Maldives felt the pinch of the global economic turndown quite severely, particularly in the budget and midrange categories, with many travellers cancelling their holidays in the wake of economic uncertainty. Even more harmful was the 2014 tumble of the ruble, which led to many Russian visitors cancelling holidays in 2015. The sky-rocketing Chinese market has remained strong, however, with hundreds of thousands of Chinese middle-class visitors now swelling resort numbers, bringing a totally new demographic to the country's tourism industry.

Income tax was introduced to the Maldives in 2012 – the first time most Maldivians had ever had to pay tax in their life. As well as generating important income for the government, it was also aimed at getting the population to have more of a stake in their society.

The other major field of industry is fishing. Previous policies helped to mechanise the fishing fleet, introduce new packing techniques and develop new markets, which has seen the Maldives remain a major fish supplier to markets in Asia and the Middle East. Nevertheless, the fishing industry is vulnerable to international market fluctuations. Most adult males have some experience in fishing, and casual employment on fishing boats is something of an economic backstop. Men are unlikely to take on menial work for low pay when there is a prospect that they can get a few days or weeks of relatively well-paid work on a fishing boat or dhoni. The 2009 ban on all shark fishing has earned the Maldives valuable environmental credibility, but has unsurprisingly been unpopular with fishermen, many of whom hunted sharks in Maldivian waters for sale to China.

Trade and shipping (nearly all based in Male) is the third-biggest earner; nearly all food is imported and what little domestic agriculture there is accounts for less than 6% of GDP. Manufacturing and construction make up 17% of GDP: small boat yards, fish packing, clothing and a plastic-pipe plant are modern enterprises, but mostly it's cottage industries producing coconut oil, coir (coconut-husk fibre) and coir products such as rope and matting. Some of the new industrial activities are on islands near Male while others, such as fish-packing plants, are being established in the outer atolls.

Religion

Islam is the religion of the Maldives, and officially there are no other religious groups present. All Maldivians are Sunni Muslims. No other religions or sects are permitted, though it's no problem to bring religious items for your own use into the country.

The Maldives observes a liberal form of Islam, like that practised in India and Indonesia. Maldivian women do not observe purdah, although the large majority wear a headscarf. Ironically this has been driven by religious freedom and fashion more than anything else. Until the election of President Nasheed in 2008, the media was strictly controlled and religious broadcasts were not common. Since the onset of more liberal attitudes towards freedom of speech, religious programming has become extremely popular, and young women throughout the country (though not in resorts) have reverted to covering their heads in large numbers, making it fashionable and not always just a sign of particular religious devotion.

> Officially only Muslims may become citizens of the Maldives. It is possible for foreigners to convert and later become Maldivian nationals, although this is extremely rare.

There have been worrying signs of radicalisation all over the country in recent years; a high profile case saw a 15-year-old rape victim sentenced to 100 lashes for 'fornication', a sentence that was eventually quashed by the High Court after a global outcry, but which highlighted how justice works in Maldives under Sharia'a Law. A pro-IS march in Male in 2014 and a significant number of Maldivians fighting with IS in Syria are further examples of how radicalised the country has become.

Prayer Times

The initial prayer session is in the first hour before sunrise, the second around noon, the third in the mid-afternoon around 3.30pm, the fourth at sunset and the final session in the early evening.

IDOLATRY

Most countries prohibit the importation of things like narcotics and firearms, and most travellers understand such restrictions, but when you're forbidden to bring 'idols of worship' into the Maldives, what exactly does that mean? The Maldives is an Islamic nation, and it is sensitive about objects that may offend Muslim sensibilities. A small crucifix, worn as jewellery, is unlikely to be a problem, and many tourists arrive wearing one. A large crucifix with an obvious Christ figure nailed to it may well be prohibited. The same is true of images of Buddha – a small decorative one is probably OK, but a large and ostentatious one may not be.

Maldivian authorities are concerned about evangelists and the objects they might use to spread their beliefs. Inspectors would not really be looking for a Bible in someone's baggage, but if they found two or more Bibles they would almost certainly not allow them to be imported. It would be unwise to test the limits of idolatrous imports – like customs people everywhere, the Maldivian authorities take themselves very seriously.

Learn more about the amazing development of Hulhumale island, the artificial island next to Male that will provide the future base for the government and much of the city's population in the face of rising sea levels, at www.hdc.com.mv.

The call to prayer is delivered by the *mudhim* (muezzin). In former days, he climbed to the top of the minaret and shouted it out. Now the call is relayed by loudspeakers on the minaret and the *mudhim* even appears on TV. All TV stations cut out at prayer time, although only TVM (the national channel) cuts out for the entire duration – satellite channels just have their broadcasts interrupted to remind Muslims to go to the mosque.

Shops and offices close for 15 minutes after each call. Some people go to the mosque, some kneel where they are and others do not visibly participate. Mosques are busiest for the sunset prayers and at noon on Fridays.

Ramazan

This month of fasting, which begins at the time of a particular new moon and ends with the sighting of the next new moon, is called Ramazan in the Maldives. The Ramazan month gets a little earlier every year because it is based on a lunar calendar of 12 months, each with 28 days. Ramazan begins on 6 June in 2016, 27 May in 2017 and 16 May in 2018.

During Ramazan Muslims do not eat, drink, smoke or have sex between sunrise and sunset. Exceptions to the eating and drinking rule are granted to young children, pregnant or menstruating women, and those who are travelling. It can be a difficult time for travel outside the resorts, as teashops and cafes are closed during the day, offices have shorter hours and people may be preoccupied with religious observances or the rigours of fasting. Visitors should avoid eating, drinking or smoking in

WOMEN IN SOCIETY

In the 14th century, long before the call for equality gained momentum, the Maldives was ruled by women. Three queens reigned; one, Sultana Khadija, held the throne for 33 years from 1347 to 1379. The shift from monarchy to a constitutional republic barred women from the post of president, and this clause was only removed by the 2008 constitution.

Traditional lifestyle, especially on the islands away from the capital, dictated gender-specific roles for women and men. Women tended to their children and household duties during the day, and cooked fish in the evenings. Men spent the day fishing and then rested in the evenings. Modernisation and development changed the traditional way of life and conferred a double burden on many women – income generation plus domestic responsibilities. More opportunities and better education mean that more women are ready to join the workforce or take up income-generating activities at home. This has become a necessity rather than a choice for most women living in Male, as rising expenses and changing lifestyles demand a dual income to meet basic family expenses.

Traditionally, a woman could choose a suitor and name a bride-price *(rhan)*. The bride-price is paid by the husband to the wife, at the time of marriage or in instalments as mutually agreed, but must be repaid in full if there's a divorce. The wedding itself is a low-key affair, but is often followed by a large banquet for all family and friends, who can easily number in the hundreds.

Women in the Maldives can, and do, own land and property but in general women have a fraction of the property that men do. While inheritance generally follows Islamic Shari-ia'a law in the Maldives, land is divided according to civil law, whereby a daughter and son inherit equal shares of land.

There is little overt discrimination between the sexes. Although it's a fully Muslim society, women and men mingle freely and women enjoy personal liberty not experienced by women in most Muslim societies. However, Islam is used as a tool by some patriarchs to counter gender equality, even as they proclaim that Islam grants equality to women and men.

Aishath Velezinee is a Maldivian writer, researcher and women's rights advocate.

public, or in the presence of those who are fasting. After a week or so, most Muslims adjust to the Ramazan routine and many say they enjoy it. There are feasts and parties long into the night, big breakfasts before dawn and long rests in the afternoon.

Kuda Eid, the end of Ramazan, is a major celebration that is marked by three days of public holidays. The celebrations begin when the new moon is sighted in Male and a ceremonial cannon is fired to mark the end of Ramazan. There are large feasts in every home for friends and family, and in the atolls men participate in frenzied *bodu beru* (big drum) ceremonies and other dancing, often all night. At this time, it's polite to wish locals 'Eid Mubarak'.

Local Beliefs

On the islands people still fear *jinnis,* the evil spirits that come from the sea, land and sky. They are blamed for everything that can't be explained by religion or education.

To combat jinnis there are *fandhita,* which are the spells and potions provided by a local *hakim* (medicine man), who is often called upon when illness strikes, if a woman fails to conceive or if the fishing catch is poor.

The hakim might cast a curing spell by writing phrases from the Quran on strips of paper and sticking or tying them to the patient or writing the sayings in ink on a plate, filling the plate with water to dissolve the ink, and making the patient drink the potion. Other concoctions include *isitri,* a love potion used in matchmaking, and its antidote *varitoli,* which is used to break up marriages.

Sport

Soccer is the most popular sport and is played all year round. On most islands, the late-afternoon match among the young men is a daily ritual, although volleyball and cricket are also common. There's a football league in Male, played between club teams with names such as Valencia and Victory, and annual tournaments against teams from neighbouring countries. Matches are also held at the National Stadium in Male.

Cricket is played in Male for a few months each year, beginning in March. Volleyball is played indoors, on the beach and in the waterfront parks. The two venues for indoor sport are the Centre for Social Education, on the west side of Male, and a newer facility just east of the New Harbour, used for basketball (men and women), netball, volleyball and badminton.

Traditional games include *bai bala,* where one team attempts to tag members of the other team inside a circle, and a tug-of-war, known as *wadhemun. Bashi* is a women's game, played on something like a tennis court, where a woman stands facing away from the net and serves a tennis ball backwards, over her head. There is a team of women on the other side who then try to catch it.

Thin mugoali (meaning 'three circles') is a game similar to baseball and has been played in the atolls for more than 400 years. The *mugoali* (bases) are made by rotating on one foot in the sand through 360 degrees, leaving a circle behind. You'll sometimes see *bashi* in Male parks or on village islands in the late afternoon, but traditional games are becoming less popular as young people are opting for international sports.

The Maldives has participated in the Olympics since 1988, but have yet to win any medals. Unsurprisingly, the team has never taken part in the winter Olympics.

MALDIVIAN WAY OF LIFE SPORT

Marine Life in the Maldives

The world beneath the water is one of the most compelling reasons to visit the Maldives, and whether you're diving on a reef thriving with life or walking across your resort's lagoon on a wooden walkway, you'll find yourself seeing many of the spectacular and unusual creatures for which the Maldives is famous. The Maldives' combination of amazingly clear and warm water, rich marine life, and good environmental protection ensures that anyone with an interest in the underwater world won't go home disappointed.

Life on the Reef

Despite its total size of 90,000 sq km, the Maldives is 99% water, and has just 298 sq km of land, effectively making it smaller than Andorra.

Reefs are often referred to as the rainforests of the sea, and rightly so – even though they take up just 0.1% of the ocean's surface, they are home to around a quarter of all underwater species. Reefs are created by the calcium carbonate secreted by corals, and are most commonly found in shallow, warm waters, making the Maldives a perfect environment for these complex and delicate ecosystems.

As well as the many types of coral, there are various shells, starfish, crustaceans and worms living directly on the reef. Then there are the 700 species of fish that directly or indirectly live off the reef, which can be divided into two types: reef fish, which live inside the atoll lagoons, on and around coral-reef structures; and pelagics, which live in the open sea but come close to the reefs for food. These include some large animals, such as turtles, whales and dolphins that are very popular with divers. For more on Maldives' marine life, see p58.

Coral

These are coelenterates, a class of animal that also includes sea anemones and jellyfish. A coral growth is made up of individual polyps – tiny tube-like fleshy cylinders. The top of the cylinder is open and ringed by waving tentacles (nematocysts), which sting and draw any passing prey inside. Coral polyps secrete a calcium-carbonate deposit around their base, and this cup-shaped skeletal structure is what forms a coral reef – new coral grows on old dead coral and the reef gradually builds up.

The whale shark is an evolutionary oddity, skipping almost the whole food chain to ensure its survival: despite being the biggest fish in the water, it feeds solely on plankton.

Most reef building is done by hermatypic corals, whose outer tissues are infused with zooxanthellae algae, which photosynthesises to make food from carbon dioxide and sunlight. The zooxanthellae is the main food source for the coral, while the coral surface provides a safe home for the zooxanthellae – they live in a symbiotic relationship, each dependent on the other. The zooxanthellae give coral its colour, so when a piece of coral is removed from the water, the zooxanthellae soon die and the coral becomes white. If the water temperature rises, the coral expels the algae, and the coral loses its colour in a process called 'coral bleaching', something that happened in the Maldives during the El Niño weather incident in 1997–98, and the legacy of which can still be seen in places today.

Polyps reproduce by splitting to form a colony of genetically identical organisms – each colony starts life as just a single polyp. Although each polyp catches and digests its own food, the nutrition then passes between the polyps to the whole colony. Most coral polyps only feed at night; during the day they withdraw into their hard limestone skeleton, so it is only after dark that a coral reef can be seen in its full, colourful glory, which is the reason so many divers like to do night dives.

Hard Corals

These *Acropora* species take many forms. One of the most common and easiest to recognise is the staghorn coral, which grows by budding off new branches from the tips. Brain corals are huge and round with a surface looking very much like a human brain. They grow by adding new base levels of skeletal matter then expanding outwards. Flat or sheet corals, like plate coral or table coral, expand at their outer edges.

Soft Corals

These are made up of individual polyps, but do not form a hard limestone skeleton. Lacking the skeleton that protects hard coral, it would seem likely that soft coral would fall prey to fish, but they seem to remain relatively immune either due to toxic substances in their tissues or to the presence of sharp limestone needles. Soft corals can move around and will sometimes engulf and kill off a hard coral. Attractive varieties include fan corals and whips. Soft corals thrive on reef edges washed by strong currents.

Megafauna

As on an African wildlife safari, it is the big animals that divers most hope to see in the Maldives. Alongside vast shoals of reef fish, the Maldives is home to a huge variety of megafauna, from turtles, dolphins and manta rays to the mighty whale shark, the largest fish in the ocean.

Sharks

Juvenile reef sharks can be seen without getting into the water: they love to swim about in the warm water of the shallow lagoon right next to the beach and eat small fish all day long. They're tiny – most are around 50cm long – but are fully formed sharks, and so can scare some people! They don't bite, although feeding or provoking them still isn't a good idea.

Get out into the deeper water and adult sharks are visible, but you'll have to go looking for them. The most commonly seen shark in the Maldives are white-tip and grey-tip reef sharks. The white-tip reef shark is a small, nonaggressive, territorial shark, rarely more than 1.5m long and often seen over areas of coral or off reef edges. Grey-tip reef sharks are also timid, shallow-water dwellers and often grow to over 2m in length.

Other species are more open-sea dwellers, but do come into atolls and especially to channel entrances where food is plentiful. These include the strange-looking hammerhead shark and the whale shark, the world's largest fish species, which is a harmless plankton eater. Sharks pose little danger to divers in the Maldives – there's simply too much else for them to eat.

Stingrays & Manta Rays

Among the most dramatic creatures in the ocean, rays are cartilaginous fish – like flattened sharks. Ray feeding is a popular activity at many resorts and it's quite something to see these muscular, alienesque creatures jump out of the water and chow down on raw steak. Stingrays are sea-bottom feeders, and are equipped with crushing teeth to grind the molluscs and crustaceans they sift out of the sand. They are occasionally found in the shallows, often lying motionless on the sandy bottom of

---

Hammerhead sharks are among the most spectacular underwater creatures in the Maldives. Your best chance of seeing them is early in the morning in Northern Ari and Rasdhoo Atolls.

MARINE LIFE IN THE MALDIVES LIFE ON THE REEF

The whale shark is the largest fish in the world – they regularly reach up to 12m in length and are one of the biggest diving attractions when they cruise the kandus in May.

Male sharks show their interest in females by biting them on the sides, often causing wounds, even though the female shark skin has evolved to be thicker than the male equivalent!

lagoons. A barbed and poisonous spine on top of the tail can swing up and forward, and will deliver a very painful injury to anyone who stands on one, but you're unlikely to get close to it as the sound of you approaching will probably frighten it away first.

Manta rays are among the largest fish found in the Maldives and a firm favourite of divers. They tend to swim along near the surface and pass overhead as a large shadow. They are quite harmless and, in some places, seem quite relaxed about divers approaching them closely. Manta rays are sometimes seen to leap completely out of the water, landing back with a tremendous splash. The eagle ray is closely related to the manta, and is often spotted by divers.

Male and female shark populations live in same-sex groups and rarely meet, save for mating.

Turtles

Five of the seven species of marine turtles are found in the Maldives, with green and hawksbill turtles being the most commonly spotted. Turtles nest on sandy beaches across the islands from May to October, particularly in Shaviyani Atoll. Although the animals are protected, there are reports of fishermen catching turtles and harvesting turtle eggs and several charities are actively promoting turtle conservation in the islands.

Whales & Dolphins

Whales dwell in the open sea, and so are not found in the atolls, but may be spotted on dive safaris or boat trips. Species seen in the Maldives include beaked, blue, Bryde's dwarf, false killer, melon-headed, sperm, and pilot whales. Specialised whale-watching trips are available, but sightings are not common.

By contrast, dolphins are extremely common throughout the Maldives, and you're very likely to see them, albeit fleetingly. These fun-loving, curious creatures often swim alongside boats, and also swim off the side of reefs looking for food. Most resorts offer dolphin cruises, which allow you to see large schools up close. Species known to swim in Maldivian waters include bottlenose, Fraser's, Risso's, spotted, striped and spinner dolphins.

Anemonefish are so-called as they cover themselves in a special mucous from the anemone, which protects them from its sting.

Reef Fish of the Maldives

You don't have to be a hardcore diver to enjoy the rich marine life of the Maldives. Hundreds of fish species can be spotted by anyone with a mask and snorkel. On almost any dive or snorkelling trip in Maldives you're pretty certain to see several types of butterflyfish, angelfish, parrotfish, rock cod, unicornfish, trumpetfish, bluestripe snapper, Moorish idol and Oriental sweetlips, but as well as these, you'll inevitably see far less common ones.

For a comprehensive online guide to the fish of the Maldives, visit www.popweb.com/maldive. For more information, try *Photo Guide to Fishes of the Maldives* by Rudie H Kuiter (Atoll Editions), the classic guide to the fish of the Maldives.

Anemonefish

Young male anemonefish living within the anemone are under the control of a single dominant female. When she dies, the largest male fish changes sex and replaces her as the dominant female.

Maldives anemonefish are around 11cm long, orange, dusky orange or yellow, with differences in face colour and the shape and thickness of the head bar marking. Their mucous coating protects them from the venomous tips of sea anemone tentacles, allowing them to hide from predators among the anemones' tentacles. In return for this protection, they warn the anemones of the approach of fish such as butterflyfish, which feed on the tentacle tips. Juveniles are lighter in colour than adults, and have greyish or blackish pelvic fins.

Angelfish

Of the many species, 14 are found in the Maldives, mostly found in shallow water, though some inhabit reef slopes down to 20m. They can be seen individually or in small groups. Small species are around 10cm, the largest around 35cm. They feed on sponges and algae. Regal (or empress) angelfish have bright yellow bodies with vertical dark blue and white stripes, and grow up to 25cm. The emperor, or imperial, angelfish are larger (to 35cm) and live in deeper water, with almost horizontal blue-and-yellow lines and a dark blue mask and gill markings; juveniles are quite different in shape and markings.

Boxfish

These unusual looking and highly poisonous fish are sometimes encountered by divers in the Maldives. They usually grow up to half a metre in length and feed on worms and other invertebrates on the reef and ocean floor. Boxfish are literally boxed in by a thick external skin, with holes for moving parts such as the eyes, gills and fins. That, coupled with their poisonous flesh, makes them formidable creatures. It's a joy to see them swimming, their tiny fins moving their large bodies effortlessly across the reef.

Butterflyfish

There are over 30 species in the Maldives; they are common in shallow waters and along reef slopes, singly, in pairs or in small schools. Species vary in size from 12cm to 30cm when mature, with a flattened body shape and elaborate markings. Various species of this carnivorous fish have specialised food sources, including anemones, coral polyps, algae and assorted invertebrate prey. Bennett's butterflyfish, bright yellow and 18cm long, is one of several species with a 'false eye' near the tail to make predators think it's a larger fish facing the other way. Spotted butterflyfish, which grow to 10cm long, are camouflaged with dark polka dots and a dark band across its real eye.

The sea snake is an air-breathing reptile with venom 20 times stronger than any snake on land. Basically, don't touch them if you're lucky enough to see any!

Flutemouth

The smooth flutemouth is very common in shallow waters in the Maldives, often occurring in small schools. They are very slender, elongated fish, usually around 60cm in length, but deep-sea specimens grow up to 1.5m. Flutemouths (cornetfish) eat small fish, often stalking prey by swimming behind a harmless herbivore. The silver colouring seems almost transparent in the water, and it can be hard to spot flutemouths even in shallow, sandy lagoons.

Flying Gurnard

These beautiful fish feature wing-like fins that make them look like smalls rays from afar, something it uses to its advantage when trying to catch prey, as well as to defend itself by frightening off would be attackers. Juveniles even have a pattern on their fins that looks like an eye, a good defence tactic. Flying Gurnards usually don't grow to more than 30cm and feed on bottom-feeder fish.

Groupers

This large reef fish is commonly seen on the reef, normally alone, and it can be very skittish when approached by divers. Most commonly spotted are black groupers with blue spots or red groupers with green or blue spots; they tend to be around 40cm to 60cm in length. Groupers feed on mobile invertebrates and small fish, generally hunting in the evening when other species on the reef are looking for a place to sleep for the night. Groupers are cunning hunters and juveniles often mimic wrasses to get close to prey.

MARINE LIFE IN THE MALDIVES LIFE ON THE REEF

Jacks & Trevallies

These fast silver fish are formidable hunters. While they spend much of their time in the open ocean, they feed on reefs, preying on confused fish that stray too far from safety. With 20 different kinds of jacks and trevallies in the Maldives, it's common to see them hunting on the reef. The giant trevally truly lives up to its name and can measure up to 1.7m.

Lionfish

These attractive fish are firm favourites with divers and are easily recognised by their long and thin fanlike fins, which deliver a very painful sting and are used to trap prey. Raised fins can be a sign of alarm – in such a case stay clear and don't corner the fish, as it may attack. Usually reddish brown in colour and growing only to 20cm, lionfish are commonly seen on the reef, although they are experts at camouflage, and so are often missed even by experienced divers.

Moray Eel

Moray eels' bodies are almost entirely made up of muscle, which they employ when hunting to twist and crush their prey, much like a constrictor.

A common sight on the reefs of the Maldives, these large, usually spotted eels are routinely seen with their heads poking out of holes on the reef edge. Those on reefs visited by divers tend to be extremely easy to approach, but will withdraw entirely into their holes (or swim away altogether) if humans come too close. They can also deliver an extremely strong bite, so do not feed or provoke them. Growing up to 2m long, they are one of the most easily spotted large creatures on the reef.

Moorish Idol

The Moorish idol is commonly seen on reef flats and reef slopes in the Maldives, often in pairs. Usually 15cm to 20cm long, it is herbivorous, feeding primarily on algae. They are attractive, with broad vertical yellow-and-black bands, pointed snouts, and long, streamer-like extensions to the upper dorsal fin.

Parrotfish

More than 20 of the many parrotfish species are found in Maldives – they include some of the most conspicuous and commonly seen reef fish. The largest species grow to more than a metre, but those around 50cm long are more typical. Most parrotfish feed on algae and other organisms growing on and around a hard-coral structure. With strong, beaklike mouths they scrape and bite the coral surface, then grind up the coral chunks, swallowing and filtering to extract nutrients. Snorkellers often hear the scraping, grinding sound of parrotfish eating coral, and notice the clouds of coral-sand faeces that parrotfish regularly discharge. Colour, pattern and even sex can change as parrotfish mature – juveniles and females are often drab, while mature males can have brilliant blue-green designs. Bicolour parrotfish start life white with a broad orange stripe, but the mature males (up to 90cm) are a beautiful blue, with hot-pink highlights on the scale edges, head, fins and tail. Green-face parrotfish grow to 60cm, with the adult male identified by its blue-green body, bright green 'face' and white marks on fins and tail. Heavybeak (or steephead) parrotfish can be 70cm long, and have a distinctive rounded head.

Pipefish have a very unusual mating system. The female deposits the egg into the sperm on the underside of the male's body, where fertilisation occurs and the pregnant male then incubates the eggs for a month before hatching.

Pufferfish

There are 18 species of the aptly named pufferfish in the Maldives. These incredible creatures have poisonous flesh (which can kill a human if eaten without the correct preparation) and the amazing power to inflate themselves like a balloon when attacked or feeling threatened. Pufferfish vary enormously in colour and size, though Bennett's pufferfish, with its green, orange and blue pattern is the most beautiful. The scribbled pufferfish, one of the largest seen in Maldivian waters, is the most commonly seen.

Rock Cod

Hundreds of species are currently classified as *Serranidae,* including rock cod and grouper, which are common around reefs. Smaller species reach 20cm; many larger species grow to 50cm and some to over a metre. Rock cod are carnivorous, feeding on smaller fish and invertebrates. Vermillion rock cod (or coral grouper) are often seen in shallow waters and near the coral formations in which they hide; they are a brilliant crimson colour covered with blue spots and are up to 40cm long.

RISE & RISE OF THE ATOLLS

A coral reef is not, as many people believe, formed of multicoloured marine plants. It is a living colony of coral polyps – tiny, tentacled creatures that feed on plankton. Coral polyps are invertebrates with sac-like bodies and calcareous or horny skeletons. After extracting calcium deposits from the water around them, the polyps excrete tiny, cup-shaped, limestone skeletons. These little guys can make mountains.

A coral reef is the rock-like aggregation of millions of these polyp skeletons. Only the outer layer of coral is alive. As polyps reproduce and die, the new polyps attach themselves in successive layers to the skeletons already in place. Coral grows best in clear, shallow water, and especially where waves and currents from the open sea bring extra oxygen and nutrients.

Charles Darwin put forward the first scientific theory of atoll formation based on observations of atolls and islands in the Pacific. He envisaged a process where coral builds up around the shores of a volcanic island to produce a fringing reef. Then the island sinks slowly into the sea while the coral grows upwards at about the same rate. This forms a barrier reef, separated from the shore of the sinking island by a ring-shaped lagoon. By the time the island is completely submerged, the coral growth has become the base for an atoll, circling the place where the volcanic peak used to be.

This theory doesn't quite fit the Maldives, though. Unlike the isolated Pacific atolls, Maldivian atolls all sit on top of the same long, underwater plateau, around 300m to 500m under the surface of the sea. This plateau is a layer of accumulated coral stone over 2000m thick. Under this is the 'volcanic basement', a 2000km-long ridge of basalt that was formed over 50 million years ago.

The build-up of coral over this ridge is as much to do with sea-level changes as it is with the plateau subsiding. When sea levels rise the coral grows upwards to stay near the sea surface, as in the Darwin model, but there were at least two periods when the sea level actually dropped significantly – by as much as 120m. At these times much of the accumulated coral plateau would have been exposed, subjected to weathering, and 'karstified' – eroded into steep-sided, flat-topped columns. When sea levels rose again, new coral grew on the tops of the karst mountains and formed the bases of the individual Maldivian atolls.

Coral grows best on the edges of an atoll, where it is well supplied with nutrients from the open sea. A fringing reef forms around an enclosed lagoon, growing higher as the sea level rises. Rubble from broken coral accumulates in the lagoon, so the level of the lagoon floor also rises, and smaller reefs can rise within it. Sand and debris accumulate on the higher parts of the reef, creating sandbars on which vegetation can eventually take root. The classic atoll shape is oval, with the widest reefs and most of the islands around the outer edges.

Geological research has revealed the complex layers of coral growth that underlie the Maldives, and has shown that coral growth can match the fastest sea-level rises on record, some 125m in only 10,000 years – about 1.25cm per year. In geological terms, that's fast.

Snapper

There are 28 species of snapper that have been documented in the Maldives, mostly in deep water. Small species are around 20cm and the largest grow to 1m (snapper, themselves carnivorous, are popular with anglers as a fighting fish and are excellent to eat). Blue-striped snapper, commonly seen in schools near inshore reefs, are an attractive yellow with blue-white horizontal stripes. Red snapper (or red bass) are often seen in lagoons.

Pilot fish can often be seen swimming alongside sharks or other large pelagic fish, with whom they swim to eat scraps of whatever the larger fish kills. In return the pilot fish eats parasites on the larger fish.

Surgeonfish

The surgeonfish are so named for the tiny scalpel-sharp blades that are found on the sides of their bodies, near their tails. When they are threatened they will swim beside the intruder swinging their tails to inflict cuts, and can cause nasty injuries. Over 20 species of surgeon, including the powder-blue surgeonfish, are found in the Maldives, often in large schools. The adults range from 20cm to 60cm. All species graze for algae on the sea bottom or on coral surfaces.

Sweetlips

Only a few of the many species are found in the Maldives, where they inhabit outer-reef slopes. Some species grow up to 1m, but most are between 50cm and 75cm; juveniles are largely herbivorous, feeding on algae, plankton and other small organisms; older fish hunt and eat smaller fish. Oriental sweetlips, which grow to 50cm, are superb-looking, with horizontal dark and light stripes, dark spots on fins and tail, and large, lugubrious lips. Brown sweetlips are generally bigger, duller and more active at night.

Sea urchins are rare in the sandy shallows of the lagoons, but numerous deeper on the reefs – wearing fins or other protective footwear is always a good idea to avoid their nasty needles.

Triggerfish

There are over a dozen species in the Maldives, on outer-reef slopes and also in shallower reef environments. Small species grow to around 25cm and the largest species to over 75cm. Triggerfish are carnivorous. Orange-striped triggerfish (30cm) are common in shallow reef waters. Titan triggerfish have yellow and dark-brown crisscross patterning and grow up to 75cm; they can be aggressive, especially when defending eggs, and will charge at divers. The clown triggerfish (up to 40cm) is easily recognised by its conspicuous colour pattern, with large, round, white blotches on the lower half of its body.

Unicornfish

From the same family as the surgeonfish, unicornfish grow from 40cm to 75cm long (only males of some species have the horn for which the species is named), and are herbivores. Spotted unicornfish are very common blue-grey or olive-brown fish with narrow dotted vertical markings (males can change their colours for display, and exhibit a broad white vertical band); their prominent horns get longer with age. Bignose unicornfish (or Vlaming's unicorn) have only a nose bump for a horn.

Wrasse

The hump on the head of a Napoleon wrasse becomes larger and more pronounced as the fish ages.

Some 60 species of this large and very diverse family can be found, some on reefs, others on sandy lagoon floors, others in open water. The smallest wrasse species are only 10cm; the largest over 2m. Most wrasse are carnivores; larger wrasse will hunt and eat small fish. Napoleonfish (also called Napoleon wrasse) are the largest wrasse species, often seen around wrecks and outer-reef slopes; they are generally green with fine vertical patterning. Large males have a humped head.

Environmental Issues & Responsible Travel

Adrift in the middle of the Indian Ocean and almost totally reliant on the marine environment for its food, the Maldives is a country where environmental issues play a larger than normal role in everyday life. Moreover, lying at such a low level above the sea makes the Maldives one of the most vulnerable places on earth to rising sea levels, and its fragile and unusual ecology means that responsible and thoughtful travel is important for anyone who cares about the impact of their holiday on locals.

However you spend your time in the country, you will never be far removed from the environmental issues. Resorts use enormous amounts of electricity and water, their imported food (not to mention guests) have significant environmental consequences, and in some cases they are not particularly responsible about their sewage disposal or energy use. We take into account a resort's environmental policy and highlight resorts that have implemented particularly sustainable and ecologically sound practices.

Environmental Issues

As a small island nation in a big ocean, the Maldives had a way of life that was ecologically sustainable for centuries, but certainly not self-sufficient. The comparatively small population survived by harvesting the vast resources of the sea and obtaining the other necessities of life through trade with the Middle East and Asia.

In the modern age the Maldives' interrelationship with the rest of the world is greater than ever, and it has a high rate of growth supported by two main industries: fishing and tourism. Both industries depend on the preservation of the environment, and there are strict regulations to ensure sustainability. To a great extent, the Maldives avoids environmental problems by importing so many of its needs. This is, of course, less a case of being environmentally friendly than just moving the environmental problems elsewhere.

Bluepeace (www.bluepeacemaldives.org) is an organisation campaigning to protect the Maldives' unique environment. Its comprehensive website and blog is a great place to start for anyone interested in the ecology of the Maldives and the most pressing environmental issues of the day.

Global Warming

Along with Tuvalu, Bangladesh and parts of the Netherlands, the Maldives has the misfortune to be one of the lowest-lying countries in the world at a time in history when sea levels are rising. Indeed, its highest natural point – said to be Mount Villingili, at a whopping 5.1m – is the lowest in any country in the world. Thanks in part to its crusading former president, the Maldives has become a byword around the world for the human consequences of global warming and rising sea levels, as an entire nation seems set to lose its way of life and may even be forced to

Bodu raalhu (big wave) is a relatively regular event in the Maldives, when the sea sweeps over the islands, causing damage and sometimes even loss of life.

Beach erosion is a constant problem facing most islands in the Maldives. Changing currents and rising sea levels mean that beaches shrink and grow, often unpredictably, with the resulting sandbags holding the beach in place often marring that perfect white-sand beach photo.

The depletion of freshwater aquifers is one of the Maldives' biggest environmental problems. As all fresh water comes from rainwater collected below ground and from desalination, water conservation is extremely important.

leave for good the islands it calls home. While the political will to get an international agreement on how best to combat climate change may finally be within sight, the Maldives has long been making contingency plans in the likely event that whatever the international community does will be too little, too late.

These contingency plans range from an already well-established project to reclaim land on a reef near Male to create a new island 2m above sea level, to a plan to set aside a portion of the country's annual billion-dollar tourism revenue for a sovereign wealth fund to purchase a new homeland for the Maldivians if rising sea levels engulf the country in decades to come. Both options are fairly bleak ones – the prospect of moving to the new residential island of Hulhumale is not one relished by most Maldivians, who are attached to their home islands and traditional way of life, but the prospect of the entire country moving to India, Sri Lanka or even Australia (as has been suggested) is an even more sobering one.

Perhaps because of its perilous situation, the Maldives has become one of the most environmentally progressive countries in the world. Before its dramatic collapse in 2012, the Nasheed government pledged to make the country carbon neutral within a decade, managed to impose the first total ban on shark hunting anywhere in the world and made ecotourism a cornerstone of its tourism strategy. The successive governments of Presidents Waheed and Yameen have focused far less on a progressive environmental agenda, but it's certain that environmental issues will continue to play a prominent role in Maldivian politics.

In the long term it's simply not an option to protect low-lying islands with breakwaters, and if the sea continues to rise as predicted then there is no long-term future for much of the country. There have been bold efforts made to ensure the survival of the human population of the Maldives in the future in the worst case scenario when waters wash over many of the lower-lying islands. Most obviously this includes the land reclamation project that has created 2m-high Hulhumale island next to the airport, which one day will house around half the country's population and all of the government.

If the day does indeed come when waters engulf the entire country, then in theory the government's sovereign wealth fund may be used to buy land elsewhere in the world for at least some, if not all, of the Maldivian population. India and Sri Lanka are the most likely destinations due to proximity and similarities in culture, climate and cuisine, but Australia is also frequently mooted given its large amount of free space.

The 2011 film *The Island President* is a fascinating documentary that followed the progress (or frankly, lack of progress) of former president Nasheed as he lobbied internationally for an agreement to curtail global warming and prevent the Maldives from being one of the first victims

THE MALDIVES' VOLCANIC PAST

The geological formation of the Maldives is fascinating and unique. The country is perched on the top of the enormous Laccadives-Chagos ridge, which cuts a swath across the Indian Ocean from India to Madagascar. The ridge, a meeting point of two giant tectonic plates, is where basalt magma spews up through the earth's crust, creating new rock. These magma eruptions created the Deccan Plateau, on which the Maldives sits. Originally the magma production created huge volcanoes that towered above the sea. While these have subsequently sunk back into the water as the ocean floor settled, the coral formations that grew up around these vast volcanoes became the Maldives, and this explains their idiosyncratic formation into vast round atolls.

AN ALTERNATIVE GEOGRAPHY

While the Maldives has appeared in the *Guinness Book of Records* as the world's flattest country, with no natural land higher than 2.4m above sea level, it's also one of the most mountainous countries in the world. Its people live on peaks above a plateau that extends 2000km from the Lakshadweep Islands near India to the Chagos Islands, well south of the equator. The plateau is over 5000m high and rises steeply between the Arabian Basin in the northwest and the Cocos-Keeling Basin in the southeast. Mountain ranges rise above the plateau, and the upper slopes and valleys are incredibly fertile, beautiful and rich with plant and animal life. The entire plateau is submerged beneath the Indian Ocean and only scattered, flat-topped peaks are visible at the surface. These peaks are capped not with snow, but with coconut palms.

of the world's rising sea levels. It's well worth watching to see just what an enormous challenge it is for such a tiny country to be heard on the international stage, regardless of the urgency of its message.

Fisheries

Net fishing and trawling is prohibited in Maldivian waters, which include an 'exclusive economic zone' extending 320km beyond all the atolls, meaning foreign craft cannot fish using these methods in the country's waters either. All fishing is by pole and line, with over 75% of the catch being skipjack or yellowfin tuna. The no-nets policy helps to prevent over-fishing and protects other marine species, such as dolphins and sharks, from being inadvertently caught in nets – something that has catastrophic implications for marine biodiversity elsewhere around the world.

The local tuna population appears to be holding up despite increased catches, and Maldivian fisheries are patrolled to prevent poaching. But the tuna are migratory, and can be caught without limit in international waters using drift nets and long-line techniques.

The small but active shark-meat trade was still claiming thousands of sharks a year until a nationwide ban was introduced in 2009. Shark numbers have been recovering ever since.

The Nasheed government banned the hunting of reef sharks in 2009, extending the ban to all sharks a year later. The ban was intended to arrest the plummeting number of sharks, whose fins were sold by local fishermen to Asian markets. This move has been widely celebrated by environmentalists, and while shark numbers are rising, there's a long way still to go before shark populations rebuild fully.

Tourism

Tourism development is strictly regulated and resorts are established only on uninhabited islands that the government makes available. Overwhelmingly, the regulations have been effective in minimising the impact on the environment – the World Tourism Organization has cited the Maldives as a model for sustainable tourism development.

Construction and operation of the resorts does use resources, but the vast majority of these are imported. Large amounts of diesel fuel are used to generate electricity and desalinate water, and the demand for hot running water and air-conditioning has raised the overall energy cost per guest.

An excellent organisation to look out for is the nonprofit environmental protection NGO Ecocare (www.ecocare.mv), whose comprehensive website gives interesting accounts of environmental problems and current campaigns.

Extraordinarily, most resorts simply pump sewage directly out into the sea. While an increasing number of resorts do treat their own sewage and dispose of it responsibly, the majority still do not. New resorts are now required to do so by law, but the older resorts can still get away with this negligent behaviour.

Efficient incinerators must be installed to get rid of garbage that can't be composted, but many resorts request that visitors take home plastic bottles, used batteries and other items that may present a disposal problem.

The Maldives has a very small proportion of arable land – just 13% – meaning that fish and imported foods make up the bulk of most people's diets.

When the first resorts were developed, jetties and breakwaters were built and boat channels cut through reefs without much understanding of the immediate environmental consequences. In some cases natural erosion and deposition patterns were disrupted, with unexpected results. More structures were built to limit damage and sand pumped up to restore beaches. This was expensive and it marred the natural appearance of islands. Developers are now more careful about altering coasts and reefs. Environmental studies are required before major works can be undertaken.

Responsible Travel

Given the strictures of travelling to the Maldives, in most cases your chances to be a truly responsible tourist are limited. First, you're almost certain to arrive in the country by long-haul flight, with all the emissions that entails. Second, you'll be using electricity-thirsty air-conditioning wherever you go, eating imported food and drinking expensively desalinated water (or even more costly imported water). Nevertheless, there are a few things you can do to lessen your carbon footprint and care for the local environment.

First of all, choose your resort carefully. We have given resorts with excellent sustainability credentials a sustainable icon in the reviews – these are resorts with the best environmental records in the country. This can mean anything from having a comprehensive recycling program, using home-grown food, not using plastic bottles, using ecologically sound wood for their buildings and serving only sustainably sourced food in their restaurants, to running environmental education programs for the local community, stimulating coral growth on the reef and donating money to offset the carbon footprint of its guests. If in doubt, contact your resort directly before you book with them and ask them for some information on their environmental record – any good resort will very happily provide this, and if they don't, then don't book with them.

Other things you can do to be a responsible visitor to the Maldives include taking home any plastic bottles or batteries you bring with you, respecting rules about not touching coral when diving or snorkelling, picking up any litter you may see on the beach, using water and air-conditioning judiciously, avoiding imported mineral water and drinking desalinated water instead, not replacing your towels daily and not buying souvenirs made from turtle-shell or coral, which can still be found in many places.

Wildlife

Stand still on a Maldivian beach for a minute or two and you'll see a surprising amount of wildlife: the ubiquitous hermit crabs scurrying across the warm sands; cawing crows in the palm trees, their call instantly recognisable; juvenile sharks chasing schools of little fish through the shallows; majestic flying foxes swooping over the islands during the late afternoon. You will rapidly realise that the Maldives is a fun place for nature lovers, and that's before you get to the amazing variety of life down on the reef. The best thing about wildlife in the Maldives is that it's almost universally safe. Who said this wasn't paradise?

Animals

One of the most unforgettable sights in the Maldives is giant fruit bats flying over the islands to roost in trees at dusk. Their size and numbers can make it quite a spectacle. Colourful lizards and geckos are very common and there is the occasional rat, usually euphemistically dismissed as a 'palm squirrel' or a 'Maldivian hamster' by resort staff.

The mosquito population varies from island to island, but it's generally not a big problem except after heavy rains. Nearly all the resorts spray pesticides daily to get rid of those that are about. There are ants, centipedes, scorpions and cockroaches, but they're no threat to anyone.

Local land birds include crows (many of which are shot by resorts on regular culls), the white-breasted water hen and the Indian mynah. There are migratory birds, such as harriers and falcons, but waders like plover, snipe, curlew and sandpiper are more common. Thirteen species of heron can be seen in the shallows (nearly every resort has one or two in residence) and there are terns, seagulls and two species of noddy.

WATER, WATER, EVERYWHERE

Ensuring a supply of fresh water has always been imperative for small island communities. Rainwater quickly soaks into the sandy island soil and usually forms an underground reservoir of fresh water, held in place by a circle of salt water from the surrounding sea. Wells can be dug to extract the fresh ground water, but if water is pumped out faster than rainfall replenishes the supply, then salty water infiltrates from around the island and the well water becomes brackish.

One way to increase the freshwater supply is to catch and store rainwater from rooftops. This wasn't feasible on islands that had only small buildings with roofs of palm thatch, but economic development and the use of corrugated iron has changed all that. Nearly every inhabited island now has a government-supported primary school, which is often the biggest, newest building on the island. The other sizable building is likely to be the mosque, which is a focus of community pride and the social centre of every island. Along with education and spiritual sustenance, many Maldivians now also get their drinking water from the local school or the mosque.

Expanding tourist resorts required more water than was available from wells or rooftops, and as resorts grew larger, tourists' showers became saltier. Also, the ground water became too salty to irrigate the exotic gardens that every tourist expects on a tropical island. The solution was the desalination of sea water using 'reverse osmosis' – a combination of membrane technology and brute force.

Now every resort has a desalination plant, with racks of metal cylinders, each containing an inner cylinder made of a polymer membrane. Sea water is pumped into the inner cylinder at high pressure and the membrane allows pure water to pass through into the outer cylinder from which it is piped away. Normally, when a membrane separates fresh water from salt water, both salt and water will pass through the membrane in opposite directions to equalise the saltiness on either side – this process is called osmosis. Under pressure, the special polymer membrane allows the natural process of osmosis to be reversed.

Small, reliable desalination plants have been a boon for the resorts, providing abundant fresh water for bathrooms, kitchens, gardens and, increasingly, for swimming pools. Of course, it's expensive, as the plants use lots of diesel fuel for their powerful pumps and the polymer membranes need to be replaced regularly. Many resorts ask their guests to be moderate in their water use, while a few are finding ways to recycle bath and laundry water onto garden beds. Most have dual water supplies, so that brackish ground water is used to flush the toilet while desalinated sea water is provided in the shower and the hand basin.

Is desalinated water good enough to drink? If a desalination plant is working properly, it should produce, in effect, 100% pure distilled water. The island of Thulusdhoo, in North Male Atoll, has the only factory in the world where Coca-Cola is made out of sea water. In most resorts, the water from the bathroom tap tastes just fine, but management advises guests not to drink it. The precariousness of Maldives' water supply was highlighted in late 2014, when a fire at Male's only desalination plant left the city without running water for an entire week.

Turtles

Most turtle species are endangered worldwide. Four species nest in the Maldives: green, olive ridley, hawksbill and loggerhead. Leatherback turtles visit Maldivian waters, but are not known to nest. Turtle numbers have declined in the Maldives, as elsewhere, but they can still be seen by divers at many sites. The catching of turtles and the sale or export of turtle-shell products is now totally prohibited, and you should report it if you come across it.

Turtles are migratory and the population can be depleted by events many miles from their home beach, such as accidental capture in fishing nets, depletion of sea-grass areas and toxic pollutants. Widespread collection of eggs and the loss of nesting sites are both problems in the Maldives today, although both the government and various environmental foundations have done a lot to educate locals about the importance of turtle protection. Nevertheless, turtle eggs are a traditional food and are used in *velaa folhi,* a special Maldivian dish, which is still legally made today.

Resort development has reduced the availability of nesting sites, while artificial lights confuse hatchling turtles, which are instinctively guided into the water by the position of the moon. Beach chairs and boats can also interfere with egg laying and with hatchlings. Some attempts are being made to artificially improve the survival chances of hatchlings by protecting them in hatching ponds and cages in some resorts with professional marine biologists in residence.

Maldivian turtles are protected, but they are still caught illegally. The charity Eco-care Maldives has campaigned to raise awareness of the turtles' plight. See www.ecocare.mv.

National Parks

There are 25 Protected Marine Areas in the Maldives, usually popular diving sites where fishing of any kind is banned. These are excellent as they have created enclaves of marine life that's guaranteed a safe future. There's also the Hanifaru Huraa Unesco World Biosphere Reserve (p98) in Baa Atoll, one of the country's most important and fully protected feeding grounds for manta rays and whale sharks.

The Maldives first Marine National Park was officially formed in 2012, but its boundaries remained undetermined in 2015, and progress has been decidedly slow following the change of government after the 2012 coup. However, in theory the park will cover the Edu Faru archipelago, nine uninhabited islands in Noonu Atoll, and will be by far the biggest reserve in the country, enjoying full national park status.

In 2009 the Maldivian government set aside large areas of Baa and Ari Atolls as Marine Protected Areas for the breeding of endangered whale sharks, manta rays and reef sharks.

Aside from the new Marine National Park, there are no specially designated island reserves in the Maldives. However, the vast majority of the islands in the Maldives are uninhabited and permission from the government is needed to develop or live there. With some of the tightest development restrictions in the world, the Maldives' future as pristine wilderness in many parts is assured.

Arts, Crafts & Architecture

Despite the Maldives being a small country with a widely dispersed population, Dhivehi culture has thrived in isolation from the rest of the world, finding expression in Maldivian arts and crafts, and retaining a strong national identity even in the modern age. Islamic beliefs, Western and Indian fashions, pop music and videos have all shaped local culture, but on public occasions and festivals the celebrations always have a recognisably local, Maldivian style. *Bodu beru* remains vibrant, rock bands sing Dhivehi lyrics, and traditional crafts are surviving in the face of modernity. It's actually remarkable that such a tiny population maintains such a distinctive culture in a globalised world.

Arts

Song & Dance

Bodu beru means 'big drum' in Dhivehi and gives its name to the best-known form of traditional music and dance in the country. It tends to be what resorts put on once a week as an exponent of local culture, but despite this sanitised framing, a performance can be very sophisticated and compelling. Dancers begin with a slow, nonchalant swaying and swinging of the arms, becoming more animated as the tempo increases and finishing in a rhythmic frenzy. In some versions the dancers even enter a trance-like state. There are four to six drummers in an ensemble and the sound has strong African influences.

However, these performances are not just to be found in resorts. If you're staying on an inhabited island, you'll often hear the *bodu beru* being played as groups of young men hang out and dance together after sundown. Witnessing it can be an fantastic experience, as the dancing becomes more and more frenetic as the night goes on, and there's no chance that this performance is for tourists.

Apart from *bodu beru,* the music most visitors will experience at resorts will rarely be a highlight. Local rock bands often perform in the bars in the evening, where they usually do fairly tacky covers of old favourites as well as performing their own material. They may incorporate elements of *bodu beru* in their music, with lots of percussion and extended drum solos when they're in front of a local audience. Some popular contemporary bands are Seventh Floor, Mezzo and Zero Degree Atoll.

Since 2012, the government has consistently harassed music fans attending live events in and around Male. On the pretext of catching drug users, the police have arrested and detained scores of people over the past few years.

Literature

Despite the unique Maldivian script that dates from the 1600s, most Maldivian myths and stories come from an oral tradition and have only recently appeared in print. Many are stories of witchcraft and sorcery, while others are cautionary tales about the evils of vanity, lust and greed, and the sticky fates of those who transgressed. Some are decidedly weird

In 2012 an Islamist mob attacked Male's National History Museum and destroyed around 30 priceless carvings depicting Buddha, effectively wiping out all significant pre-Islamic relics in the Maldives.

The government plans to properly excavate the country's large number of pre-Islamic Buddhist sites in a bid to attract travellers interested in more than just beaches and diving.

and depressing, and don't make good bedtime reading for young children. Male bookshops sell quite a range of local stories in English. Again, most of these are legends of the past, many overlaid with Islamic meaning. Novelty Press published a small book called *Mysticism in the Maldives,* which is still available in some shops.

Alternatively, if you're looking for thematic beach reading, you could always try the Hammond Innes thriller *The Strode Venturer,* which is set in the Maldives, or for some real escapist fun and a great behind-the-

LOCAL VOICE: EAGAN MOHAMED BADEEU

Eagan Mohamed Badeeu is a commercial artist living and working in Male. He produces paintings of Maldives that can be seen in galleries and resorts around the country.

What can visitors expect from the Maldivian art scene? Souvenirs, such as the traditional Maldivian lacquered vases, jewellery and other craftwork, do still tend to dominate the art scene, but in fact most of this is imported and little is locally made. Beyond the touristy stuff there is an emerging art scene, which was boosted by the founding of the National Art Gallery in Male, currently the only space where Maldivian artists can show their work. Most painted themes portray the natural beauty of the islands, though more contemporary and conceptual art styles are also becoming popular.

Is there a big artistic tradition in the Maldives? The Maldives has a rich culture and tradition of craftsmanship, especially for stone carving and lacquer work – the Old Friday Mosque in Male, for example, is a masterpiece of both, with the complicated floral and symmetrical patterns showing us how creative these craftsmen were. Our ancestors used organic dyes to colour the traditional *feyli* (Maldivian sarong) and *thundu kunaa* (reed mats), but there is no evidence of paintings in our tradition before the early 20th century.

You paint a lot of traditional Maldivian scenes. Are you worried that some of these traditions will be lost in the future? Yes, for me it is sad to see the dredged concrete harbours taking over from the timber jetties of our islands. Thirty years ago I remember young people sailing small dhonis for fun, learning how to use the ocean currents and the monsoon winds to navigate. However, today a young Maldivian is more likely to circle the island on a motorcycle than in a dhoni! Most of our traditions will be lost in the future, so it's up to us to keep traditions passed on by our forefathers alive for the next generation.

You must have travelled a lot in your country; do you have a favourite part of the Maldives? My favourite part of the country is Haa Dhaalu Atoll in the north Maldives. I particularly love the island of Hanimaadhoo, which has a charming old village and a thick palm and banyan tree forest. Most of all, the lovely people there are very friendly. The island of Kulhuduffushi, the capital of Haa Dhaalu, is another favourite of mine. The islanders are famous for celebrating Eid by performing lots of traditional dances, and people travel there to see them.

What is your favourite thing about Maldivian village life? I like to sit in a *holhuashi* (small beach hut) and chat with the island folk. On any island the *holhuashi* is where the village men gather to talk politics and play cards and chess. For me the most interesting time of the day is when the fishermen return with the day's catch. People gather on the beach to clean and buy the fish before the village women prepare a delicious *garudia* (fish broth) with rice, lime and chillies.

Does life vary strongly between the rural areas in Maldives and the bigger towns? Which do you prefer? Of course – Male is now the world's most densely populated island, with all the problems of any big city, while rural islands are quiet, spacious and clean. Despite this, many families blindly migrate from their islands to Male. If it were possible, I would do the opposite as I'd love to live in the atolls – this is actually the dream of many people living in the capital!

SITTING IN THE MALDIVES

The Maldives has two unique pieces of furniture. One is the *undholi,* a wooden platform or netting seat that's hung from a tree or triangular frame. Sometimes called a bed-boat, the *undholi* is a sofa, hammock and fan combination – swinging gently creates a cooling movement of air across the indolent occupant.

The *joli* is a static version – net seats on a rectangular frame, usually made in sociable sets of three or four. Once made of coir rope and wooden sticks, these days steel pipes and plastic mesh are now almost universal – it's like sitting in a string shopping bag, but cool; you'll see these curious and ingenious inventions all over inhabited islands.

---

scenes look at one of the country's top resorts, Imogen Edwards-Jones' *Beach Babylon* is a good pick.

Visual Arts

There is no historical tradition of painting in the Maldives, but demand for local art (however fabricated) from the tourist industry has created a supply in the ultra-savvy Maldivian market, with more than a few locals selling paintings to visitors or creating beach scenes for hotel rooms.

The National Art Gallery in Male puts on an exhibition of Maldivian art every few years. It combines photography, painting and some conceptual art, and is well worth a visit if it happens to coincide with your time in Male. Some local names to look out for are Eagan Badeeu, Ahmed Naseer and Hassan Shameem.

Some islands were once famous for wood and stone carving – elaborate calligraphy and intricate intertwining patterns are a feature of many old mosques and gravestones. A little of this woodcarving is still done, mainly to decorate mosques. The facade of the Majlis building in Male is decorated with intertwined carvings, for example.

Crafts

Mats

Natural-fibre mats are woven on many islands, but the most famous are the ones known as *thundu kunaa,* made on the island of Gadhdhoo in Gaaf Dhaal Atoll. This was once an endangered art form, but renewed interest thanks to the increase in tourism has arguably saved it from disappearing. A Danish researcher in the 1970s documented the weaving techniques and the plants used for fibre and dyes, and noted that a number of traditional designs had not been woven for 20 years. Collecting the materials and weaving a mat can take weeks, and the money that can be made selling the work is not much by modern Maldivian standards. Some fine examples now decorate the reception areas of tourist resorts, and there's a growing appreciation of the work among local people and foreign collectors.

Lacquer Work

Traditionally, lacquer work *(laajehun)* was for containers, bowls and trays used for gifts to the sultan – some fine examples can be seen in the National Museum in Male. Different wood is used to make boxes, bowls, vases and other turned objects. Traditionally the lathe is hand-powered by a cord pulled round a spindle. Several layers of lacquer are applied in different colours. They then harden, and the design is incised with sharp tools, exposing the bright colours of the underlying layers. Designs are usually floral motifs in yellow with red trim on a black background (most likely based on designs of Chinese ceramics). Production of lacquer work

> The crown jewel of Maldivian arts and crafts is the unique dhoni boat, which anyone travelling in Maldives will have the chance to see and, normally, travel on as well. Made entirely from wood, and having evolved from the Arab dhow, the dhoni is a most uniquely Maldivian creation and something that all locals are proud of.

Coconut palm oil is a traditional product that has been widely used in Maldives, most commonly as a fuel for lamps before electricity. Today many islanders make shampoo, soap and lotions from the oil that they sell to tourists.

is a viable cottage industry in Baa Atoll, particularly on the islands of Eydhafushi and Thulhaadhoo.

Jewellery

Ribudhoo Island in Dhaalu (South Nilandhoo Atoll) is famous for making gold jewellery, and Hulhudheli, in the same atoll, for silver jewellery. According to local belief, a royal jeweller brought the goldsmithing skills to the island centuries ago, having been banished to Ribudhoo by a sultan. It's also said that the islanders plundered a shipwreck in the 1700s, and reworked the gold jewellery they found to disguise its origins.

Architecture

A traditional Maldivian village is notable for its neat and orderly layout, with wide sandy streets in a regular, rectangular grid. Houses are made of concrete blocks or coral stone joined with mortar, and the walls line the sides of the streets. Many houses will have a shaded courtyard in front, enclosed by a chest-high wall fronting the street. This courtyard is an outdoor room, with *joli* (net seats) and *undholi* (wooden seats), where families sit in the heat of the day or the cool of the evening. A more private courtyard behind, the *gifili,* has a well and serves as an open-air bathroom.

Mosques tend to be the most interesting and attractive buildings you'll see on inhabited islands. Some date back to the 16th century and are extremely impressive examples of craftsmanship both for their coral-carved exteriors and their teak and lacquer-work interiors, although in most cases you'll have to view the insides from the doorway, as non-Muslims are not normally allowed to enter mosques in the Maldives.

Male has several very beautiful 16th and 17th century mosques, as well as its impressive, modern Grand Friday Mosque, the city's most striking and, arguably, iconic building – its large golden dome is visible for miles around.

One island that is particularly worth visiting to see traditional Maldivian architecture is Utheemu, in the very far northern atoll of Haa Alifu. Here you'll find the best example of a 16th-century Maldivian nobleman's house. Although rather hyperbolically called Utheemu Palace, the building is nevertheless fascinating to tour for its interiors and interesting outer design.

Taste of the Maldives

Your culinary experience in the Maldives could be, depending on your resort, anything from haute cuisine ordered from a menu you've discussed with the chef in advance to bangers and mash at the all-you-can-eat buffet in the communal dining room. What it's unlikely to be in either case is particularly Maldivian, given the dislocation from local life experienced in resorts. However, anyone staying in Male or on an inhabited island should take advantage of this opportunity to try real Maldivian food. This is easily done by visiting the so called teashops or hotels, where delicious 'short eats' (called *hedhikaa* in Dhivehi) are served up to an all-male crowd of locals, but where foreigners, including accompanied women, will normally be very welcome. Maldivian cuisine is unsurprisingly simple due to the lack of variety provided by local agriculture. However, it is nevertheless testament to a nation's historical survival on a relatively small, but bountiful, amount of locally occurring ingredients.

Staples & Specialities

Essentially all that grows in the Maldives are coconuts, yams, mangoes, papayas and pineapples; the only other locally occurring product is fish and seafood, which explains the historical simplicity of Maldivian cuisine. However, as trade with the Indian subcontinent, Africa, Arabia and the Far East have always brought other, more exciting influences, the result is far less bland than it could be.

Kavaabu are small deep-fried dough balls with tuna, mashed potato, pepper and lime – a very popular 'short eat'.

The Indian influence is clear in local cuisine above all; Maldivian food is often hot and spicy. If you're going to eat local food, prepare your palate for spicy fish curry, fish soup, fish patties and variations thereof. A favourite Maldivian breakfast is *mas huni,* a healthy mixture of tuna, onion, coconut and chilli, eaten cold with *roshi* (unleavened bread, like an Indian chapati) and tea.

'Maldive fish', is a big export of the Maldives, a tuna product that is cured on the islands and often sold abroad, where it is widely used as a supporting ingredient in Sri Lankan cooking. It is also used as the principal ingredient of several Maldivian dishes such as *mas huni.*

For snacks and light meals, Maldivians like *hedhikaa,* a selection of finger foods. In homes the *hedhikaa* are placed on the table and everyone helps themselves. In teashops this is called 'short eats' – a choice of things like *fihunu mas* (fish pieces with chilli coating), *gulha* (fried dough balls filled with fish and spices), *keemia* (fried fish rolls in batter) and *kuli boakiba* (spicy fish cakes). Sweets include little bowls of *bondi bai* (rice pudding), tiny bananas and *zileybee* (coloured coils of sugared, fried batter). Generally, anything small and brown will be savoury and contain fish, and anything light or brightly coloured will be sweet.

Bis hulavuu is a popular snack – a pastry made from eggs, sugar and ghee and served cold. You may well be invited to try some if you visit an inhabited island.

A main meal will include rice or *roshi* or both, plus soups, curries, vegetables, pickles and spicy sauces. In a teashop, a substantial meal with rice and *roshi* is called 'long eats'. The most typical dish is *garudia,* a soup made from dried and smoked fish, often eaten with rice, lime and chilli. The soup is poured over rice, mixed up by hand and eaten with the fingers. Another common meal is *mas riha,* a fish curry eaten with rice or *roshi* – the *roshi* is torn into strips, mixed on the plate with the curry and condiments, and eaten with the fingers. A cup of tea accompanies the meal, and is usually drunk black and sweet.

The Maldivian equivalent of the after-dinner mint is the areca nut, chewed after a meal or snack. The little oval nuts are sliced into thin sections, some cloves and lime paste are added, the whole lot is wrapped in an areca leaf, and the wad is chewed whole. It's definitely an acquired taste, and the kind of thing that few foreigners try more than once!

Drinks

The only naturally occurring fresh water in the Maldives is rainwater, which is stored in natural underground aquifers beneath each island. This makes getting water quite a feat, and water conservation has always been extremely important in Maldivian culture, to the extent that the Maldives Tourism Law states that no water resources may be diverted from an inhabited island to supply a resort. All resorts have their own desalination plants to keep visitors supplied with enough water for their (by local standards incredibly wasteful) water needs. Most resorts include a bottle or two of drinking water for each guest per day; though in many cheaper resorts, you'll need to pay for each one, which can add up quickly.

The main local drinks other than rainwater are imported tea and toddy tapped from the crown of the palm trunk at the point where the coconuts grow. Every village has its toddy man *(raa veri)*. The *raa* is sweet and delicious if you can get over the pungent smell. It can be drunk immediately after it is tapped from the tree, or left to become a little alcoholic (though not too much!) as the sugar ferments.

Fermented *raa* is of course the closest most Maldivians ever get to alcohol; the Maldives is strictly dry apart from the resorts (and Maldivian staff cannot drink alcohol even there). This may be a consideration if you're planning to travel independently in the country and stay in guesthouses on inhabited islands – your holiday will have to be totally dry, with alcohol available only by visiting a nearby resort, stepping aboard a live aboard dive boat or swinging by the hotel near Male's international airport.

Despite the ban on alcohol, nonalcoholic beer is very popular in Male. Soft drink, including the only Coca-Cola made from salt water anywhere in the world (desalinated, of course), is available all over the country at prices much lower than in resorts. Outside resorts the range of drinks is very limited. Teashops will always serve *bor feng* (drinking water) and, of course, *sai* (tea). Unless you ask otherwise, tea comes black, with *hakuru* (sugar). *Kiru* (milk) isn't a common drink, and is usually made up from powder, as there are no cows in the Maldives.

Where to Eat & Drink

In budget resorts you won't usually have any choice about where to eat, as most cheaper resorts have just one restaurant. Midrange places typically have two or more to afford some variety, and top-end resorts often boast three or more. Buffets (nearly always for breakfast, sometimes for lunch and dinner too) allow for lots of different cuisines and plenty of choice, while à la carte dining is more popular for lunch and dinner, and is nearly always the case in finer establishments.

In Male, where there's a much broader choice, the most obvious place for authentic Maldivian 'short eats' is in a teashop. In recent years traditional teashops (confusingly sometimes also called 'hotels') have modernised so that they look less forbidding and are now more pleasant places at which to eat. Larger towns elsewhere will also have teashops and these are a great way to sample real Maldivian food. If you're staying on a small or medium-sized inhabited island though, most guesthous-

Don't be fooled by beer in Male – it's all nonalcoholic, even if it doesn't look it. For those gasping for the real thing, you'll need to cross the lagoon to the airport island where alcoholic beer is widely available.

Maldivians love their coffee. You can get very good espresso, latte or cappuccino anywhere in Male, as well as at most resorts and guesthouses.

Wine is available in the better resorts. Expect to pay extraordinary mark-ups; you'll do well to find anything under US$50. It's illegal to bring wine into the country (luggage is X-rayed on arrival to check for bottles).

TRAVEL YOUR TASTEBUDS

If you feel like trying something both exotic and dear to the Maldivian people, go for *miru-hulee boava* (octopus tentacles). This is not commonly found in resorts or in Male, but is often prepared in the atolls as a speciality should you be lucky enough to visit an inhabited island. The tentacles are stripped and cleaned, then braised in a sauce of curry leaves, cloves, garlic, chilli, onion, pepper and coconut oil – delicious.

es will provide all your meals as part of the room price because so few islands have sufficient or decent-enough restaurants for you to eat comfortably elsewhere. Even in places where independent travel is now well established, such as Maafushi, there is still a dearth of eating options, and nearly everything has to be found in guesthouses or hotels.

Vegetarians & Vegans

Vegetarians will have no problem in resorts (although at cheaper resorts where there may be a set meal rather than a buffet spread, veggies will often be stuck with an unimaginative pasta dish or a ratatouille). In general, resorts are well prepared for all types of diet, and in better resorts the chef may cook you a dish by request if what's on offer isn't appealing. Vegans will find the Maldives quite a challenge, though soy milk is on offer in most resorts and the buffet allows each diner to pick and mix. On inhabited islands things won't be so easy – fish and seafood dominate menus in the islands, so those who don't eat fish will have trouble.

Eating with Kids

In resorts menus sometimes have kids' sections, giving youngsters a choice of slightly less sophisticated foods, ranging from spaghetti to fish fingers and chicken nuggets. Even if there's nothing dedicated to the kids' tastes, resort buffets are usually diverse enough to cater to even the fussiest eaters. However, it's always best to check what resorts offer before booking a holiday with young kids. We've heard complaints from travellers about the poor availability of child-suitable foods even at the very best resorts. Note that baby-food products are not on sale in resorts, so bring whatever you will need for the trip.

Habits & Customs

There's not a huge amount of etiquette to worry about if you eat in Male or resorts. If you're lucky enough to be entertained in a local house you should obey some basic rules. That said, Maldivians are very relaxed and as long as you show respect and enjoyment, they'll be glad to have you eating with them.

When going to eat, wait to be shown where to sit and wait for the *kateeb* (island chief) or the male head of the household to sit down before you do. Take a little of everything offered and do so only with your right hand, as the left hand is considered unclean by Muslims. Do ask for cutlery if you find it hard to roll your food into little balls like the Maldivians do; this is quite normal for foreigners.

Survival Guide

Directory A–Z

Accommodation

Ouch. That's most people's reaction to Maldivian resort prices, and it's fair to say this is not and will never be a cheap place to stay. Even budget resorts and guesthouses cost more than most top-end places in India or Sri Lanka.

Our accommodation reviews are divided into three price groups: budget, midrange and top end. For each option a room rate is quoted for the high season (December to March, outside Christmas and New Year), with the normal meal plan with which rooms are sold. There are almost no single rooms in resorts, so singles are nearly always doubles for single occupation, with a similar price tag to a double room. Therefore we just list the standard room price (r) in the cheapest accommodation category, which is for two people unless otherwise stated. Prices usually include a service charge (normally 10% to 12%), GST (12%) and the government bed tax (US$8 per person per night).

BOOK YOUR STAY ONLINE

For more accommodation reviews by Lonely Planet authors, check out http://lonelyplanet.com/hotels. You'll find independent reviews, as well as recommendations on the best places to stay. Best of all, you can book online.

Resorts

The vast majority of travellers will stay at one of the roughly 110 self-contained island resorts throughout the Maldives.

Each resort is on its own island and provides accommodation, meals, and activities for its guests, ranging from the most basic beach huts, with a buffet three times a day and a simple diving school, to vast water villas with every conceivable luxury, à la carte dining and all kinds of activities, from kiteboarding to big-game fishing.

Most resorts have a range of room categories, so for simplicity we generally give the rate for the cheapest room. However, be warned, these prices are nothing more than a guideline. They are rack rates, and so booking through a travel agent will get you access to far better deals and lower rates.

Budget resorts (up to US$350 per room per night) tend to be busier and more basic in their facilities and level of sophistication than more expensive resorts. Few budget resorts are being built

these days, so those that do exist tend to date from the 1980s or '90s and are often in need of a lick of paint.

Midrange resorts (from US$350 to US$750 per night) are noticeably slicker and have a better standard of facilities and accommodation, all carried off with some style, and are luxurious at the top end of the bracket.

Top-end resorts (more than US$750 per night) are currently what the Maldives is all about. The standards in this category range from the very good to the mind-bogglingly luxurious.

Booking resorts through travel agents is nearly always cheaper than doing so directly, with some amazing deals to be had compared with the eye-watering rack rates. However, increasingly some resorts offer great deals via their websites, so it's always worth checking online. Last-minute deals can also prove good value.

Guesthouses

Previous laws prohibited the construction of hotels and guesthouses on most of the islands inhabited by locals. This law was changed in 2009 and guesthouses have now sprung up on inhabited islands throughout the Maldives. They offer a totally different experience to staying in a resort, far more contact with local life and far cheaper accommodation, but staying in one also entails certain restrictions, particularly with regards to alcohol and attire.

Hotels in Male

As hotels in Male are far cheaper than those of island resorts, we've used a separate price breakdown for the capital's hotels: budget (under US$80), midrange (US$80 to US$150) and top end (over US$150). These apply also to hotels on Hulhumale, the man-made extension island of the capital, 2km away.

Safari Boats

Live-aboard safari boats allow you to travel extensively throughout the country, visiting great dive sites, desert islands and small local settlements usually too remote to see travellers. Live-aboards also range from simple to luxurious, and you get what you pay for. The advantage is that you can visit many places otherwise off-limits to resort travellers, dive in pristine waters and enjoy a very sociable atmosphere. Prices range from bargain basement to exorbitant, depending on the facilities available.

Business Hours

Male is really the only place you have to worry about business hours in the Maldives. The resorts are far more flexible, as they have to cater round the clock to visitors.

The Maldivian working week runs from Sunday to Thursday, with Friday and Saturday being the weekend. Friday, a day of rest and prayer for most Maldivians, is like Sunday in some Christian countries, with most businesses closed.

Typical business hours outside resorts are as follows:

Banks 8am-1.30pm Sun-Thu

Businesses 8am-6pm Sun-Thu

SLEEPING PRICE RANGES

CATEGORY	RESORTS	HOTELS IN MALE
$ budget	<US$350	<US$80
$$ midrange	US$350-750	US$80-150
$$$ top end	>US$750	>US$150

Government offices 7.30am-2pm Sun-Thu

Restaurants noon-10pm Sat-Thu, 4-11pm Fri

Nearly all Male businesses stop several times a day for prayers, which can be frustrating for shoppers, as businesses suddenly close for 15 minutes to half an hour. Teashops can open very early or close very late. During Ramazan the places where locals eat will probably be closed during daylight hours, but will bustle after dark.

Children

Part of the appeal of staying on a desert island is the fact that there isn't much to do apart from relax, which can be limiting for children. Younger kids will enjoy playing in the water and on the beach, but older children and teenagers may find resort life a little confining after a few days, and they may get bored.

Families should look for resorts that offer lots of activities. Kayaking and fishing trips are always popular, and many places also offer courses in sailing, windsurfing and other watersports.

The minimum age for scuba diving is 10 years, but most resorts offer a 'bubble blowers' introduction for younger kids, which is very popular, and supervised snorkelling is always possible.

Kids clubs – for those aged 12 and under – and clubs for teenagers are very common in bigger, smarter resorts. These are free and the kids clubs run activities all day long, while teenagers are generally able to do what they want – even if it means playing computer games in a darkened air-conditioned room. Where resorts have good kids clubs or a generally welcoming child-friendly policy, we've included the child-friendly icon (🌴).

Although exotic cuisine is sometimes on the menu, you'll always find some standard Western-style dishes that kids will find appealing. Young children are more susceptible to sunburn than adults, so bring sun hats and plenty of sunblock. Lycra swim shirts are an excellent idea – they can be worn on the beach and in the water and block out most UV radiation.

Climate
Male

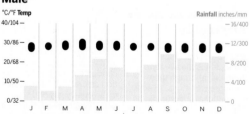

Practicalities

Note that some resorts do not encourage young children – check with the resort before you book. Children under five are often banned from honeymoon resorts and there is normally a minimum age requirement of 10 or 12 years for water villas, given the obvious safety issues. Where kids are welcome, it's no problem booking cots and organising high chairs in restaurants, and there's often a babysitting service as well. Baby supplies are available in Male, but usually not in resorts, so bring all the nappies and formula you'll need for the duration of the holiday. Outside resorts, breast-feeding should only be done in private.

Customs Regulations

The immigration cards issued to you on your flight to Male include a great list of items that are banned from the republic. Alcohol, pornography, pork, narcotics, dogs, firearms, spear guns and 'idols of worship' cannot be brought into the country and you're advised to comply. Baggage is always X-rayed and may be searched carefully, and if you have any liquor it will be taken and held for you till you're about to leave the country. This service will not extend to other prohibited items, and the importation of multiple bibles (one for personal use is fine), pornography and, in particular, drugs, will be treated very seriously. The export of turtle shell, or any turtle-shell products, is forbidden.

Electricity

Electricity supply is 220V to 240V, 50Hz AC. The standard socket is the UK-style three-pin, although there are some variations, so an international adaptor can be useful, though most resorts supply adaptors for non-UK travellers.

230V/50Hz

Embassies & Consulates

The few existing foreign representatives in Male are mostly honorary consuls with limited powers; most countries have no diplomats in Maldives at all. In an emergency contact your country's embassy or high commission in Colombo, Sri Lanka. If you lose your passport in Maldives, you'll generally need to be deported to Sri Lanka or India in order to receive a replacement.

Gay & Lesbian Travellers

By Maldivian law all extra-marital sex is illegal, but there is no specific mention of homosexuality in the country's legal index. This grey area means that while gay life does certainly exist in Maldives, it's all generally conducted with great discretion online. In 2013 an attack on an openly gay and secularist blogger Hilath Rasheed in Male, in which assailants slit his throat with a box cutter, revealed the level of homophobia at some levels of society. Rasheed amazingly survived the attack and now lives in Sri Lanka.

Of course in the country's resorts, things are very different. Same-sex couples will be able to book a double room with no questions asked (from budget to luxury, Maldivian hotel staff are the model of discretion), and it's common to see same sex-couples enjoying Maldivian holidays. Public displays of affection may embarrass Maldivian resort staff, but won't result in anything but blushes on their part. In Male and on inhabited islands discretion is key and public displays of affection should not be indulged in by anyone, gay or straight – the Maldives remains an extremely conservative place.

Insurance

A travel-insurance policy to cover theft, loss and medical problems is highly recommended. Some policies offer lower and higher medical-expense options; the higher ones are chiefly for countries that have high medical costs, and this would be a good idea for a Maldives trip.

Some policies specifically exclude 'dangerous activities', which can include diving, so check your policy carefully if you plan to dive, though anyone diving in Maldives is automatically obliged to buy Maldivian diving insurance as part of the package.

Worldwide travel insurance is available at www. lonelyplanet.com/bookings. You can buy, extend and claim online anytime – even if you're already on the road.

Internet Access

All resorts have internet access for guests. Sadly this is still used in a small minority of places as a way to fleece (there really is no other word for it) guests who want to be online, with some resorts charging as much as US$10 per hour for access. The good news is that in the vast majority of places there is now free wi-fi at least somewhere on the island, if not always in each room, for which sometimes there's an additional charge for wi-fi access. Do check with your resort before booking, though, as wi-fi charges can add up if you need to be online for your entire trip. Most resorts also have terminals connected to the internet (in nearly all cases free) for the use of guests without their own laptops or smartphones. All guesthouses have free wi-fi.

In Male internet cafes are now obsolete, but free wireless is offered in all hotels and at many restaurants and cafes.

Legal Matters

➡ Alcohol is illegal outside resorts – you're theoretically not even allowed to take a can of beer out on a boat trip. Some foreign residents in the capital have a liquor permit, which entitles them to a limited amount per month, strictly for personal consumption at home.

➡ Illicit drugs are around, but are not widespread. Penalties are heavy. 'Brown sugar', a semirefined form of heroin, has become a problem among some young people in the capital and even in some outer islands.

➡ Apart from the police and the military, there is a chief on every atoll and island who must keep an eye on what is happening, report to the central government and be responsible for the actions of local people.

➡ Resorts are responsible for their guests and for what happens on their island. If a guest sunbathes or goes swimming in the nude, the

resort can be fined, as well as the visitor.

Maps

Put simply, the Maldives is a nightmare to map. The islands are so small and scattered that you're forever trying to distinguish between the tiny islands and the reefs that surround them. Another problem is scale – the country is over 800km from north to south, but the largest island is only about 8km long, and most are just a few hundred metres across.

For anyone doing a serious amount of travel, especially diving, *Maps of the Maldives* (Atoll Editions, 2007) is indispensable and in a very practical book form, alleviating the need to fold out a vast map. It includes everything from shipwreck sites to Protected Marine Area plans. It's somewhat rare and dated now, but can still be found at some bookshops in Male, or ordered online at www.atolleditions.com.au.

Money

The currency of the Maldives is the rufiyaa (Rf), which is divided into 100 larees. Notes come in denominations of 500, 100, 50, 20, 10, five and two rufiyaa, but the last two are uncommon. Coins are in denominations of two and one rufiyaa, and 50, 25 and 10 larees. Most resort and travel expenses will be billed in dollars, and most visitors never even see rufiyaa, as US dollars are accepted everywhere. If you're staying in a resort, all extras (including diving costs) will be billed to your room, and you pay the day before departure. Resorts accept cash and credit cards, and unless specified US dollars are preferred (although some European-oriented resorts use the euro as their default currency).

ATMs

There are a large number of ATMs in Male – nearly all allow you to withdraw funds from international accounts.

Look for the major banks on Boduthakurufaanu Magu, a few blocks beyond the airport ferry. Note that while you can do cash advances on credit cards over the counter at Male airport and at most resorts, internationally compatible ATMs outside Male are rare, save at the airport, and should not be relied upon.

Cash

It's perfectly possible to have a holiday in the Maldives without ever touching cash of any sort, as in resorts everything will be chalked up to your room number and paid by credit card on departure. You won't need Maldivian rufiyaa unless you're using local shops and services. Even these will usually take dollars, though you'll be given change in rufiyaa.

Be aware that there are restrictions on changing rufiyaa into foreign currency. If you take out cash in rufiyaa from an ATM, you won't be able to change the remainder back into US dollars or any other foreign currency. Therefore if you need lots of local currency, exchange foreign cash for rufiyaa at a bank and keep the receipt to be allowed to change the remainder back at the airport.

Credit Cards

Every resort takes major credit cards including Visa, Amex and MasterCard. A week of diving and drinking could easily run up a tab over US$2000, so ensure your credit limit can stand it. Guesthouses are less well-equipped for credit cards, so check before you travel if yours will accept them.

Tipping

Tipping is something of a grey area in the Maldives, where a 10% to 12.5% service tax is added to nearly everything from minibar drinks to snorkelling excursions. In many places this would mean that you don't need to tip any further, but it's still the case that people serving you personally will often expect something. While it's obviously impossible to tip everyone who carries your bag (that would be about five people between

---

THOSE UNPRONOUNCEABLE ATOLLS

Confusingly enough, the 26 atolls of the Maldives are divided for official purposes into 21 administrative districts, which are named by the letters of the Thaana alphabet and as such are a lot easier to pronounce. Note that this usage is not used for North and South Male Atolls, North and South Ari Atoll and Addu Atoll in the far south, so we also use their traditional name instead of Kaafu, Alif and Seenu. The following table gives both traditional and administrative names for most parts of the country; those marked with an aterisk are the names used in this book.

ADMINISTRATIVE NAME	ATOLL NAME
Alifu	Ari Atoll*
Baa*	South Maalhosmadulu Atoll
Dhaalu*	South Nilandhe Atoll
Faafu*	North Nilandhe Atoll
Gaafu Alifu*	North Huvadhoo Atoll
Gaafu Dhaalu*	South Huvadhoo Atoll
Gnaviyani*	Fuvahmulah Atoll
Haa Alifu*	North Thiladhunmathee Atoll
Haa Dhaal*	South Thiladhunmathee Atoll & Maamakunudhoo Atoll
Kaafu	Male Atoll*
Laamu*	Hadhdunmathee Atoll
Lhaviyani*	Faadhippolhu Atoll
Meemu*	Mulaku Atoll
Noonu*	South Miladhunmadulu Atoll
Raa*	North Maalhosmadulu Atoll
Seenu	Addu Atoll*
Shaviyani*	North Miladhunmadulu Atoll
Thaa*	Kolhumadulu Atoll
Vaavu*	Felidhe Atoll

arrival at the airport and your hotel room), it's good form to leave a tip for your room staff and in smarter resorts your *thakuru* (butler). Give any tips to the staff personally, not to the hotel cashier – US dollars, euros and local currency are equally acceptable. There's no need to tip bar staff or waiting staff, as that will be added to your bill automatically. In Male the fancier restaurants usually add a 10% service charge, so you don't need to tip. Tipping is not customary in local teashops.

Travellers Cheques

Banks in Male will change travellers cheques and cash in US dollars, but other currencies are trickier. Most will change US-dollar travellers cheques into US dollars cash with a commission of US$5. Changing travellers cheques to Maldivian rufiyaa should not attract a commission. Some of the authorised moneychangers around town will exchange US-dollar or euro travellers cheques at times when the banks are closed.

Post

Postal services are quite efficient, with mail to overseas destinations delivered promptly. A high-speed Express Mail Service (EMS) is available to many countries from Male's **main post office** (Map p54; ☑ 331 5555; Boduthakurufaanu Magu; ⊚ 9am-7.30pm Sun-Thu, 10am-3.30pm Sat). Parcel rates can be quite expensive and will have to clear customs at the main post office. At the resorts you can buy stamps and postcards at the shop or the reception desk. Generally there is a mailbox near reception, and there's a full post office at Male Airport too.

Public Holidays

If you're in a resort, Maldivian holidays will not affect you –

service will be as normal. Christmas, New Year, Easter and European school holidays will affect you more – they're the busiest times for tourists and bring the highest resort prices.

If a holiday falls on a Friday or Saturday, the next working day will be declared a holiday 'on the occasion of' whatever it was. Most Maldivian holidays are based on the Islamic lunar calendar and the dates vary from year to year.

National Day A commemoration of the day Mohammed Thakurufaanu and his men overthrew the Portuguese on Male in 1578. It's on the first day of the third month of the lunar calendar.

Huravee Day The day the Malabars of India were kicked out by Sultan Hassan Izzuddeen after their brief occupation in 1752. Usually around July.

Ramazan Known as Ramazan or *roarda mas* in the Maldives, the Islamic month of fasting is an important religious occasion that starts on a new moon and continues for 28 days. Expected starting dates for the next few years are: 7 June 2016, 27 May 2017, and 16 May 2018. The exact date depends on the sighting of the new moon in Mecca and can vary by a day or so either way.

Kuda Eid Also called Id-ul-Fitr or Fith'r Eid, this occurs at the end of Ramazan, with the sighting of the new moon, and is celebrated with a feast.

Bodu Eid Also called Eid-ul Al'h'aa (Festival of the Sacrifice), 66 days after the end of Ramazan, this is the time when many Muslims begin the pilgrimage (haj) to Mecca.

Martyr's Day Commemorates the death of Sultan Ali VI at the hands of the Portuguese in 1558. Usually around December.

Prophet's Birthday The birthday of the Prophet Mohammed is celebrated with three days of eating and merriment. The approximate start dates for the next few years are 12 December 2016, 1 December 2017 and 21 November 2018.

The following are fixed holiday dates:

New Year's Day 1 January

Independence Day Celebrates the ending of the British protectorate (in 1965) on 26 and 27 July.

Victory Day Celebrates the victory over the Sri Lankan mercenaries who tried to overthrow the Maldivian government in 1988. A military march is followed by lots of schoolchildren doing drills and traditional dances, and more entertaining floats and costumed processions on 3 November.

Republic Day Commemorates the second (current) republic, founded in 1968 on 11 November. Celebrated in Male with lots of pomp, brass bands and parades. Sometimes the following day is also a holiday.

Telephone

➡ There are two telephone providers operating in the Maldives: Dhiraagu and Ooredoo.

➡ Both providers offer good coverage, although given the unique geography of the country there are still lots of areas without coverage in the atolls.

➡ You can buy a local SIM card for around US$10 and use it in your own phone if it's unlocked (check with your provider before you leave) – this becomes worth the price almost immediately if you're using your phone locally. There are offices of both providers at the airport, so it's easy to pick up a local SIM on your way to your resort.

➡ All resorts have telephones, either in the rooms or available at reception. Charges vary from high to astronomical, starting around US$15 for three minutes; our advice is to avoid them and stick to Skype instead.

➡ The international country code for the Maldives is ☑ 960. All Maldives numbers have seven digits and there are no area codes.

➡ To make an international call, dial ✆00.

Time

The Maldives is five hours ahead of GMT, in the same time zone as Pakistan. When it's noon in the Maldives, it's 7am in London, 8am in Berlin and Rome, 12.30pm in India and Sri Lanka, 3pm in Singapore and 4pm in Tokyo.

Around half of Maldivian resorts operate one hour ahead of Male time to give their guests the illusion of extra daylight in the evening and a longer sleep in the morning. This can make it tricky when arranging pick-up times and transfers, so always check whether you're being quoted Male time or resort time.

Toilets

Male public toilets charge Rf2. On local islands, you may have to ask where the *fahana* is, although many people still use the town beach as a public latrine and rubbish dump. In general you're better off using toilets in cafes and restaurants in Male – they're usually cleaner and free.

Tourist Information

The official tourist office is the **Maldives Tourism Promotion Board** (www. visitmaldives.com), which has a somewhat informative website and a desk at the airport in Male. However, most tourism promotion is done by private travel agents, tour operators and resorts.

Travellers with Disabilities

At Male International Airport, passengers must use steps to get on and off planes, but it should be no problem to get assistance for mobility-challenged passengers.

Transfers to nearby resorts are by dhoni or speedboat and a person in a wheelchair or with limited mobility will need assistance, which the crews will always be happy to provide. Transfer to more distant resorts is often by seaplanes, which can be more difficult to access, but again staff are quite experienced in assisting passengers in wheelchairs or with limited mobility.

All resorts have ground-level rooms, few steps, and reasonably smooth paths to beaches, boat jetties and all public areas, but some of the more rustic and 'ecofriendly' resorts have a lot of sand floors. Staff – something there's never a shortage of in the Maldives – will be on hand to assist disabled guests. When you decide on a resort, call them directly and ask about the layout. It's usually a good idea for guests to advise their tour agency of any special needs, but if you want to find out about specific facilities, it's best to contact the resort itself.

Many resort activities are potentially suitable for disabled guests. Fishing trips and excursions to inhabited islands should be easy, but uninhabited islands may be more difficult to disembark on. Catamaran sailing and canoeing are possibilities, especially if you've had experience in these activities. Anyone who can swim will be able to enjoy snorkelling. The **International Association for Handicapped Divers** (www. iahd.org) provides advice and assistance for anyone with a physical disability who wishes to scuba dive.

As no dogs are permitted in the Maldives, it's not a destination for anyone dependent on a guide dog.

Visas

The Maldives issues a 30-day stamp on arrival to holders of all passports. Citizens of India, Pakistan, Bangladesh or Nepal are given a 90-day stamp. If you want to stay longer you'll either need to apply for an extension to the 30-day stamp or leave the country when your 30 days is up, then return. You should know the name of your resort or hotel and be able to show a return air ticket out of the country if asked by immigration officials.

Visa Extensions

To apply for an extension, go to the **Department of Immigration & Emigration** (✆332 3910; Ameer Ahmed Magu; ◷9am-3pm Sun-Thu), near Jumhooree Maidan in Male. Fill in the Application for Permit Extension form, which will need to be co-signed by a local sponsor. The main requirement is evidence that you have accommodation, so it's best to have your resort, travel agent or guesthouse manager act as a sponsor and apply on your behalf. Have your sponsor sign the form, and bring it back to the office, along with your passport, a passport photo and your air ticket out of the country. You have to have a confirmed booking for the new departure date before you can get the extension – fortunately, the airlines don't ask to see a visa extension before they'll change the date of your flight. You'll be asked to leave the documents at the office and return in a couple of days to pick up the passport with its extended visa (get a receipt for your passport). Extensions are for a maximum of 30 days.

Volunteering

There are few volunteering opportunities in the Maldives, but those that do exist tend to be worthwhile projects involving sustainable development, wildlife protection and teaching. Bear in mind that for the most part, volunteers will be living on small, remote islands without many creature comforts, and will also be expected to raise money to fund their trip. The **Maldivian High Commission** (☑44 207 224 2135; www.maldiveshighcommission.org; 22 Nottingham Place, London W1U 5NJ) can help with some placements and its webpage is useful for those considering volunteer work. Some excellent organisations that offer volunteering opportunities include the following:

➡ www.maldives whalesharkresearch.org

➡ www.volunteermaldives. com

➡ www.atollvolunteers.com

Women Travellers

Culturally, resorts are European enclaves and visiting women will not have to make too many adjustments. Topless bathing and nudity are strictly forbidden, but bikinis are perfectly acceptable on resort beaches.

In Male reasonably modest dress is appropriate – shorts should cover the thighs and shirts should cover the shoulders and not be very low cut. Local women don't go into teashops in Male, but a foreign woman with a male companion will not cause any excitement.

In more out-of-the-way parts of the country, quite conservative dress is in order. It is very unlikely that a foreign woman would be harassed or feel threatened on a local island, as Maldivian men are conservative and extremely respectful. They are very closed, small communities, and the fact that a foreign woman would be associated with a local sponsor should give a high level of security.

Work

There is an enormous work market for foreigners in the Maldives, as almost 50% of resort staff generally come from abroad (a Maldivian law stipulates that 50% of all resort staff must be Maldivian). Resorts are keen to hire people with a background in the hospitality industry, including managers, administrators, divemasters, masseurs, biologists, chefs, sommeliers and yoga instructors, and the positions tend to be well compensated and provide for plenty of 'off-island' time.

Transport

GETTING THERE & AWAY

Entering the Country

Entering the Maldives is simple and hassle-free. However, you must know the name of your resort, hotel or guesthouse, so if you haven't got accommodation pre-arranged for your first night, pick a place to write down on the immigration form.

Passport

There are no restrictions on foreign nationals entering the country. Visas are not needed for visits of 30 days or less.

Air

Airports & Airlines

Almost every visitor to the Maldives arrives at Male's **Ibrahim Nasir International Airport** (☑331 5366; www.macl.aero), on the island of Hulhule, 2km across the water from the capital island, Male. It's a decent but rather aged terminal awaiting an upgrade to a world-class airport terminal that has been on the cards for years, but whose progress has been agonisingly slow. There are three further airports in the country that can take international flights, on the islands of Hanimaadhoo,

Maamigili and Gan, though in practice they only receive regular domestic flights from Male, private jets and the odd charter flight, and none of them has at present any scheduled international arrivals.

The national carrier is **Maldivian** (www.maldivian.aero), connecting the Maldives internationally to various cities in China and India, as well as to all domestic terminals from the capital. A second domestic airline, **FlyMe** (www.flyme.mv), operates flights that are often cheaper than those on Maldivian, though its network is not so comprehensive, nor are its flights as frequent, focusing as they do on their private airstrip at Maamigili in Ari Atoll.

The international carriers serving Male are a mixture of scheduled and charter airlines. Some airlines only fly in certain seasons and many change services frequently in line with traveller demand.

Air India (www.airindia.com)

Austrian (www.aua.com)

Bangkok Airways (www.bangkokair.com)

British Airways (www.ba.com)

Emirates (www.emirates.com)

Etihad (www.etihadairways.com)

Japan Airlines (www.jal.com)

Malaysia Airlines (www.malaysiaairlines.com)

Mega Maldives Airlines (www.megamaldivesair.com)

Oman Air (www.omanair.com)

Qatar Airways (www.qatar-airways.com)

Singapore Airlines (www.singaporeairlines.com)

SriLankan Airlines (www.srilankan.aero)

Transaero (www.transaero.ru)

Turkish Airlines (www.turkishairlines.com)

Tickets

If you're on a package, you'll usually have little or no choice about the airline you fly, as it will be part of the package. However, packages without flights are available, so in those cases it pays to shop around for both scheduled and charter deals. More and more chartered airlines are selling flight-only seats and these can be good deals, so check their websites as well as those of scheduled carriers. The other advantage of charter flights is that you can fly direct from Western Europe to Male, without the change in the Middle East that is common for scheduled airlines.

Flights can be booked online at lonelyplanet.com/bookings.

Sea

International Connections

While it may look like an obvious transport route, there are no scheduled boat connections between either India or Sri Lanka and the Maldives, nor do cargo ships generally take paying passengers. You might be lucky if you ask around in Colombo, Sri Lanka, or Trivandrum in India, but it's unlikely.

Yacht

Yachts and super-yachts cruise Maldivian waters throughout the year – this is, after all, a playground for the rich and super rich. However, with the Maldives being somewhat out of the way, this is not a standard port of call, and most people fly here to meet their craft. The negatives for yacht captains include the maze of reefs that can make Maldives a hazardous place to cruise, the high fees for cruising permits, the bureaucracy that attends any journey, the restrictions on where yachts can go and the absence of lively little ports with great eating options and waterfront bars: the Caribbean this is not.

A large marina has been built at Island Hideaway in the far north of the country, and this is the only place currently set up for servicing yachts in a professional way. Addu, in the far south, has a sheltered anchorage, a lux-ury resort and refuelling and resupply facilities.

The three points where a yacht can get an initial 'clear in' are Uligamu (Haa Alifu) in the north, Hithadhoo/Gan (Addu Atoll) in the south, and Male. Call in on VHF channel 16 to the National Security Service (NSS) Coastguard and follow instructions. If you're just passing through and want to stop only briefly, a 72-hour permit is usually easy to arrange. If you want to stay longer in Maldivian waters, or stop for provisions, you'll have to do immigration, customs, port authority and quarantine checks, and get a cruising permit. This can be done at any of the three clear-in facilities.

If you want to stop at Male, ensure you arrive well before dark, go to the east side of Viligili island, between Viligili and Male, and call the coastguard on channel 16. Officially, all boats require a pilot, but this isn't usually insisted upon for boats under 30m. Carefully follow the coastguard's instructions on where to anchor, or you may find yourself in water that's very deep or too shallow. Then contact one of the port agents, such as **Island Sailors** (☏333 2536; www.islandsailors.com) or **Real Sea Hawks Maldives** (☏330 5922; www.realseahawksmaldives.com).

Port agents can arrange for port authority, immigration, customs and quarantine checks, and can arrange repairs, refuelling and restocking. After the initial checks you'll be able to cross to the lagoon beside Hulhumale, the reclaimed land north of the airport. This is a good anchorage. The bigger supermarkets, such as **Fantasy Store** (Map p54; Fareedhee Magu; ⊘9am-10pm Sat-Thu, 2.30-10pm Fri; ✺), have quite a good range of provisions at relatively reasonable prices.

Before you leave Maldivian waters, don't forget to 'clear out' at Uligamu, Hithadhoo or Male.

GETTING AROUND

Air

Airlines in the Maldives

Air is the main way to cover long distances in the Maldives. There are nine regional airports in the country, all of which are linked to the capital by regular flights, and several more are in the planning stages. Domestic flights are run by the national carrier **Maldivian** (www.maldivian.aero) and privately owned **FlyMe** (www.flyme.mv). Flights fill up fast, so reserve in advance (booking online is currently only possible on Maldivian) to ensure you get the flight you want.

Seaplane

The use of seaplanes means that almost every corner of the country can be reached by air, given that they don't

---

CLIMATE CHANGE & TRAVEL

Every form of transport that relies on carbon-based fuel generates CO2, the main cause of human-induced climate change. Modern travel is dependent on aeroplanes, which might use less fuel per kilometre per person than most cars but travel much greater distances. The altitude at which aircraft emit gases (including CO2) and particles also contributes to their climate change impact. Many websites offer 'carbon calculators' that allow people to estimate the carbon emissions generated by their journey and, for those who wish to do so, to offset the impact of the greenhouse gases emitted with contributions to portfolios of climate-friendly initiatives throughout the world. Lonely Planet offsets the carbon footprint of all staff and author travel.

require a runway. Many travellers use the services of the two charter seaplane companies, **Trans Maldivian Airways** (☎334 8400; www.transmaldivian.com) and **Maldivian** (www.maldivian.aero). Both fly tourists from the seaplane port next to Male International Airport out to resorts on 18-seater DeHavilland Twin Otter seaplanes. Normally each resort has a contract with just one of the carriers, though some resorts have their own seaplane, which they operate independently.

All seaplane transfers are made during daylight hours, and offer staggering views of the atolls, islands, reefs and lagoons. The cost is between US$200 and US$600 return, depending on the distance and the deal between the resorts, and it's generally included in the package price. If you book independently, the seaplane will be charged as an extra.

Charter flights for sightseeing, photography and emergency evacuation can also be arranged. Call either companies for rates and availability. Note that cargo capacity on the seaplanes is limited to 20kg in most cases, with extra weight charged at a premium, and some heavy items may have to wait for a later flight.

Boat

For short hops, boat is nearly the only option for getting around, given Maldivian geography and its 1800 islands, only a few of which are connected to each other by causeways.

Dhoni Charters

In Male, go along the waterfront to the eastern end of Boduthakurufaanu Magu by the airport ferry jetty and you'll find many dhonis waiting in the harbour. Some of these are available for charter to nearby islands. The price depends on where you want to go, for how long, and on your negotiating skills – somewhere between Rf1000 and Rf2000 for a day is a typical rate, but if you want to start at 6am and go nonstop for 12 hours, it could be quite a bit more. You can also charter a dhoni at most resorts, but it will cost more (anything from US$400 to US$800 per day) and you'll only get one if they're not all being used for excursions or diving trips.

Ferry

The Nasheed government introduced a public ferry network in 2010, and while it's not without its faults, all the inhabited islands in the country are now connected by ferry to at least somewhere else, even if it is just a couple of times a week to another island in the atoll. This means that if you have plenty of time, independent travel around the Maldives is now possible. These ferries will not, however, help you travel between resorts, as they only stop at inhabited islands. To reach resorts you'll still need to do so by far pricier speedboat or seaplane transfers.

We have included basic information about ferry routes, but for specific timings you'll need to check with the guesthouse you're heading to (and unless you know someone on the island in question, you'll need to be heading to an island with a guesthouse on it, unless it's just a day trip). Some, but by no means all timetables are online at www.mtcc.com.mv.

Ferries are cheap and relatively slow compared to speedboats. They are time-tabled, but are also prone to delays due to bad weather or technical problems, so ferries are for those with plenty of time and patience.

Speedboat

Resorts in North and South Male Atoll, as well as some in Ari Atoll, offer transfer by speedboat, which costs anything from US$80 to US$400 return depending on the distance. This is generally included in the package price, but for independent travellers it's charged as an extra on leaving the resort.

Most big travel agencies can organise the charter of launches from Male, which, if you can afford it, is absolutely the best way to get around. **Inner Maldives** (☎300 6886; www.innermaldives.com.mv) has good-value launches for charter at around US$500 per day, excluding the (substantial) fuel prices. For the price you'll get the services of the captain and a couple of crew members for a 10-hour day. If chartering a boat for the day, standard practice is for the client to pay for the tank to be refuelled on arrival back at Male. Another well-priced and reliable company to hire launches from in Male is **Nazaki Marine** (☎332 8219; www.nazaki.com).

Car & Motorcycle

The only places where visitors will need to travel by road are in the island cities of Male, Fuvahmulah and Hulhumale, and between a few islands in Laamu and Addu Atoll that are connected by causeways. Taxis are available in all these places, and driving is on the left.

Health

The Maldives is not a dangerous destination, with few poisonous animals and – by regional standards – excellent health care and hygiene awareness. Staying healthy here is mainly about being sensible and careful.

BEFORE YOU GO

Insurance

Make sure that you have adequate health insurance and that it covers you for expensive evacuations by seaplane or speedboat, and for any diving or water-sports risks.

Recommended Vaccinations

The only vaccination officially required by the Maldives is one for yellow fever if you're coming from an area where yellow fever is endemic. Malaria prophylaxis is not necessary.

Medical Checklist

Be aware that in resorts all medical care will be available only through the resort doctor or, when the resort doesn't have a doctor in residence, from a nurse or a member of staff with access to basic medical supplies. Bringing a few basic supplies such as plasters for small cuts is a good idea, as is mosquito repellent for the evenings on most islands. Mosquito nets are often provided by resorts where there is a consistent mosquito problem, but bringing your own is a good idea if they're not included and you normally suffer from bites.

IN THE MALDIVES

Availability & Cost of Health Care

Most resorts have a resident doctor, or share one with another nearby resort. However, if you are seriously unwell it will be necessary to go to Male, or to the nearest atoll capital with a hospital if you're in a far-flung resort. The Maldivian health service relies heavily on doctors, nurses and dentists from overseas, and facilities outside the capital are very limited. The country's main hospital is the **Indira Gandhi Memorial Hospital** (☏333 5211; www.mhsc.com.mv; Buruzu Magu) in Male. Male also has the **ADK Private Hospital** (☏331 3553; www.adkhospital.mv; Sosun Magu), which offers high-quality care at high prices, but as it's important to travel with medical insurance to the Maldives, the cost shouldn't be too much of a worry. The capital island of each atoll has a government hospital or at least a health centre – these are being improved, but for any serious problem you'll have to go to Male.

Dengue Fever

Mosquitoes vary from non-existent to very troublesome depending on which island you're on and what time of year it is. In general, mosquitoes aren't a huge problem because there are few areas of open fresh water where they can breed. However, they can be a problem at certain times of the year (usually after heavy rainfall), so if they do tend to annoy you, use repellent or burn mosquito coils, available from resort shops at vast expense (bring your own just in case). Dengue fever, a viral disease transmitted by mosquitoes, occurs in Maldivian villages but is not a significant risk on resort islands or in the capital.

Diving Health & Safety

Health Requirements

Officially, a doctor should check you over before you do a course, and fill out a form full of diving health questions. In practice, most dive schools will let you dive or do a course if you're under 50 years old and complete a

DRINKING WATER

Tap water in the Maldives is all treated rain water and it's not advisable to drink it, not least as it has generally got an unpleasant taste. Nearly all resorts supply drinking water to their guests for free – some cheaper resorts make you pay for it, though. Either way, it's a far better option.

medical questionnaire yourself, but the check-up is still a good idea. This is especially so if you have any problem at all with your breathing, ears or sinuses. If you are an asthmatic, have any other chronic breathing difficulties or any inner-ear problems, you shouldn't do any scuba diving. Be aware that most dive centres will not let you dive if you are taking any regular medicine for other ailments.

Diving Safely

The following laws apply to recreational diving in the Maldives, and divemasters should enforce them:

➡ Maximum depth is 30m – this is the law in the Maldives.

➡ Maximum time is 60 minutes.

➡ No decompression dives.

➡ Each diver must carry a dive computer.

➡ Obligatory three-minute safety stop at 5m.

➡ Last dive no later than 24 hours before a flight, including seaplanes.

Decompression Sickness

This is a very serious condition – usually, though not always, associated with diver error. The most common symptoms are unusual fatigue or weakness; skin itch; pain in the arms, legs (joints or mid-limb) or torso; dizziness and vertigo; local numbness, tingling or paralysis; and shortness of breath. Signs may also include a blotchy skin rash, a tendency to favour an arm or a leg, staggering, coughing

spasms, collapse or unconsciousness. These symptoms and signs can occur individually, or a number of them can appear at one time.

The most common causes of decompression sickness (or 'the bends' as it is commonly known) are diving too deep, staying at depth for too long or ascending too quickly. This results in nitrogen coming out of solution in the blood and forming bubbles, most commonly in the bones and particularly in the joints or in weak spots such as healed fracture sites.

Avoid flying after diving, as it causes nitrogen to come out of the blood even faster than it would at sea level. Low-altitude flights, like a seaplane transfer to the airport, can be just as dangerous because the aircraft are not pressurised.

The only treatment for decompression sickness is to put the patient into a recompression chamber. That puts a person back under pressure similar to that of the depth at which they were diving so nitrogen bubbles can be reabsorbed. The time required in the chamber is usually three to eight hours. There are decompression chambers at both Baros and Kuramathi resorts.

Insurance

All divers must purchase compulsory Maldivian diving insurance before their first dive in the Maldives. This will automatically be done at the dive school where you do your first dive, and is not expensive. This remains valid for 30 days, no matter where in the country you dive.

In addition to normal travel insurance, it's a very good idea to take out specific diving cover, which will pay for evacuation to a recompression facility and the cost of hyperbaric treatment in a chamber. Evacuation is normally by chartered speedboat or seaplane, both of which are very expensive. **Divers Alert Network** (DAN; www.diversalertnetwork.org) is a nonprofit diving-safety organisation. It can be contacted through most dive shops and clubs, and it offers a DAN TravelAssist policy that provides evacuation and recompression coverage.

Environmental Hazards

Most of the potential danger (you have to be extremely unlucky or very foolhardy to actually get hurt) lies under the sea.

Anemones

These colourful creatures are poisonous, and putting your hand into one can give you a painful sting. If stung, consult a doctor as quickly as possible; the usual procedure is to soak the sting in vinegar.

Coral Cuts & Stings

Coral is sharp stuff and brushing up against it is likely to cause a cut or abrasion. Most corals contain poisons and you're likely to get some in any wound, along with tiny grains of broken coral. The result is that a small cut can take a long time to heal. Wash any coral cuts very thoroughly with fresh water and then treat them liberally with antiseptic. Brushing against fire coral or the feathery hydroid can give you a painful sting and a persistent itchy rash.

Sea Urchins

Sea urchins generally grow on reefs, and most resorts remove them if they're a danger to casual waders in the shallows, though the waters are generally so clear that it's easy to spot them. Watch out though, as the spines are long and sharp, break off easily and once embedded in your flesh are very difficult to remove.

Stingrays

These rays lie on sandy sea beds, and if you step on one, its barbed tail can whip up into your leg and cause a nasty, poisoned wound. Sand can drift over stingrays, so they can become all but invisible while basking on the bottom. Fortunately, stingrays will usually glide away as you approach. If you're wading in the sandy shallows, try to shuffle along and make some noise. If stung, bathing the affected area in hot water is the best treatment; medical attention should be sought to ensure the wound is properly cleaned.

Stonefish

These fish lie on reefs and the sea bed, and are well camouflaged. When stepped on, their sharp dorsal spines pop up and inject a venom that causes intense pain and sometimes death. Stonefish are usually found in shallow, muddy water, but also on rock and coral sea beds.

Bathing the wound in very hot water reduces the pain and effects of the venom. An antivenene is available, and medical attention should be sought, as the after-effects can be long lasting.

Other Conditions
Heat Exhaustion

Dehydration and salt deficiency can cause heat exhaustion. Take the time to acclimatise to high temperatures, drink sufficient liquids and don't do anything too physically demanding.

Salt deficiency is characterised by fatigue, lethargy, headaches, giddiness and muscle cramps; salt tablets may help, but adding extra salt to your food is better.

Heatstroke

This serious condition can occur if the body's heat-regulating mechanism breaks down and the body temperature rises to dangerous levels. Long, continuous periods of exposure to high temperatures and insufficient fluids can leave you vulnerable to heatstroke.

The symptoms are feeling unwell, not sweating very much (or at all) and a high body temperature (39°C to 41°C, or 102°F to 106°F). Where sweating has ceased, the skin becomes flushed and red. Severe, throbbing headaches and lack of coordination will also occur, and the sufferer may be confused or aggressive. Hospitalisation is essential, but in the interim get victims out of the sun, remove their clothing, cover them with a wet sheet or towel and then fan continuously. Give them fluids if they are conscious.

Travelling with Children

The Maldives is an exceptionally safe destination for children, with almost no medical dangers from the environment. The biggest worry, as with all travellers, will be the strength of the sun. Ensure than kids are well covered with waterproof sunscreen (it's best to bring this with you as the mark up in the resorts can be huge) and that they take it easy during the first few days.

Traveller's Diarrhoea

A change of water, food or climate can all cause a mild bout of diarrhoea, but a few rushed toilet trips with no other symptoms is not indicative of a serious problem. Dehydration is the main danger with any diarrhoea. Fluid replacement and rehydration salts remain the mainstay in managing this condition.

Language

The language of the Maldives is Dhivehi (also commonly written as 'Divehi'). It is related to an ancient form of Sinhala, a Sri Lankan language, but also contains some Arabic, Hindi and English words. There are several dialects throughout the country.

English is widely spoken in Male, in the resorts, and by educated people throughout the country. English is also spoken on Addu, the southernmost atoll. On other islands, especially outside the tourism zone, generally only Dhivehi is spoken.

The Romanisation of Dhivehi is not standardised, and words can be spelt in a variety of ways. This is most obvious in Maldivian place names, eg Majeedi is also spelt Majidi, Majeedhee and Majeedee; Hithadhoo also becomes Hithadhu and Hitadhu; and Fuamulak can be Fua Mulaku, Foahmmulah or Phoowa Moloku.

DHIVEHI SCRIPT

Dhivehi has its own script, Thaana. It was introduced by the Maldivian hero Thakurufaanu during the Islamic revival of the late 16th century. Dhivehi shares Arabic's right-to-left appearance for words (and left-to-right for numbers). The list below shows the letters of the Thaana alphabet and their closest English equivalents, and a few words to show the way the letters combine.

ސ (h) ށ (sh) ނ (n) ރ (r) ބ (b)
ޅ (lh) ކ (k) އ (a) ވ (v) މ (m)
ފ (f) ތ (t) ދ (dh) ހ (th) ލ (l)
ގ (g) ޏ (gn) ސ (s) ދ (d) ޒ (z)
ޓ (t) ޔ (y) ޕ (p) ޖ (j) ޗ (ch)

palm tree	ruh	ރުށް
cat	bulhaa	ބުޅާ
egg	bis	ބިސް

BASICS

Hello.	a-salam alekum
Hi.	kihine
Goodbye.	vale kumu salam
See you later.	fahung badaluvang
Peace.	salam
How are you?	haalu kihine?
Very well. (reply)	vara gada
Fine./Good./Great.	barabah
OK.	enge
Yes.	aa
No.	noo
Thank you.	shukuria
I/me	aharen/ma
you	kale
she/he	mina/ena
What did you say?	kike tha buni?
What is that?	mi korche?
How much is this?	mi kihavaraka?
I'm leaving.	aharen dani
Where are you going?	kong taka dani?
How much is the fare?	fi kihavare?
bathroom	gifili
cheap	agu heyo
dance	nashani
eat	kani
enough	heo
(very) expensive	(vara) agu bodu
go	dani
inside	etere
little (people/places)	kuda
mosquito (net)	madiri (ge)
name	nang/nama
now	mihaaru

outside	berufarai
sail	duvani
sleep	nidani
stay	hunani
swim	fatani
toilet	fahana
walk	hingani
wash	donani
water (rain/well)	vaare/valu feng

EATING & DRINKING

I'm a vegetarian.	aharen ehves baavatheh ge maheh nukan
What is the local speciality?	dhivehi aanmu keumakee kobaa?
What is this?	mee ko-on cheh?
The meal was delicious.	keun varah meeru
Thank you for your hospitality.	be-heh-ti gaai kamah shukuriyya

PEOPLE & PLACES

atoll chief	atolu verin
evil spirit	jinni
father	bapa
fisherman	mas veri
foreigner (tourist/expat)	don miha
friend	ratehi
island chief	kateeb
mother	mama
prayer caller	mudeem
religious leader	gazi
toddy man	ra veri
VIP, upper-class person	befalu

atoll	atolu
house	ge
island	fushi/rah
lane, small street	golhi/higun
mosque	miskiiy
reef/lagoon	faru
sandbank	finolhu
street	magu

TIME, DAYS & NUMBERS

day	duvas
night	reggadu
today	miadu
tomorrow	madamma
tonight	mire
yesterday	iye
Monday	horma
Tuesday	angaara
Wednesday	buda
Thursday	brassfati
Friday	hukuru
Saturday	honihira
Sunday	aadita
1	eke
2	de
3	tine
4	hatare
5	fahe
6	haie
7	hate
8	ashe
9	nue
10	diha
11	egaara
12	baara
13	tera
14	saada
15	fanara
16	sorla
17	satara
18	ashara
19	onavihi
20	vihi
30	tiris
40	saalis
50	fansaas
60	fasdolaas
70	hai-diha
80	a-diha
90	nua-diha
100	sateka

GLOSSARY

bai bala – traditional game where one team tries to tag another inside a circle

bashi – traditional women's team game played with a tennis ball, racket and net

BCD – buoyancy control device; a vest that holds air tanks on the back and can be inflated or deflated to control a diver's buoyancy and act as a life preserver; also called a buoyancy control vest (BCV)

bodu beru – literally 'big drum'; made from a hollow coconut log and covered with stingray skin; *bodu beru* is also Maldivian drum music, often used to accompany dancers

chew – wad of areca nut wrapped in an areca leaf, often with lime, cloves and other spices; commonly chewed after a meal

Dhiraagu – the Maldives telecommunications provider, it is jointly owned by the government and the British company Cable & Wireless

Dhivehi Raajje – 'Island Kingdom'; what Maldivians call the Maldives

dhoni – Maldivian boat, probably derived from an Arabian dhow; formerly sail-powered, many dhonis are now equipped with a diesel engine

divemaster – male or female diver qualified to supervise and lead dives, but not necessarily a qualified instructor

faru – also called *faro*; ring-shaped reef within an atoll, often with an island in the middle

feyli – traditional sarong, usually dark with light-coloured horizontal bands near the hem

finolhu – sparsely vegetated sand bank

fushi – island

garudia – a soup made from dried and smoked fish, often eaten with rice, lime and chilli.

giri – coral formation that rises steeply from the atoll floor and almost reaches the surface; see also *thila*

hawitta – ancient mound found in the southern atolls; archaeologists believe these mounds were the foundations of Buddhist temples

hedhikaa – finger food; also called 'short eats'

hingun – wide lane

house reef – coral reef adjacent to a resort island, used by guests for snorkelling and diving

inner-reef slope – where a reef slopes down inside an atoll; see also *outer-reef slope*

joli – also called *jorli*; net seat suspended from a rectangular frame; typically there are four or five seats together outside a house

kandu – sea channel connecting the waters of an atoll to the open sea; feeding grounds for pelagics, such as sharks, stingrays, manta rays and turtles; good dive sites, but subject to strong currents

kateeb – chief of an island

long eats – a substantial meal with rice and *roshi*

magu – wide street

mas – fish

miskiiy – mosque

mudhim – muezzin; the person who calls Muslims to prayer

munnaaru – minaret, a mosque's tower

NSS – National Security Service; the Maldivian army, navy, coastguard and police force

outer-reef slope – outer edge of an atoll facing open sea, where reefs slope down towards the ocean floor; see also *inner-reef slope*

PADI – Professional Association of Diving Instructors; commercial organisation that sets diving standards and training requirements and accredits instructors

pelagic – open-sea species such as sharks, manta rays, tuna, barracuda and whales

raa veri – toddy seller

Ramazan – Maldivian spelling of Ramadan, the Muslim month of fasting

Redin – legendary race of people believed by modern Maldivians to have been the first settlers in the archipelago and the builders of the pre-Islamic *hawittas*

reef flat – shallow area of reef top that stretches out from a lagoon to where the reef slopes down into the deeper surrounding water

roshi – unleavened bread

short eats – finger food; also called *hedhikaa*

STO – State Trading Organisation

Thaana – Dhivehi script; the written language unique to the Maldives

thila – coral formation that rises steeply from the atoll floor to within 5m to 15m of the surface; see also *giri*

thundu kunaa – finely woven reed mats, particularly those from Gaafu Dhaalu

undholi – wooden seat, typically suspended under a shady tree so the swinging motion provides a cooling breeze

Wataniya – Kuwaiti mobile phone provider operating one of the Maldives' two networks

Behind the Scenes

SEND US YOUR FEEDBACK

We love to hear from travellers – your comments keep us on our toes and help make our books better. Our well-travelled team reads every word on what you loved or loathed about this book. Although we cannot reply individually to your submissions, we always guarantee that your feedback goes straight to the appropriate authors, in time for the next edition. Each person who sends us information is thanked in the next edition – the most useful submissions are rewarded with a selection of digital PDF chapters.

Visit **lonelyplanet.com/contact** to submit your updates and suggestions or to ask for help. Our award-winning website also features inspirational travel stories, news and discussions.

Note: We may edit, reproduce and incorporate your comments in Lonely Planet products such as guidebooks, websites and digital products, so let us know if you don't want your comments reproduced or your name acknowledged. For a copy of our privacy policy visit lonelyplanet.com/privacy.

OUR READERS

Many thanks to the travellers who used the last edition and wrote to us with helpful hints, useful advice and interesting anecdotes:
Barney Smith, Johann Schelesnak, Juan Miguel Mariatti, Kevin Callaghan

AUTHOR THANKS
Tom Masters

A huge thanks first of all to Moritz Estermann, who was my companion for much of my trip, and who provided excellent guidance on fine food and wine, was an expert with pillow menus and remained positive through some of the worst weather I've ever seen in Maldives. Thanks also to Paul Roberts, Shauna Aminath, Aaron Sein, Allo Saeed, Zuhair Mohammed, Ahmed Naseer and Ali Rilwan. I owe a huge debt of thanks also to all the resort managers, press officers and guesthouse owners who made great efforts to help me reach their properties, often going way beyond the call of duty; they are sadly way too numerous to name in person, but they know who they are.

ACKNOWLEDGMENTS

Climate map data adapted from Peel MC, Finlayson BL & McMahon TA (2007) 'Updated World Map of the Köppen-Geiger Climate Classification', *Hydrology and Earth System Sciences*, 11, 163344.

Cover photograph: Hammock on tropical beach, Maldives; Sakis Papadopoulos, Corbis

THIS BOOK

This 9th edition of Lonely Planet's *Maldives* guidebook was researched and written by Tom Masters, who also wrote the previous two editions. This guidebook was produced by the following:

Destination Editor
Joe Bindloss

Coordinating Editor
Samantha Forge

Product Editors Penny Cordner, Bruce Evans

Senior Cartographer
David Kemp

Book Designer
Katherine Marsh

Assisting Editors Melanie Dankel, Jeanette Wall

Cartographer Gabe Lindquist

Cover Researcher
Naomi Parker

Thanks to Kate Chapman, Chris Love, Anne Mason, Claire Naylor, Kirsten Rawlings

Index

Map Pages **000**
Photo Pages **000**

RESORTS

NOTES

Map Legend

Sights

- Beach
- Bird Sanctuary
- Buddhist
- Castle/Palace
- Christian
- Confucian
- Hindu
- Islamic
- Jain
- Jewish
- Monument
- Museum/Gallery/Historic Building
- Ruin
- Shinto
- Sikh
- Taoist
- Winery/Vineyard
- Zoo/Wildlife Sanctuary
- Other Sight

Activities, Courses & Tours

- Bodysurfing
- Diving
- Canoeing/Kayaking
- Course/Tour
- Sento Hot Baths/Onsen
- Skiing
- Snorkelling
- Surfing
- Swimming/Pool
- Walking
- Windsurfing
- Other Activity

Sleeping

- Sleeping
- Camping

Eating

- Eating

Drinking & Nightlife

- Drinking & Nightlife
- Cafe

Entertainment

- Entertainment

Shopping

- Shopping

Information

- Bank
- Embassy/Consulate
- Hospital/Medical
- Internet
- Police
- Post Office
- Telephone
- Toilet
- Tourist Information
- Other Information

Geographic

- Beach
- Hut/Shelter
- Lighthouse
- Lookout
- Mountain/Volcano
- Oasis
- Park
- Pass
- Picnic Area
- Waterfall

Population

- Capital (National)
- Capital (State/Province)
- City/Large Town
- Town/Village

Transport

- Airport
- Border crossing
- Bus
- Cable car/Funicular
- Cycling
- Ferry
- Metro/MRT/MTR station
- Monorail
- Parking
- Petrol station
- Skytrain/Subway station
- Taxi
- Train station/Railway
- Tram
- Underground station
- Other Transport

Routes

- Tollway
- Freeway
- Primary
- Secondary
- Tertiary
- Lane
- Unsealed road
- Road under construction
- Plaza/Mall
- Steps
- Tunnel
- Pedestrian overpass
- Walking Tour
- Walking Tour detour
- Path/Walking Trail

Boundaries

- International
- State/Province
- Disputed
- Regional/Suburb
- Marine Park
- Cliff
- Wall

Hydrography

- River, Creek
- Intermittent River
- Canal
- Water
- Dry/Salt/Intermittent Lake
- Reef

Areas

- Airport/Runway
- Beach/Desert
- Cemetery (Christian)
- Cemetery (Other)
- Glacier
- Mudflat
- Park/Forest
- Sight (Building)
- Sportsground
- Swamp/Mangrove

Note: Not all symbols displayed above appear on the maps in this book

OUR STORY

A beat-up old car, a few dollars in the pocket and a sense of adventure. In 1972 that's all Tony and Maureen Wheeler needed for the trip of a lifetime – across Europe and Asia overland to Australia. It took several months, and at the end – broke but inspired – they sat at their kitchen table writing and stapling together their first travel guide, *Across Asia on the Cheap*. Within a week they'd sold 1500 copies. Lonely Planet was born.

Today, Lonely Planet has offices in Franklin, London, Melbourne, Oakland, Beijing and Delhi, with more than 600 staff and writers. We share Tony's belief that 'a great guidebook should do three things: inform, educate and amuse'.

OUR WRITER

Tom Masters

Tom is a British-born, Berlin-based travel writer who has been covering Maldives for Lonely Planet for a decade. While Maldives' incredible geography, amazing beaches and incomparable underwater world were the initial attraction, it's actually the wonderful contradictions of the Maldivian people and the confusingly closed Dhivehi culture that have kept him coming back, although the luxury hotels and amazing food aren't exactly disincentives either.

You can find him online at www.tommasters.net.

Published by Lonely Planet Publications Pty Ltd
ABN 36 005 607 983
9th edition – October 2015
ISBN 978 1 74321 012 3
© Lonely Planet 2015   Photographs © as indicated 2015
10 9 8 7 6 5 4 3 2 1
Printed in China

Although the authors and Lonely Planet have taken all reasonable care in preparing this book, we make no warranty about the accuracy or completeness of its content and, to the maximum extent permitted, disclaim all liability arising from its use.